COACHING BASEBALL SUCCESSFULLY

Andy Lopez
University of Florida

with
John Kirkgard
Westmont College

Human Kinetics

Library of Congress Cataloging-in-Publication Data

Lopez, Andy, 1953-
    Coaching baseball successfully / Andy Lopez with John Kirkgard.
        p.   cm.
    Includes index.
    ISBN 0-87322-609-7
    1. Baseball--Coaching. I. Kirkgard, John II. Title
    GV875.5.L67 1996
    796.357'07'7--dc20   95-52858
                                          CIP

ISBN: 0-87322-609-7

Developmental Editor: Jan Colarusso Seeley; **Assistant Editor:** Lynn M. Hooper; **Editorial Assistant:** Amy Carnes; **Copyeditor:** Jim Kestner; **Proofreader:** Bob Replinger; **Indexer:** Barbara Cohen; **Typesetter and Layout Artist:** Tara Welsch; **Text Designer:** Keith Blomberg; **Photo Editor:** Boyd LaFoon; **Cover Designer:** Jack Davis; **Photographer (cover):** Stephen Morton; **Photographer (cover inset):** University of Florida; **Photographers (interior):** Adrian Dennis, M. Bradley Elliott, Bob Libby Photography, University of Florida, Pepperdine University, and Westmont College; **Illustrator (line drawings):** John Hatton; **Illustrator (mac art):** Jennifer Delmotte; **Printer:** Versa Press

Printed in the United States of America   10 9 8 7 6 5 4 3 2 1

Human Kinetics
Web site: http://www.humankinetics.com

United States: Human Kinetics
P.O. Box 5076, Champaign, IL 61825-5076
1-800-747-4457
e-mail: humank@hkusa.com

Canada: Human Kinetics, Box 24040, Windsor, ON N8Y 4Y9
1-800-465-7301 (in Canada only)
e-mail: humank@hkcanada.com

Europe: Human Kinetics, P.O. Box IW14, Leeds LS16 6TR, United Kingdom
(44) 1132 781708
e-mail: humank@hkeurope.com

Australia: Human Kinetics, 57A Price Avenue, Lower Mitcham, South Australia 5062
(08) 277 1555
e-mail: humank@hkaustralia.com

New Zealand: Human Kinetics, P.O. Box 105-231, Auckland 1
(09) 523 3462
e-mail: humank@hknewz.com

To my children, Kristi Louise, Kerri Lynne, Michael Andrew, and David Arthur Lopez. Each of you is a very special gift from the Lord.

Contents

Foreword

I coached baseball at the major-league level for 27 years, and people always ask how I stayed so enthusiastic. I give them three reasons. One, my love of the game. Two, the enjoyment and satisfaction of working with players. And three, the competition each season to be the best.

All three of these factors are important to effective coaching, as Andy Lopez makes clear in *Coaching Baseball Successfully*. Andy's enthusiasm for the game is as apparent in the pages that follow as it is when you see him work with his team on the field.

If you're enthused about what you do, you'll make the time and the effort to do it well. And doing it well means continuing to learn and improve, no matter how many years you've coached. Even at the major-league level, the challenge is to better yourself—to improve your knowledge and skills each season.

Andy Lopez's enthusiasm has translated into high achievement as a coach. He had the desire to do what it takes to climb the ranks from the high school to junior college to major college level. At each level his teams have excelled, reaching championship form. And Andy kept learning all along the way.

In *Coaching Baseball Successfully* Coach Lopez presents the stuff from which champi-

onships are made: good teaching of skills and strategies; good practice coaching; good philosophy, communication, and motivation; good game coaching; and good evaluation of performance. If you already have covered all these bases, you're probably pretty successful. But my guess is that—like every other baseball coach and manager—you could improve in one or more of these areas.

You are fortunate in that for at least part of each day during the season, the ballpark is your office and your classroom. Be as organized as the top CEOs and as instructive as the best teachers. Take your job seriously, but remember to put the development of your athletes ahead of personal honors. This book will help. Even if you use only three or four key ideas from *Coaching Baseball Successfully* next season, you'll be a better coach.

Coaching young men is an important job. Take the opportunity to learn from Coach Lopez's experiences. With enough enthusiasm, discipline, preparation, knowledge, and skill, you too will be highly successful.

George "Sparky" Anderson
Former Manager,
Detroit Tigers and Cincinnati Reds

Acknowledgments

I would like to thank John Kirkgard for his great friendship, as well as his pride of workmanship in putting the material for this book into manuscript form; Mike Zapolski and Steve McClain for their expert assistance throughout the book; and every coach, player, professional scout, and institution that have been a positive influence in my life.

To Dr. Isaac Canales, who in June of 1982 challenged me to be a man of God.

To my sister, Teresa Connelly, and my brother, John Lopez, for their love and direction toward their younger brother; my mother, Consuelo Morales Lopez, and my father, Arturo Lopez, for their patient, kind, yet strong, hands of guidance and love; and my wife, Linda, who possesses the wisdom, love, patience, and support to enable me to pursue a career in baseball.

Above all to my Lord and Savior Jesus Christ. If I have accomplished anything at all it is by his grace. —Jer. 9:23

Introduction

In my home and office libraries, I have dozens of instructional baseball books, many of which I have used to develop my approach to coaching. So why write another? I saw a need for a baseball book that goes beyond the technical, beyond even the fundamentals of the game, a book that would lend itself to the fundamentals of life and to the development of players as people and athletes. As coaches we often get overly concerned with the trivial aspects of our jobs and lose sight of the impact we have on the lives of those around us.

Much of the success with which I have been blessed comes as the result of an emphasis on my athletes becoming men. Over the years our desire is for our players to develop into successful husbands and fathers and leaders in the community, business world, their churches, and other organizations.

"If you have run with men on foot and they have worn you out, how then can you compete with the horses of excellence?" (Jeremiah 12:5). Much of my philosophy comes from a sound belief in biblical principles and my faith in God. The statement from the Book of Jeremiah serves as a constant reminder of the standard of excellence for which I should strive in my relationships with my family, friends, peers, athletes, and also in my profession.

Coaching Baseball Successfully covers the fundamental skills, strategies, and drills of the game. In addition, I've included sections that transcend the *X*s and *O*s of baseball. The coaching philosophy section of this book applies to anyone in a position to manage and motivate others. It is interesting for me to observe friends in the business world applying these principles with their employees. Philosophy, communication, motivation, and program development are essentials of

leadership, and they are covered in Part I. From these guiding principles, effective coaches establish their specific ideas and methods for coaching.

Part II covers planning, an essential ingredient in any coach's success. From preseason administrative details to actual examples of practice plans, this section presents the process and people involved in planning, preparing, and organizing for a successful season.

The bulk of the book focuses on baseball techniques and tactics, and the keys to teaching them to players. Parts III and IV deal with every offensive and defensive area of the game. Baseball skills and how to teach them are a constant, but strategy often changes with the personnel you have. I try to give you the basics, and then I help you to develop a strategy that will work best with the athletes on your club.

Part V takes you from the practice field into the game itself. Featured here are methods of scouting, personnel management, game day motivation, and specific game strategies. I also offer suggestions about an area in which we can all improve—how to win *and* lose with dignity.

The last section explains how, when, what, and who a coach should evaluate. The ability to correctly evaluate your athletes' on-field performance and off-field conduct is a valuable skill for any coach. Unless you can monitor and pin-point problem areas, you'll never have a top-flight program.

The ideas in this book are those that I have used throughout my career. My practice plans today at Florida are much the same as those I used early in my career at Mira Costa High School (Manhattan Beach, CA), at California State University, Dominguez Hills (Carson, CA), and Pepperdine University (Malibu, CA).

My experiences at all three levels of coaching (high school and NCAA Divisions I and II) have been similar. At Mira Costa, our ball club reached the final California Interscholastic Federation (CIF) championship game played in Dodger Stadium. It happened in our fifth year. At Cal State Dominguez Hills, the program developed into a contender for the NCAA Division II championship, finishing third nationally in 1988, our fifth year at that school. In my fourth year at Pepperdine, we had the privilege to play for and win the NCAA Division I championship. The content of *Coaching Baseball Successfully* is an approach that has been proven successful at all levels of the game of baseball. I trust it will be applicable to your coaching situation.

It is my sincere desire and prayer that in some way this book will have an impact on your life, that it will not only develop your knowledge of baseball, but also impress upon you the importance of having a positive impact on those around you. Above all else, I would like this book to honor the Lord, to whom I give full credit for my life, my abilities, and all my blessings.

Part I

Coaching Foundation

## Chapter 1

Developing a Baseball Coaching Philosophy

Becoming a baseball coach was not always my goal. I did not grow up with a passion to coach at the major college level and to win a national championship. On the contrary, I had many career paths from which to choose. Professional baseball was an option. Selling life insurance was my first career pursuit. I also desired to be a youth pastor. It was a combination of these other pursuits, coupled with my upbringing as a child influenced by godly parents, that encompasses the development of my coaching philosophy.

Each coach must have a philosophy to be successful. Knowledge of the game and its fundamentals only takes your ball club so far without the foundation of a consistent philosophy. Each coach's philosophy will be different, influenced by a lifetime of experiences and information.

In this chapter I'll share my coaching philosophy, describing some of my background and highlighting what I believe are the keys to an approach that results in consistent success. I won't try to change your way of thinking or your way of doing things, but you might just find something you can use.

Roots of a Coaching Philosophy

How we choose to work with people and our perspective of coaching develop well before we make out our first lineup card. So it's not surprising that my mom's and dad's personalities, how and where I was raised, my social experiences as a youth, and my playing career helped shape my philosophy.

Parents' Influence

My parents have had the greatest influence on my approach to life. They both immigrated to the United States from Mexico and met while working in the cannery industry in the Port of Los Angeles, San Pedro, California.

My father and mother are both godly people. They are humble and hard working. They have a phenomenal work ethic. They have taught me much, including the basics of what is now a part of my coaching philosophy. I learned that nothing will ever be handed to you, to deal with people honestly, to work hard and put in a full day's work, to put your name on everything you do, and if you are going to do something, do it right.

My father served in the South Pacific during World War II. Despite being a quiet, humble man of God, he was a successful soldier and was promoted to the rank of sergeant. As quickly as he was promoted, he was demoted, not because he wasn't doing a good job but because he would not yell at his men!

I don't ever remember my dad raising his voice as I grew up, yet he was a powerful leader. He is a man I love dearly and if I have any patience or poise in my life it's because of my father.

On the other hand, Mom is a fighter! I still remember her chasing me down the street with discipline on her mind. In front of all my friends she caught me and gave me a good (and no doubt deserved) spanking. I was 13 at the time, and I am still not sure how she caught me. But her determination and wisdom in knowing her son needed the foolishness driven from him is a strong memory that will always remain with me.

It is interesting that although my mom is a strong, brave woman, she is also afraid of many things. She fears flying, driving, and the water to name a few. Yet from her I've learned that it's okay to be scared, as long as you pursue your fears and conquer them. I'll never forget her flying to Omaha, Nebraska,

to see us play in the College World Series. She overcame yet another fear so she could be there.

 TAKING CARE OF DETAILS

When I was nine, I remember my parents taking me to the Blue Chip Stamp Store in San Pedro and getting a brand new baseball glove. My world was complete except that I was still learning the importance of taking care of my school clothes, putting toys away, and things of that nature. Just weeks after I received the glove, I left it outside one night. My mom desired to teach me a valuable lesson and said I would get the glove back when I showed I was really ready to handle the responsibility. For a long time I was forced to borrow gloves every practice and game I played. When the glove was finally returned to me, I had learned the lesson of taking care of things that are given to me. I can't remember the last thing I have lost. I don't lose keys; I don't lose notes; I don't miss appointments. I'm on time. My parents taught me the importance of details.

Street Experiences

My parents raised me in San Pedro, California, a small port town outside of Los Angeles, which bred a pretty good group of ballplayers. Brian Harper (Twins), Joe Amalfitano (Dodgers), Garry Maddox (Phillies), and Alan Ashby

(Astros) are a few of the prominent names. More than any other sport, baseball was big in our city.

Yet baseball was not the sole interest in my life. I was also involved with a gang called the Persuasions, and we hung out together on the city streets. There were about 12 of us involved. I was with this gang for 2-1/2 years between the ages of 15 and 17. Even though I was younger than most of the other members, I remember being the leader. I became streetwise, and my perspective on life was shaped by these experiences. I did what was necessary to survive on the streets, actions of which I am not proud.

I grew up living with con men. There wasn't much truth in the streets. So I grew up doubting the sincerity of most people. Because of this experience, I attempt to be as honest with others as possible.

God gave me the option of athletics, which allowed me a way off the streets. A gang lifestyle is a dead end, literally. Some of the Persuasions are no longer alive. It's sad to see the degree to which gangs have grown and harmed today's society.

Playing Career

Despite the street influence, I was fortunate to have the option of athletics and pursued it with a passion. I was successful in my years at San Pedro High School, and upon graduating in 1971 I pursued my athletic career at Los Angeles Harbor Junior College. I was fortunate to make some all-state teams and then went on to play at UCLA in 1974-75. The Detroit Tigers made me their ninth-round draft pick in 1975.

My playing career was unique. I was a shortstop, yet I caught in high school and at UCLA. I caught about 30 games for UCLA as a junior. I played short, third, center field, and like everyone else, I pitched as a youngster. In fact, first base is the only position I never played.

My street personality surfaced in negotiations with the Tigers. Since my collegiate eligibility was over, the Tigers negotiated with me from the perspective that they felt I had no other options. Call it stubbornness, but I did not appreciate being told I had no options other than to sign the contract. I

thought I did and decided to walk away from professional baseball.

At that time I had one more quarter term of school needed for my degree at UCLA, and was fortunate enough to be asked by Coach Jim O'Brien to assist him at L.A. Harbor Community College. This is where my coaching career began. Lord only knew then that my career would take me to Mira Costa High School (1978-82), California State University at Dominguez Hills (1982-88), Pepperdine University (1988-93), and the University of Florida in 1994.

First Coaching Job

Some people know at an early age exactly what they want to do for a career. Others bounce from job to job, praying that the next position will be the dream job. I have pursued and interviewed for only one job in my life. Believe it or not, it was an insurance sales position. I did the interview, took the test, and tried everything to convince the company that I was the man for the job, but they still didn't hire me. About that time, a career in coaching and teaching began looking much more attractive.

My first head coaching job at Mira Costa lasted five years. During that time I realized three important things that affected my coaching philosophy and probably have much to do with why I have continued to coach through all of these years:

• I was blessed with an ability to communicate with my players. If there's one single thing that I enjoy about coaching, it is being able to interact on a daily basis with the young men on my team.

• I gained confidence that I could coach. The team's success, including playing for the California Interscholastic Federation (CIF) 4A championship in my fifth season, removed even my own doubts that I could do the job.

• I came to know the Lord Jesus Christ personally in my life. Among other things, this has helped me to better prioritize my work and to give greater value to the well-being of others. It is these three experiences that are the deep roots of any success I have experienced.

Coaching Mentors

Coaching did not come to me automatically. I have been fortunate to have access to fine coaches and to their knowledge of the game. I have learned from many. In fact, I have *had* to learn from many. Following only one year as an assistant, I became a head coach. Most would consider this very little experience! It has been quite necessary to draw upon the knowledge of other coaches throughout my career.

My coach at San Pedro High School was Jerry Lovarov. Although I was ignorant of it at the time, Jerry taught me the importance of allowing good players to play. His team was loaded with good players. He let us play and we were successful. He did not overcoach us. We won three high school championships in my time there and always played in the city playoffs. He showed wisdom in letting us play, which is now part of my philosophy—to let good players play and to not overcoach them.

A gentleman who was way ahead of his time was my junior college coach, Norm Jacot. He was an outstanding hitting instructor, one of the better I have been around. Back in the early '70s and before VCRs became popular and affordable, Norm showed us films of our swings to help us correct hitting flaws. He was innovative and he left me with an openness to new ideas and innovations.

Jerry Kindall, at the University of Arizona, has been a great example for me. A few years back he went through a tragic time in losing his wife to Lou Gehrig's disease, and I remember watching him very closely. I wanted to see how he handled a life situation that was far more difficult than any game experience. Anybody knows that during a game you can feel the crunch. If you allow it, you can feel the pressure. So I watched Coach. I observed the way he handled himself and how he handled his clubs. He is a very consistent man. I don't think I have ever been able to detect whether he has won or lost after a game when I've played him. His body language is on an even keel. He is competitive yet poised. I admire that and have tried to emulate that over the last seven or eight years.

Jim O'Brien, the first coach I worked for at L.A. Harbor, was a tremendous influence on my competitive approach. By the sheer force of his personality he showed me how to compete. I have met few men with as intense a desire to come out on top as Coach O'Brien. His focus was simply to be the best. He wanted his clubs to be the very best. His clubs always played hard and excelled. I would say Jim introduced me to a new level of competitiveness.

Several coaches have instilled in me the importance of sharing time and knowledge with others. You will find it difficult to improve without the ability to pursue others in your field and seek their insight. Dennis Rogers, currently at Riverside City College, comes to mind. He has a unique background, having been part of several outstanding baseball programs, such as the Oakland A's and the Pittsburgh Pirates. He played and coached under John Scolinos. Dennis and I get together yearly to share ideas. The late Joe Hicks, a legend in southern California, also confirmed the value of getting help from other coaches.

Finally, I must come back to John Scolinos (Cal Poly Pomona). I would like to emulate this man. He is a gentleman who takes his faith in God seriously yet still competes hard. He also influences his players beyond the field and into their daily lives. He is a consistent man, unwavering in his beliefs. I have seen him win national championships and have seen him lose 30 to 40 games. By his response you could not tell the difference. These are all qualities that someday I would like to have attributed to me.

Every coach I have played for and every coach I have played against has been a source of learning for me. From Coach Lovarov's lesson of letting his players play to Coach Scolinos's unwavering class and dignity, I have continued to learn from other individuals.

Pursue ideas of others and adapt them to your approach. If you can learn at least one thing from an individual, which is often the case, do it. Consider, for example, a drill that my college teammate Dave Norris taught me in 1974. It involves spreading the feet, putting the bat on the shoulder, and pulling every pitch to develop quickness in the hands.

Where he got that drill I do not know, but I still use it today.

Developing a Philosophy

If you believe that a philosophy must have no apparent inconsistencies, then you'll be disappointed to learn that mine mixes intense competition with gentle communication. But these two components *can* coexist in an overall philosophy.

In the Gospel of Matthew, Jesus tells his disciples that he is sending them out among the wolves, and therefore they must be as shrewd as serpents yet as gentle as doves (Matthew 10:16). It is this balance that best describes my approach to coaching.

Do not take this wrong. I am not saying coaches are a pack of wolves, but the profession is a competitive one, and the setting in which we work is a competitive arena. There-

fore, I try to get our players to be tough competitors (as shrewd as serpents) to compete on a daily basis. On the other hand, I insist that we also show humility, class, and compassion (as gentle as doves). These are valuable behaviors that our society fails to nurture like it should.

Adhering to this competitive yet compassionate philosophy is much like walking a tightrope between two distinct beliefs. Yet it is a tightrope I have tried to walk at all levels of coaching, day by day, often minute by minute.

Keeping Baseball in Perspective

Let me give you another example of walking a tightrope. Our goal is to win a national championship. Within that goal I make a very important statement regarding our time on the field. The statement is this: "It's not life or death for the next two hours, it's *more* important than that." Then I take the concept further by making sure my athletes understand that when practice or the game is over, baseball becomes what it truly is—trivial. The results are trivial. The game is trivial relative to the bigger issues of life, trivial in the sense that it cannot consume you at the sacrifice of other important aspects of your life.

Is it a contradiction to say that baseball is more important than life or death, and then to claim it is trivial? No. It's a matter of when and in what situation you take one of these two perspectives and how well you integrate them into your athletic, social, academic, family, and religious lives.

We need the full effort on the field. If a player has a family problem, it can't affect him. If he just flunked a test, he can't be affected by it. If he broke up with his girlfriend, he can't be affected. Actually nothing should take him out of his game, not a thing for the next two hours. But when the two hours end, the game cannot destroy the player's life. In its purest sense it's just a game.

⚾ REAL LIFE OR DEATH

I had an experience that illustrates the previous points, an event that I would have traded the national title for along with every coaching win I have ever had. My wife was found to have a tumor in her throat, and the first diagnosis was that the growth was malignant. Thank God it was benign. But during the three days prior to surgery I would have traded my accomplishments for her health.

The day before the surgery, I met with a recruit's family and worked as hard as I ever had to get the commitment. The athlete signed a letter of intent. The only reason that I did a good job in that situation was that I tried to live my philosophy. Baseball is not life or death; it's more than life or death at a given moment.

After I left my office and was driving home, I realized it did not really matter if the recruit committed or not. What really mattered was that my wife be healthy. The recruiting process was important only when it was taking place. It was trivial relative to the essential aspects of life.

I want to teach my athletes not to be double minded. This philosophy works well off the field, too. If someone wants to be an athlete, he should not confuse the issues. When he shows up for practice, he should be an athlete. When he's in the classroom, he should be a student. When he's on a date, he should focus on his relationship with the other person.

For about two or three hours every day during practice, I demand that all players and coaches be completely focused. As a coach, I must also separate my work and family times—and be absorbed in each when the time calls for it.

Winning in Life

I do not believe my value as a human being is dictated by my win-loss record. I do not believe having won a national title makes me a genius. I want to be in the group of coaches who are driven to be successful yet are driven to do things right, driven to develop young athletes into solid citizens later in life. Yes, I want to win another national title, but my value as a father, husband, Christian, and coach is not a direct result of winning 40 games every year. I hope I can teach that to my athletes.

All of us in coaching know that some of our colleagues base their success and worth as a coach and as a person on how big a number they have in their win column. How many wins? How many championships? Their phi-

losophy: "Let's do whatever it takes to win regardless of long-term consequences." This perspective is rooted in ego and self-promotion.

I strive to be a part of the coaching community that says, "Let's be successful; let's develop athletes; let's mold young men to grow up mature and do things right." We need to understand that baseball is trivial and say to ourselves, "I'm not going to base my self-worth on this. I'm not going to destroy my life. I'm not going to destroy my marriage. I'm not going to destroy my relationship with my kids. I'm simply not going to allow this white ball with red seams to control my life."

Be Yourself

The single most important suggestion I can make to a young coach developing a philosophy is to be yourself. You have to be comfortable in your approach to coaching.

I have the utmost respect for former UCLA basketball coach John Wooden. When I was younger, I thought I would adopt Coach Wooden's coaching style. As I watched him, I admired the way he sat on the bench: poised and quiet, the only hint of anxiety the rolled-up program clutched tightly in one hand. Be calm and collected like Coach Wooden and you'll succeed, I thought. So I tried it; the ex-gang member from San Pedro tried to imitate the gentlemanly, Midwestern demeanor of Saint John Wooden. It didn't work. The style wasn't comfortable for me. I tend to raise my voice occasionally and show emotion often. That's who I am. And I'm sure that my approach might be uncomfortable for other coaches.

The key to being yourself is to know yourself. Discover who you are. What are your strengths? Your weaknesses? What do you stand for? These questions need to be answered as you develop your own philosophy of coaching. I would like to challenge anyone reading this book to examine why you do what you do. Combine your roots, personality, and the direction you have received from your coaching mentors to develop your philosophy.

It might be comforting to note that I did not answer most of these questions until well into my coaching career. Now I humbly be-

lieve I know who I am as a coach, my strengths and weaknesses. I discovered much of this while I was at California State University at Dominguez Hills—ironically, not because of success but because of failure. Hard times do bring out character.

Benefiting From a Balanced Philosophy

How does a balanced philosophy work? I'm convinced that the most tangible results come when you begin setting objectives for your athletes and for yourself.

We begin establishing objectives with our athletes with two simple rules: Be on time and do things right. Being on time is a very easy rule. Doing things right is a day-to-day process that influences one's social life, athletics, and academics.

Social Maturity

I work at a university that demands a high level of ethics. I am proud of that, and we like to think none of our athletes is involved in drinking, drugs, or anything that would be titled a social detriment. Yet the reality of the '90s is that I do have athletes who are in-

volved in these areas. I am not proud of it and do teach alternatives.

Looking at myself, it is obvious that there is wrong in my life. The reason I accepted the Lord back in 1980 was that I could not correct the wrong in my life alone. This is the wonderful concept of grace, the opportunity to change despite many mistakes. So I have a sensitive spot in my heart if one of my athletes is caught drinking or in an uncomfortable situation. I know I was given an opportunity to change and took advantage of it. I want my athletes to be provided the same opportunity.

From a social standpoint, I try to educate our athletes that the quicker they get into a mature state of mind, the better off they will be. I'll address the ball club on the field and say, "You must play like men. If you play like boys, you will get beat." I can then relate it socially, "If you act like a boy, you're going to end up in trouble. You must act like a man." Show me some mature qualities on the field and off the field. I used this approach at both the high school and college levels.

Many coaches would be able to produce a page of rules and expectations, 15 to 20 rules long. I do not have that. I basically say, "Let's do things right." It is my job to expose them to what I now know to be right after four decades on this earth—what is right and what is wrong. Our athletes need guidance not only on drugs and alcohol, but also on relationships, goals, and how to handle authority.

Unfortunately, in our society it's not cool to honor positions of authority. It's more cool to fight it, even though we know the more we fight, the tougher it gets. Even if we believe the authority is making the wrong decision, we need to honor it. I've disagreed with my athletic director at times over a denied road trip or new uniform purchases, yet I've had to honor the position of authority. Both my program and I have been blessed as a result. We try to teach social skills to our athletes on a daily basis.

Academic Integrity

Doing things right academically includes getting a degree. To get a degree, athletes need to go to class. One really can't put a dollar value on a college education. At Florida our athletes are there to get a degree. Baseball will take care of itself. We monitor our athletes' academic progress every four weeks. Although we have a study hall, it is not mandatory. If an athlete shows it needs to be mandatory, it then becomes mandatory.

I would be less than honest if I told you I didn't have players in my program who are just getting through the academic experience to get an opportunity to play pro ball. Personally, I did that my first year at UCLA. Yet it ties in to the idea of doing things the right way. I've had freshmen who were horrible students, but by their senior year they were very good students. If I had made a quick decision, dismissing them for poor academics, I would never have seen them develop into the mature individuals of their senior year. Our goals are that we want to see them get their degrees, but we also need to have patience.

Athletic Focus

No matter what it is our athletes are doing, we want them to be focused, remaining in the present tense. They are not to be in the past tense or the future tense. We make this a prominent concept in our program because

seldom do we live life in the present. Most people can't forget the past or are overly concerned about the future.

This kind of thinking can be devastating for a pitching staff. You need to get your pitchers to stay in the present tense. But what typically happens is this: A pitcher will make a pretty good pitch and then jump into the future tense and say, "Well, that was a good pitch so I'm probably going to throw an even better pitch." Instead, he hangs the next pitch and it's hit out of the park. Or the other side of the coin: He throws a poor pitch and it's crushed; it's 1-0 in the first inning. If he can't get right back into the present tense, he will stay in the past tense and one pitch will now probably dictate the next two innings. At this point, he may not get out of the third inning simply because of one pitch.

We teach staying in the present tense diligently in our program. The past tense is usually centered on guilt. The future tense is usually centered on anxiety. We believe our people have a pretty good chance of controlling the present tense.

GULF WAR FOCUS

When our country decided to react to Iraq's military aggressiveness in 1991, the effect was very close to home. The father of one of our pitchers, Jeff Myers, was in charge of one of the U.S. ground forces in Iraq. As the news was announced on the television in our clubhouse, we were stunned. Jeff and I spent considerable time behind closed doors shedding tears and praying for his father's safety.

I fondly remember Jeff's efforts during our next few workouts. He was able to separate his off-field concerns about his father's well-being and totally focus on the baseball task at hand. In fact, I might dare say they were the best workouts he had for us.

Continuing to Learn

As a coach I make it a goal to keep getting better. I read that each year John Wooden would pick one facet of the game of basketball and study it to improve in that area. I try to do the same. Each summer I will pick a part of the game and through other coaches and books immerse myself into that area. This practice keeps me constantly improving.

I also want to be constantly aware of my definition of winning. Some of this is again borrowed from Coach Wooden, but winning to me is having the peace of mind of knowing you've stayed in the present tense and you've given everything you have to give. I like Lou Holtz's description of "Win—what's important now?" Are you giving everything you have to be as good as you can be right this minute? I believe I have been a winning coach even when I have had a losing record. If you've done it right from the first day; if you've been honest, fair, and a person of integrity; if you've communicated well with your athletes, given an honest effort, and served them well; then you're a winner.

Putting Your Philosophy to Work

A coaching philosophy is only as good as the impact it has on those associated with the program. These are the qualities we try to possess and transmit throughout our program and within our players.

1. Honesty. Be honest not only within your program but also with yourself. Understand who you are and know your strengths as a coach.

2. Consistency. Be consistent in all areas during joyful times as well as difficult moments. This will allow your ball club to become familiar with your reactions to circumstances, and they can grow to trust how you will react in all situations. There is a real joy in knowing that your leader is consistent.

3. Aggressive approach. This simply means that in addition to being humble, compassionate, sincere, and honest (qualities that will make you successful in all walks of life), you must also teach aggressiveness, competitiveness, and the strength to never be intimidated by an opponent. This aggressiveness must be taught every day.

4. Inner-confidence. Develop an inner-confidence in your coaching abilities. At one time in my career I knew little about pitching. I had to decide whether to hire a pitching coach or to throw myself into the study of pitching. I chose to learn the pitching game, and by approaching it with a sincere heart I developed an inner-confidence in my ability to teach this skill.

5. Strong thinking. Athletes have told me they must wear a particular number to be successful. They believed somehow their performance was tied to wearing a favorite number. This is weak thinking. A weak thinker will concern himself with his number, the temperature at game time, field conditions, and other aspects he cannot control. Superstition is usually evident in a weak thinker. I want our athletes to have the inner-confidence that if they perform to their abilities, they will be successful. It will not matter that it is hot at game time, or that the playing surface is bad, or that they are wearing the wrong numbers. With inner-confidence comes the ability to be a strong thinker.

Summary

This chapter examined the development of my coaching philosophy. Key aspects of this philosophy are these:

- Each coach's philosophy is different, influenced by a lifetime of experiences and information.
- Learn from others. Confer with other coaches often.
- Know yourself. Discover who you are. Know what you believe and stand for.
- Coaching demands that you be competitive, but that you balance it with gentleness.
- Belong to the coaching philosophy camp that is committed to doing it right.
- Have your athletes do things right—athletically, academically, and socially.
- Make your time on the field more important than life or death, but when the game is over realize that baseball is trivial.
- Remain in the present tense at all times.
- Honesty, consistency, aggressiveness, inner-confidence, and strong thinking are important outgrowths of a positive coaching philosophy.

## Chapter 2

Communicating
Your Approach

Being a good communicator is *the* most important facet of my coaching. It is the common thread that runs through my entire program. Every day before I show up at the office or practice field, I remind myself to be a good communicator, to communicate to the players and the athletic staff. Communication is the means by which you spread your philosophy throughout the program.

Communicate in Truth

When I communicate, I communicate in truth. It is absolutely crucial that you communicate the truth. If you communicate falsehood, your athletes will read right through you. If you share the truth with them from the start of the season, someday, sometime over the course of the year, you will be able to express the truth in a situation, and it will result in an opportunity to turn the tide at that moment. It may be in the middle of a tough losing streak or at the end of the year when you must win a game to get into postseason play. But if you have not been totally honest to that point, you will find yourself trying to motivate some skeptical athletes.

Be Real

You can't fake it. Be genuine with your athletes. On those days when circumstances—budget problems, a run-in with an administrator, or maybe parents complaining their child is not playing enough—cause me to show up for practice in a sour disposition, I gather my athletes and tell them honestly what type of mood I am in. It's clear to them that this is not the day to ask favors from Coach Lopez. This is not the day to request leaving 15 minutes early. In fact, if ever there were a day to do everything perfect for the first 45 minutes of practice, this would be the day.

I don't want to be phony to my athletes. I want them to trust me. By seeing my honesty about something as simplistic as a bad mood, my athletes begin to see that I'm open and shooting straight with them. Your athletes should do the same. Encourage them to be honest with you. If an athlete confesses he has had personal or academic trouble and is down about it, then I can be more sensitive in my reaction to his practice performance.

GAINING TRUST THROUGH COMMUNICATION

Our first baseman in 1992 was Danny Melendez. He was a second-round pick for the Dodgers, All-American, and invited to the national team tryouts. He was just a great athlete. Over his three-year career he heard me say many things. At times I was brutally honest. He heard me say things like, "Melendez, you're not going at it hard! You're selling this program short, not only this program but yourself as well. And not only yourself, but also your family. Every time that you don't go hard it's a reflection on that!" Danny *knew* I would be honest with him, as I had been honest in dealing with him for the three years. He heard me speak the truth about him.

Much of that truth also consisted of positive statements and praise. Danny was a tremendous athlete for us! In Omaha, he heard me say, in front of his teammates, "You know what Melendez, you're going to have a great tournament; you're going to just go off!" He knew I'd never conned him before, so he believed it. I believed, and so did he. Danny did have a great tournament and was instrumental in our championship. He also went on to be a fine professional player.

Speak the Truth, in Love

I can be a very aggressive individual. As a result, when an athlete gives less than full effort, my response can be intense. Although the message may be strong and a player might not want to hear it, I will always speak what I believe to be the truth. The Book of Ephesians says, "Speak the truth in love," and that is what I have tried to do during my coaching career. We all know that there is more than one method of communication. There are as many styles as there are coaches. Find one that you are comfortable with and have confidence in.

It is important that my athletes understand my intent in confrontational situations. The intent is to challenge them in a way that helps them grow. For example, I might say, "Son, speaking the truth in love, I think you are playing poorly right now. How are we going to make this work?" or, "Son, I want to challenge you to be as truthful with me as I am with you: are you starting to drink a little bit?" or, "I hear you're not going to class . . . I am concerned about your two-strike hitting approach . . . I think your social behavior is starting to affect your play . . . I don't think you're going about it maturely."

These are all hard issues that need to be confronted, but if they're dealt with in truth surrounded by love, you will generally be pleased with an athlete's response. A communication has taken place that allows the athlete to respond without getting too defensive, allowing the two of you to take a positive direction and maybe solve the problem.

Avoid Angry Confrontation

During my early years as a coach, I did not have the Lord in my life, and baseball was my god. My self-esteem was directly related to my team's winning percentage. Baseball was number one, and I raised my voice much more than I do now.

I berated players back then. I attacked them verbally because my self-esteem was tied to the next win or loss, and I was going to make sure that they were successful. I intimidated them. This was in my early days of coaching, and I am not proud of my actions. It's a fact of my life, but I no longer do it.

My voice is still raised when practices aren't going well, but I no longer berate the players. Now I separate the person from the behavior. I make this very clear to my athletes. "Son, I am not mad at you, but at your behavior. I'm angry at the apparent lack of spirit for the game that has caused you to forget your assignments, to not hustle, and to be apathetic about our season. I'm not upset with you; be assured of that. But I'm ready to go to war with whatever is causing you to perform like you're performing. Realize I want you to succeed!" I try to make this clear to my athletes by communicating it to them at all times.

LOCATION AND COMMUNICATION

The distractions of Malibu are numerous. The beach environment, the great weather, the celebrities, and the L.A. lifestyle all create options for athletes other than baseball. As a result, athletes often are not at their mental best. At Pepperdine I had a name for it: the Malibu Flu. It was a sickness we could not tolerate if we were to be champions.

In Gainesville the distractions are a bit different, but the problem is the same. At the University of Florida, you're saddled with incredible expectations, resulting in a fear of failure or even success. The athletic department is very successful, which can create a spirit of fear in your athletes. We refer to this as the Gainesville Ghost, and we attack this spirit just as hard as we fought the Malibu Flu!

Some coaches communicate by not speaking. I have seen this happen. Coaches may say little to their athletes, but communicate just as effectively through body language. Athletes learn to determine if their coach is pleased or dissatisfied by body language alone.

It gets back to being comfortable with yourself. I'm comfortable with a more aggressive and competitive style. This probably results from my past gang involvement and athletic experiences. I also insist on honesty because of what I learned in the con-man environment of the streets. Get rid of the b.s. and be specific about how you want something done. That's what I do with my athletes, showing them exactly how to do it right and then letting them know specifically what was good or poor in their execution. You need to be clear.

Communication on the Field

A coach on the field is like a teacher in the classroom. Every verbal and nonverbal message you send is open to interpretation. This is the most visual expression of your communication style. You're exposed for all the world to see, so you have to be mindful of the immediate response you want to get.

Communicating With Players

There is a distinct difference between how I communicate with athletes in the early part of the year and in the later spring. During the first couple of weeks I am hard, very hard. I am more vocal than ever. If you were to ask one of my athletes, "How's Coach Lopez in the fall?" he would probably respond by saying, "He's a real stickler who raises his

voice often and seems to always be mad." Then ask the same athlete how I am in the spring. He would respond that I'm an easy-going guy, a different coach than in the fall. The stronger you are early, the less that might be needed later.

This approach is by design. The game itself is pressure, and I don't want my guys feeling any excess pressure from me during the regular season. I want them to be loose and easy. When I communicate in the spring, I communicate very slowly, very poised, in a relaxed, easy manner so that when I do raise my voice I will get the desired response quickly.

In the fall or early weeks of a season, I may raise my voice 15 times in one practice. I may raise my voice 15 times five days in a row, simply because I want to set the tempo and create the intensity necessary. A typical baseball practice is not going to get the heart rate very high, at least not compared to a ninth-inning, game-on-the-line situation. I try to get that heartbeat going so when we face a tough situation in the spring, our athletes have already experienced it and know how to respond.

One area I believe I have improved on is how I control my tone of voice. Even in a stressful situation, I will keep my tone controlled. Yes, I will raise it a few decibels when we're not playing well, but it's still controlled. Even in simple instructions I'll tend to increase my voice level to raise the athlete's heartbeat.

Communicating With Assistants

It's important that assistant coaches be given enough responsibility. I always will let them know when I need help in a certain area. We'll put our heads together to try to get some things worked out. Communicate how important assistants' input is, how vital they are to the success of the program.

We try to meet in the morning when we can within a busy schedule. I don't have a particular meeting time set for each day. But it's extremely important that assistant coaches know what the head coach is thinking. It's important to let your assistants know when you are pleased and when you're not, when it's going well and when things are not going so well. I've made a commitment to never embarrass an assistant coach in front of the ball club. That is one of the worst actions a head coach can ever take.

If I were to summarize communicating with my assistant coaches, I would once again turn to the wisdom of the scriptures. Paradox theory is one of the Lord's most fundamental teachings. He taught that if you want to be first, be last. If you want to be great, be small. If you want to be strong, be weak. I'm sensitive to my assistant coaches. I regard my assistants with high esteem. Assistant coaches' jobs are tough, without much recognition. Therefore, I attempt to give them responsibility and make them feel as important as anyone in our program.

Communicating With Umpires

Umpires are authority; therefore, it is important to treat them as such. We instruct our athletes to address an umpire by "Sir" or first name if they are on a first-name basis. To refer to an umpire by "blue" shows a lack of respect. I require the same standard of myself. Whether we like it or not, umpires are in a position of authority, and we should respond accordingly. Please understand, I do not always agree with umpires. Sometimes I will disagree with a call, and sometimes I will disagree with their mechanics. In general, though, I believe they do a great job and give an honest effort.

The best statement to make to an umpire when you have a disagreement is, "Tell me what you saw." If he answers quickly and specifically, acknowledge his call and go back to the dugout. He's trying to do the job. But if he is uncertain and hesitates when he answers, you should express concern over the call in addition to his effort. He's not doing his job.

I've never used profanity with an umpire. That is a fact of which I am proud. Yes, I've been ejected from a few games for contesting calls that I felt resulted from sloppy umpiring. But I've never used profanity in being thrown out. It should *never* happen.

🔘 RESPECT FOR THE MEN IN BLUE

I was ejected in the middle innings of a game back in 1985, and the disagreement between the umpire and me was very heated. When I returned home that night, I sat down and wrote the gentleman a letter. It went something like this: "I hope that you will accept that in a competitive situation sometimes things happen that you would not allow to happen under calmer circumstances. The next time I see you there will be no hard feelings. I hope that you will be professional because I give you my word that I will be. You had your job to do. I respect your job and although I may not agree with your action, I respect your position of authority. Looking forward to seeing you at the next ball game. Sincerely, Andy Lopez." I see this umpire regularly, and he says to this day it is the only such letter he's received in the 20 years he has been umpiring.

I do not share this as a "holier than thou" story. I share it because I think we coaches need to do it more often. Let's face it, games can get heated. But neither the players nor the assistants should question umpires: only the head coach should do that. It's my job if I feel an umpire needs to be questioned. I make the umpires aware that for two hours we approach the game as if it's more important than life or death. Umpires who've worked our games and have heard me argue calls

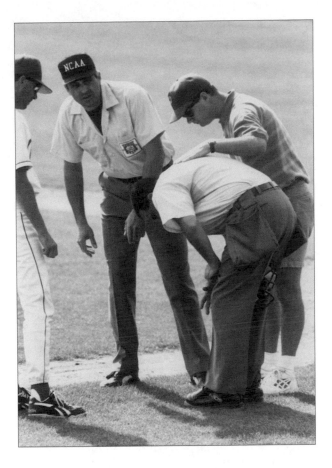

understand that. Andy Lopez is being aggressive, and an hour following the game we'll probably be able to laugh about it.

Should a coach try to intimidate umpires, to coerce them, hopefully gaining that extra edge? I don't think so. First, a good umpire will not be intimidated. Second, I read a long time ago that a team usually reflects the head coach. If you are in the business of intimidating umpires, your athletes will try to do the same.

Once again, an umpire (good or bad) is in a position of authority. If a young man observes or is taught that intimidation is a means to success, what will keep him from intimidating, say, a police officer, a bank loan officer, or any other person in a position of authority? We should be aware that we help these athletes prepare for everyday life. If we teach them to intimidate people in order to get ahead, we set them on a collision course. Someday they will run into the individual who won't be intimidated, and that young man might lose a job, may break up his marriage, or may end his career, simply because when he was 15 he saw you intimidate umpires, and thought that was how to succeed. We need to set better examples than that.

If an umpire has not hustled into position and has made a bad call, I'll let him know, *and* if he's made a good effort and a good call, I'll let him know. Several times I've gone on the field, pulled an upset player away from an umpire, and told the umpire he made a good call. Players must know where they stand. It's your job, not theirs, to express yourself about good and bad calls. Teach them not to worry about them, to focus instead on what they can control.

Communicating With Other Coaches

There are many reasons for communicating with an opposing coach, including professional activities such as scheduling, pregame arrangements, clinics, and game-day interactions.

I find it easiest to communicate with coaches who do not have their entire self-esteem wrapped up in their win-loss records. Sure, we (myself included) all have egos. But the ego is less likely to block communication if coaches base their self-esteem on more than the outcome of their games.

Take the initiative to communicate with other coaches. Good communication will create a foundation of respect when the competitive arena gets intense. It can also create a support system with some of your peers in which you can share thoughts and ideas with each other. We should also like the example it gives to our athletes over the course of the years.

Show mutual respect in your relationships with other coaches. This is developed through communication over time. I have developed great respect over the years for Arizona's Jerry Kindall. He is a class individual and has had tremendous success both on and off the field. We have similar goals for the development of our athletes and programs. Our regard for one another has grown to the point that we acknowledge praying for the other's program. Now that's respect!

Communication off the Field

Communicating within your program takes place constantly. Some of the more personal and important moments happen off the field, not only with athletes, but also with parents, community, media, and administration.

Communicating With Players

Some of the most effective times of communicating with your athletes will be off the field. In high school, I met individually with my athletes on three occasions each year. Right before the season I would meet each player and establish where he fit into our program. At this time, I would specifically define his role. Then I would meet midway through the year, usually around spring vacation, to redefine his role or continue to support what was established earlier. Finally, we would meet following season's end to explain what he needed to do to enhance or maintain his position in the program.

At the college level, I meet individually with my athletes twice a year for 15 to 30 minutes. Some go longer and some go shorter. We meet at the end of the fall season, which is typically during the first week of December, and then we meet at the end of the spring season. These meetings are important and can't be ignored. You need to discuss, on an individual basis, where each returning athlete stands within the program and what each needs to do to improve.

Typically, a small percentage of the individual player meeting time is spent talking about baseball. More often the time is spent discussing academics. Why is the athlete struggling or being successful in a particular class? Has he pursued a tutor? If I see a tendency in an athlete that may indicate his social life is becoming less disciplined, I can address it within the context of these meetings on a private basis. It's also a great time to praise an athlete personally. It's important for your athletes to realize that you understand there is more going on in their lives than chasing a ball around the baseball field. And they need to be held accountable for their activities.

These formal meetings, combined with an open-door policy, keep the lines of communication open. My office is always open for the athletes to stop by and discuss what's on their minds. An open-door policy encourages your athletes to initiate such talks.

Communicating With Parents

The area of parent communication is one of the saddest areas I've witnessed in all my years of coaching. It's probably the one area that's deteriorated more than any over my career. I wish I could say, "I've never had a problem with a parent." I cannot. And no coach is immune to the problem.

LESS THAN 24 HOURS

In 1992, we were in a Division I championship game on national network TV. That Saturday, at around 3:00 in the afternoon, the season ended with us winning a national title. Saturday evening was full of media interviews and lots of celebration.

Since we'd been in Omaha for 14 days and wanted to get back home, we took a 6:00 a.m. Sunday flight to Los Angeles.

At that time, I lived in Thousand Oaks, which is roughly 45 minutes from the airport. I arrived home by 12:00 noon, less than 24 hours after the event. At 3:00 that afternoon, the day after winning the national title and finishing with a 48-11 record, I received a phone call from a parent who began with, "I'm concerned about how you used my son this year in the program and would like to know his status for next season." I wish I could tell you I smiled and said, "Well, let's talk about it," but I did not. My response was strong and clear.

The unfortunate part was that this parent's son loved our program. Although he had not played much, he understood that he was young and that he did not fit into the everyday lineup. This experience put parental relations into perspective for me. There is absolutely no place for this type of parental involvement. Parents are to be fans and supportive of their children. They are *not* to coach.

I keep relationships with parents at a professional level now. I am cordial and friendly, but keep a healthy distance. I know some coaches can be very close with the parents of their athletes. For me, as long as the athlete is in my program, I feel the need to maintain a professional, not personal, relationship with parents. My wife understands this as well since she is more accessible, particularly on game days. No matter how close you get with parents, there always comes a time that you make an unpopular coaching decision that sours your relationship with them.

Unfortunately, I learned this the hard way. At various times we've had negative parental influences in the stands, in the community, and within the team. Parent-inspired complaints can be compared to cancer. If they aren't caught early, they'll spread.

I communicate this stance to the athletes from day one. The head coach places much less priority on developing friendships with players' families than he does on helping the players to improve on the field, to study, to graduate, and to become good citizens. My players understand that Coach Lopez has a wife and kids, a family of his own.

That is not to say that I don't want to be a part of their family. On the contrary, if a friendship develops, we will all be better for it. But the friendship probably will not develop to its fullest until the day the athlete stops playing. During the player's career, my relationship with his family is kept professional. It works. I now have great friendships with several former players' families.

KEY POINT FROM COACH K.

A friend shared a *Sports Illustrated* article in which the interviewer sat waiting for Coach Mike Krzyzewski to get off the phone. As he hung up, Coach K. smiled and explained that it was a parent of one of his athletes, concerned that he was not playing his son in his "natural" position. Keep in mind this was following a national championship year.

Coach K. responded that he was fortunate to coach athletes who had parents who were heavily involved in their sons' lives. More importantly, he went on to note that it was unfortunate that they didn't realize that at the college level it is time to allow one's son to face challenges on his own, that college is the time to start becoming a man.

I agree with Coach K.! Boys will only become men when they are given some freedom to face challenges on their own, succeed or fail, and react in an appropriate manner.

Communicating With the Community

I understand that many coaches have great booster clubs and relationships with local businesses. I understand how this can be necessary at certain levels due to financial or other considerations. Yet I had a particular experience that taught me to approach such community involvement with caution.

WITH STRINGS ATTACHED

In my years at Cal State Dominguez Hills, I was approached by a gentleman who wanted to help raise money for the program. Since we were hurting for money I said, "Please do." He raised some money and then offered to help in recruiting. He was involved with local players, so I also allowed him this opportunity. I did this because I felt this man was genuinely concerned with the program at Dominguez.

Then one day he visited my office and presented all that he had done for me and said that now it was my turn to help him. He was a summer league coach, and he wanted our top pitcher to play for his team instead of traveling to the Alaska Collegiate League for the summer. I knew the athlete and our program would benefit more if he went to Alaska and couldn't let this gentleman leverage me into having my pitcher stay local. I realized that the generosity he had shown the program came with a price.

When you communicate with the community, it is important that they realize two things. One, you definitely need and desire their support. But two, there can be no strings attached, no cost involved. That might be bold, but don't take it wrong. We all need the support of communities, administrators, admission directors, and boosters. I strive to make it very clear in my communicating with parents and community that I need their help. But our success will not be solely credited to their support; it is a joint effort. As head coach, you should *not* be controlled by any booster club, parent group, or community organization. You should be guided by *your* philosophy, experiences, and plans for your program.

Communicating With the Media

Media coverage of a program changes from level to level. Yet the impact of media coverage is similar at all levels. Quality media coverage can create interest in your program. It will give you exposure to the community (local, statewide, even national). This can influence your program by attracting possible recruits, helping to raise money, creating a positive image for your program, and improving the self-image of your athletes.

My number one recommendation with regard to the media is this: Be available. Understand that members of the media work hard at their jobs and that you can make it easier or more difficult for them. Help them do their jobs. The more accessible and more cooperative you are, the more likely you will receive the type of coverage we all believe our programs deserve. This is essential in the major media markets (e.g., southern California) where competition for exposure is high, as well as in small towns.

Another important rule is to keep the media informed. Give them as much information as you have, including statistics, schedule, upcoming events, fund-raisers, and possible special-interest stories concerning your team. The media is always looking for new angles and ideas.

If you feel you're being slighted by the coverage your program is getting, make a phone call. Set up appointments with members of your media and ask them how you can help them do their jobs better. Find out what they want from you. Be sincere and follow through. Your relationship with the media will benefit.

MASS MEDIA 1992

Playing in the same media market with the Dodgers, Angels, Lakers, Rams, UCLA, USC, and other high-profile sports programs can limit day-to-day exposure with newspapers, TV, and radio. But we were thrust into the spotlight following our national championship. Fortunately, our sports information director, Mike Zapolski, helped me handle all the media demands on my time. We did our best to honor all requests. It gave me a much better appreciation of the presence and powerful messages that can be shared through the media.

The many media opportunities following the championship season gave me the opportunity to share principles that are important in my life—things that I believe in, including views on the working profession, athletics, values, and personal faith.

The media attention has been magnified at the University of Florida. Several staff people organize not only my media contacts, but my speaking engagements as well. It is a major part of a Florida coach's life. These are all opportunities to share my faith and my belief in athletics and academics.

Communicating With Administrators

For those of us doing our coaching in the educational arena, we must also find time to be available to our administrators. They're as busy as you are, so take the initiative. Make an appointment with those who are in charge of your institution. Share your philosophies. Let them know how your program *complements* the goals of the institution. By doing so, you give your administrators the opportunity to establish confidence in you and your approach to your program.

Although involvement with teachers and administrators is important, you can't rely on them to do your job or make it any easier. At Mira Costa I discovered that it was not until the baseball program began to win that the faculty and staff wanted to be involved. If you develop a disciplined and winning program with good students and citizens, you'll get faculty support. But to reach this point, you have to address and eliminate the negative influences along the way.

CONFRONTING A PROBLEM

In 1992, we were in the top 10 in the entire nation, as high as 3rd. The only time we really dropped out of the top ten was to fall to 11th. We traveled to a three-game series in our conference and won two out of three. We won the first game 14-0; we won the second game 3-2 in a real nail biter; and we lost the last game 11-4. At the airport before the flight home I noticed six of our athletes sitting off by themselves, laughing and having a good time. The majority of my club was in another area, obviously disappointed about the results of this weekend trip. They felt like they should have won three games. Looking at the two groups of athletes, one might have thought one group had a bad weekend and the others had a great one.

More troubling to me was that the athletes who appeared most upbeat were the top players in the lineup. These were key guys! The rest of the athletes were the non-scholarship guys who weren't going to sign professional contracts and had no chance of making the Olympic team.

What these six athletes were saying by their behavior was that their future was bright regardless of the team results. Why should they care if we performed poorly and lost? They showed little concern for the club.

When we arrived on campus, I had everybody get in their practice gear except for the six athletes. They remained in their travel attire, coat and tie. There we were on the dark field (our facility had no lights) at 11:00 p.m. on a Saturday night. We had the team run a series of sprints and drills while the six players stood watching in their coats and ties.

Then I finally communicated my frustration. We had six players who had become prima donnas, and that undermined our whole program. All the star athletes were on good scholarships, but many of their teammates—who were standing before them sweating and dirty from the workout—had no scholarships and relied on financial aid to help them through. I communicated to those six athletes that they had begun to sell out their teammates, who were working at least as hard as they were. Their own interests had taken priority over the program's best interest. They thought through the painful comments and realized I had told them the truth. By confronting and correcting the problem, we reunited the club and had a great year.

Even if the truth is sometimes difficult or hurtful, honesty will mend the hurt and eliminate the scar. This honesty may be at the expense of a few, but it will result in good for the whole.

Summary

A winning coach is a communicating coach. This chapter discussed these aspects of good communication:

- Being a good communicator is the most important aspect of coaching.
- Be totally honest in your communication.
- Be firm in your communication during the early season to set the proper intensity level.
- Give assistants authority with responsibility and tell them of their importance to the program.
- Treat all umpires with the respect that a position of authority should receive. Do not try to intimidate.
- Have specific one-on-one meetings with your athletes. Communicate about areas of their lives outside baseball.
- Keep parental involvement at the professional level. Let friendships grow fully following an athlete's career.
- Ensure that community involvement comes with no strings attached.
- Help the media do their job. Be available.
- If necessary, take the initiative to communicate with administrators about your program.

Chapter 3

Motivating Players

I have been told by former players that I was a good motivator. But do not think of me as a "rah-rah" type of coach. In my programs motivation is a by-product of positive teaching and consistent rewards and punishments for all.

All MVPs

We want every one of our athletes to feel he has value. Our policy is that we never name a most valuable player at the end of the season. We may establish an outstanding offensive player, an outstanding defensive player, an outstanding pitcher or coach's award, but we never name a most valuable player. Everyone has value. Everyone has a special role. This motivates all involved because they know they are important to the team.

At the high school level we made the no-MVP concept a major issue at our very first meeting. From that point forward, we were consistent in not showing favoritism to certain top athletes. At the college level, we let players know our thinking on this from day one of recruiting, which is the first phone call. We want the athlete to know that regardless of his scholarship, he will be valuable to the program. He will be treated fairly and truthfully.

This becomes even more important to the non-scholarship player. It's easy to motivate a full-ride player: "Sign here and let's go to battle!" But it's usually the non-scholarship athletes who make or break your program.

These will be the players who give the program depth, so it's very important that they know up front and throughout the year that they have tremendous value to your ball club. Any athlete convinced he has value is a motivated athlete.

⚾ BULLPEN CATCHER

In 1992, a young man named John Sacchi was in our program. His story illustrates why we do not have an MVP. A fantastic kid who rarely played, John was an infielder who ended up being our bullpen catcher because, well, we needed one! He caught the bullpen the entire year—no complaining, no bitterness, just the willingness to play the role.

An outsider might say he'd played no role, but John had a tremendous role in getting our pitchers ready. That's not an easy task. He may not have caught the title game, but he got the pitchers ready to go into the game.

The greatest memory I have of Omaha, other than my parents being there, was watching John Sacchi celebrate. You can see him on the bottom of the pile in the celebration photograph that was published in *Sports Illustrated*: a young man with no playing time, but of great value as a person and to our program.

Rewards and Punishments

Anybody in a position of leadership realizes that some motivation is a result of rewarding or punishing those in positions below you. Most people will respond to being rewarded for desired behavior. Some need to know that punishment will result if their behavior is not acceptable.

On the Field

Our athletes are rewarded with playing time. We don't have motivational T-shirts or award stickers for their batting helmets. We don't have a player of the week. Those that do not start are rewarded with the opportunity to be on the ball club. Athletes in our programs understand their roles and understand the value of being a part of the team. Hard work and proper behavior are rewarded by being on the roster.

We reward our athletes with game day. Practices belong to the coaches. The games belong to the players. We demand so much at practice that once game day rolls around, we make it clear that it is their day to enjoy. The

game is theirs to shine in front of their parents and friends. No matter what horrible mistake players might make, we will never embarrass them in a game environment.

At practice, the coaching staff takes charge. We may raise our voices and point out players' mistakes in front of their peers if they are not getting the job done. This happens only in a practice environment, in the privacy of the ball club. It is very much like a family setting where tough love and honesty are necessary parts of growth.

I'm not big on physical punishment. We seldom run our club for punishment. (We would like running to be considered positive!) I would rather deny an athlete his practice time or playing time than to punish him physically.

If I notice an athlete not going about his practice responsibilities as well as I would like, I'll send him home. I will call him over and calmly excuse him. He won't be allowed to disrupt our practice. As soon as one athlete influences his teammates by not going at it hard, he has totally disrupted the practice. Our athletes are well aware that the coaching staff will not permit one player to bring down the whole team.

This policy motivates athletes to do things right. No one wants to be known as being unable to function with peers. Most athletes are sharp enough to realize that if they are not allowed to practice, it may eventually affect their playing time.

I do not carry punishment over to the next day. The undesired behavior is dealt with, and a change of attitude is usually the player's response. I find this approach a great motivator.

Mistakes of Omission and Commission

The great former UCLA basketball coach, John Wooden, has shared his keen insights on the subject of mistakes. Coach Wooden differentiated between mistakes of commission and omission. Mistakes of commission are active, physical mistakes. These are positive mistakes in the sense that the player who commits them is striving to do his best. Mistakes of commission are aggressive mistakes. Getting thrown out stretching a single into a double is an example. Even walking a

hitter with the bases loaded is a mistake of commission. It's a physical mistake.

Mistakes of omission include mental mistakes, lack of work ethic, and improper approach. These cannot be tolerated! Not covering on a bunt defense is an act of omission. Missing signs is omission. Throwing to the wrong base or missing a cutoff man falls in the same category. In terms of rewards and punishments, those have to be addressed so they do not continue. Mistakes of omission we punish verbally and sometimes by taking players off the field.

At Florida, believe it or not, we reward mistakes of commission. If it's an aggressive mistake, we'll reward it. I verbally reward the athlete who made an aggressive mistake. I do this because I want my team to be aggressive. I would like my players to know they have the freedom to make a physical mistake, but that there are consequences to a mental mistake. You must deal with the two differently.

Off the Field

As a younger coach, I had many more rules regarding off-field behavior than I do now—many dos and don'ts, mostly don'ts. Now I have more suggestions than rules.

I believe in making strong recommendations to our athletes as to what they should do. I would rather recommend how they should act on road trips or how they should pursue practice the next day—no threats, no black-and-white consequences. At some point in their lives, players must take responsibility for their actions. It's neither healthy nor possible for a coach to control every decision his athletes make by having a rule and penalty assigned to all options.

I strongly encourage my athletes to be on time and do things right, and doing things right includes abstaining from alcohol, drugs, smoking, and so on. Most athletes respond positively to this approach. By avoiding a rigid rule system you avoid backing yourself into a corner when it comes to enforcement. A rule system with rigid consequences forces you to discipline in a predetermined manner. I'm not afraid of disciplining my athletes. If someone fails to follow my suggestions, we will make an adjustment. I like to have flexibility while making those adjustments.

When asked by a reporter regarding his differing treatment to various athletes, former Dallas Cowboy coach Jimmy Johnson responded, "You bet I treat my athletes different. Athletes deserve to be treated different. Those that hustle and strive with diligence to do what is expected have far more grace than those that fall short of my expectations on a daily basis."

Teach, Don't Punish

Our athletes grow up in a society that does little to develop trust. Newspaper reports aren't always true. TV commercials are sometimes deceiving. Every time you hear a story, you wonder if it's legitimate.

In addition, your athletes have grown up in a society in which the single-parent family is the norm. Divorce rates are out of control. You may represent the first father-figure for several of your athletes. We're dealing with young lives that are coming from different backgrounds and fighting different wars, sometimes with no established rule system. If you come off as hard and rigid, you may needlessly run your athletes off.

Our responsibility as coaches is to teach our players that there are rules, yet to make sure there is an avenue of growth within these rules. In this environment we can teach (or suggest) what is right and what is wrong. If we can do that, think of the impact.

Institution First

I adhere 100% to whatever rules my institution sets for our student athletes. Our athletes are students first, and we make no special exceptions in that area. At Florida we have standards set for our athletes. If players fall short, they suffer the institution's consequences. Whatever my administration proposes, I am going to live by it.

If given the opportunity to have input, I will suggest an avenue in which the athlete has an opportunity to correct his wrong without losing something important to him (i.e., baseball, education). In this process we will try to teach him lessons that will help. Limit punishment and teach instead.

PUSHED TO THE LIMIT

In my second year at Pepperdine, I took away a scholarship from an athlete. He had been drinking on a road trip. We confronted him and felt we did a good job of educating him. We then gave him an opportunity to correct the wrong. Later, he was caught drinking again. We had given him every opportunity to get ahold of this problem and be accountable—counselor involvement, parental involvement, and so on. Yet he broke the rule again.

At this point, we felt he had to be responsible for his actions. We told him he could remain in the program, but would lose his scholarship at the end of the year. If it occurred again, he would be removed from the program immediately. Unfortunately, at the end of the season that's what we did.

I share this story as an example of asking athletes to be accountable while creating an environment for growth. For some kids it may be the only time that they've been in that type of situation, so I believe we need to give them a second chance.

Self-Motivated Athletes

We all want athletes who aren't preoccupied with awards. I want an athlete who has a tremendous passion for excellence, to the point where he's excelling. Every day he's challenging himself. Every day he's going about his work in a way that can only be described as self-motivated. This athlete really doesn't care about the ring that comes with the national title. He isn't focused on the certificate that says All-American. He has a drive for success, but is indifferent to the individual achievement of it all. He's an athlete who is more concerned with what he is doing (the process) than he is with what he will be when he is finished.

Coaching Motives

So how do you get your athletes motivated intrinsically? We must look at ourselves first. A lot of coaches are extrinsically motivated to moving to the next level, getting a better job, winning a championship, and getting a shoe or bat contract. Ironic, isn't it? We get on our athletes to be self-motivated, but fail to look at ourselves.

How many of us are self-motivated? By that, I mean: How many of us are motivated from a pure heart? Are you motivated to prepare your athletes for the next level of baseball and life away from baseball, or are you concerned solely with winning and moving on to another job? There's nothing wrong with wanting to move up, but don't use your athletes to get there.

Self-motivated coaches are those who do their very best in their present environments. We need to check our motives for working so hard. My motive should be to help prepare my athletes to do battle in life for the next 50 years in the workforce. This is a constant, important motivator for me.

Paint a Picture of Reality

Too many young athletes are living in a fantasy world. Their goal is to get a full scholarship or a pro contract. The truth of the matter is that very few *ever* get these opportunities.

The reality is that there are only 11 NCAA baseball scholarships per program. Even if athletes work, work, and work some more, they still may not get an athletic scholarship offer. If I were still a high school coach, I'd make sure my athletes understood that the majority of those 11 scholarships will go to pitchers. Pitching is the name of the game for all levels. So if an athlete is not a pitcher, he'd better understand the truth, and the truth is that he needs to study. He needs to be academically sound so he may become more attractive to college programs. If he qualifies for financial aid, he'd better get the paperwork done and get it done *yesterday*.

When dealing with an athlete, I might say, "If you don't play well, you'll probably not get a chance at pro ball." This may seem harsh, but I would rather be truthful than to continue to allow an athlete to live in a sugarcoated fantasy. There are so few $100,000 signees out there. If a player doesn't go about his work responsibilities properly, it will catch up to him and he may lose his spot to another recruit. He may eliminate himself by lack of motivation.

I often tell my athletes, "I'm not in the business of bursting bubbles, but here is the reality." Whether I'm speaking about pro ball, their chances to start, or an evaluation of their abilities, I want to give them a good dose of reality. Typically the message is to forget pro ball and instead get motivated to do things right (on and off the field) so players can be successful now *and* following their athletic careers.

Those who respond to the truth tend to go far beyond our expectations for them. I've been fortunate enough to see such athletes succeed. Athletes who get turned off by the truth will not perform for you in the long run. They will run home to tell Mom and Dad or their last coach to gain support for their fantasy. Those who do not accept the truth usually have someone coauthoring their fantasy. They will run into a problem somewhere down the line.

⚾ LESSON FROM PETER

There always comes a time over the course of the season when your ball club seems to be tentative. They seem hesitant as they approach the game. They need to be motivated to get more aggressive, to start doing something!

While I'm encouraging them to hustle 100% and not to be concerned about failure, I share the well-known story of Peter walking on the water. The disciples were in a boat out on a lake when a storm kicked up. They were frightened. Especially when they saw the Lord walking on the water out to meet them. When Peter realized it was Jesus, he invited himself out to meet him. Peter stepped out of the boat, but became fearful and began to sink. The moment he took his eyes off the Lord he sank.

In sharing this story with the team, I emphasize the courage it took to step out of the boat. What a great lesson. I ask the athletes to step out of their own boats, to get started and have courage. Failure may sometimes come, but it's the courage to get started that counts.

No Mind Games

My athletes *know* I won't try to fool them. When I tell them I'm pleased with their performance, they know I'm pleased. No fake motivation here. When I appear to be angry, our athletes know I'm angry. They know I'm not one to play mind games to motivate. When an athlete hears the truth in criticism or praise, he can trust what I'm saying—he gets really excited, really motivated. When he

hears the truth in criticism, he knows he must make an adjustment.

At one point in our 1992 season, I became painfully aware that our approach as a ball club was lacking. Our play was such that my focus shifted from going to Omaha to trying just to win our conference.

I met with the team and shared that they could stop thinking about the College World Series, and that I, as a coach, had to stop dreaming about the Series. We were not working hard enough. I told them we had absolutely no right to think about postseason. Our work ethic was inadequate, short of what we needed.

That might crush a ball club if I had not been truthful from the start of the year. But I had. So it quickened them a little. They took it to heart. It motivated them—no mind games, just simple truth. If I'm called a great motivator, if I've ever motivated anybody over the last 18 years, it's simply that I've told them the truth.

Designed for Failure

Baseball is a game designed for failure. The participants in the game of baseball are destined to fail. It's designed to single players out and embarrass them. It's a complex game. Failing 7 out of 10 times as a hitter, a player is considered a star. Doing it long enough, he finds himself in the Hall of Fame!

People in the stands see two opponents playing against one another, competing. But, the two teams are really playing the same opponent. The opponent is the game of baseball. We ask our players not to play against an opponent; their challenge is the game.

From a motivational standpoint, we want our athletes to make the game their focus: to understand that it is designed to make them fail *and* to challenge them to rebound from failure. Players must walk through our outfield gates each game that they suit up in a spirit that they accept the challenge of rebounding from failure. They will fail. A successful ball club or individual recognizes that and understands it is how they respond that counts. Baseball is an amazing game, full of ups and downs, made for players and coaches who can stay motivated through it all.

Summary

Motivating athletes is a must for any organization. I motivate through the following methods:

- Make every athlete valuable. Eliminate or limit the concept of MVP.
- Begin motivating with the first recruiting call or first meeting.
- Reward and punish with playing time or practice time. Physical punishment is a questionable approach.
- Reward or praise aggressive mistakes. Mistakes of commission are preferable to acts of omission.
- Make rules or suggestions, yet allow for teaching and growth opportunities within the content of your discipline. Support your institution's policies.
- Monitor your motivation as a coach; then you can check your player's motivation.
- Coach with a pure heart.
- Motivate with the truth. Lasting motivation comes from being honest with your players from day one.
- The game of baseball is designed for failure. It's how we respond to failure that separates us from others.

Chapter 4

Building a Baseball Program

Regardless of whether you are starting from scratch, rebuilding an existing program, or simply maintaining a successful one, there is far more to coaching than organizing your players. Unfortunately for most of us, the majority of our time is spent on administrative details such as fund-raising, soliciting community support, recruiting, and monitoring academics. Actual on-field coaching (which we all love most) is the area that often gets squeezed. Administrative details may be annoying, but to ensure a successful program they must be attended to.

Building a program is not easy. It takes diligent effort over time. I love the Navy Seabee slogan: "The difficult we will do im-

mediately; the impossible may take a little longer." Too often we focus on the problems and how hard we have it instead of the opportunity we have in baseball and in impacting the lives of young men. Remember what the Lord told a weary and complaining prophet Jeremiah: "If you have run with men on foot and they have worn you out, how then can you compete with the horses of excellence?" In other words, "If you think this is bad, how are you going to cope when things really get tough?"

As coaches, as well as players, we can often be satisfied with mediocrity. Going beyond average is difficult and takes much effort. However, it's a choice we make. Are we going to compete against the horses of excellence or be welcomed into the open and embracing arms of mediocrity? It's our choice!

This chapter will help us focus on areas that sometimes frustrate coaches. We will discuss getting the job, acquiring the necessary skills to be a coach, gaining support from others, hiring assistants, and organizing the recruiting process.

Getting the Job

I've never actually pursued any jobs outside of the insurance salesman position which I mentioned in chapter 1. It's amazing how the Lord has guided and blessed me throughout my coaching career. Still, there are some things you can do to put yourself in position for coaching jobs. Here are some ideas for all coaches, young and old, to keep in mind when seeking a job.

Big Time Is Where You Are

When I coached at the high school level, I was not pursuing a college job. I took my first job at Mira Costa High School with one thought in mind, to be the very best high school coach I could be. No time was wasted worrying about my next job. If a college job was a result of my hard work, fine, but it wasn't something I pursued or thought about.

When a job offer came from Cal State Dominguez Hills, an NCAA Division II program, I accepted it with one idea in mind—to be the best college coach I could be. I never pursued a Division I job. I simply wanted to be the best I could be where I was. Cal State Dominguez Hills was big-time to me.

The effort applied and success achieved at Cal State Dominguez Hills prompted the administration at Pepperdine University to approach me to be their head baseball coach. After six years at Pepperdine, the University of Florida pursued me as their new head coach. At no time was I concerned about moving on to a professional baseball position or even a college program with a bigger-time image than Pepperdine. My goal has always been to be the best where I am. And Florida is a challenging, big-time position.

If you're a freshman coach at your high school and do a good job at that level, someday you'll be the varsity coach. People will notice you. If you're the varsity coach and you do a great job, someone will notice you at the college level. If you're a college assistant, do a tremendous job and you'll move up. The coaching ladder will take care of itself.

Acquiring Tools

Supporting this concept is an even more practical thought. Prepare yourself for your next position by acquiring the necessary academic tools. Get whatever level of college education will help you be effective and employable. Some high schools want their coaches to have a teaching credential. Some colleges require head coaches to have a master's degree.

Do what needs to be done professionally so that when the opportunity comes you are prepared and qualified to accept the position. It's good to have vision and to be goal-oriented. Just remember not to let it interfere with doing a good job where you are, and pursue the necessary academic credentials.

I see many young coaches who are overzealous in meeting the right people. I see them writing notes to coaches all over the country, shaking hands with everyone they can, all with the motive of someday getting a job. It's certainly good to meet people. It's also great to send a note of appreciation or congratulations to a peer. But have sincere motives; otherwise you'll just turn off the people you're trying to impress.

"With many words and many dreams there is emptiness," reads one proverb. Don't get caught up in trying to say the right things, to the right people, at just the right time and place. Don't spend all your time dreaming of a Division I job. Make the most out of the present.

Be quality where you are! Do a great job in your current environment. Good news travels fast! By the way, the opposite is also true. Remember that good news travels fast, but bad news travels faster!

Gaining Support

You can't go it alone. Don't try to be a one-man show. Regardless of the level, you must have a supporting cast. Administrators, alumni, the community, assistant coaches, and even your players—they all must respect you. Your number one goal is to gain people's respect. The support will follow.

Administrative Support

I can probably cover this topic by sharing an experience of a good friend of mine. His first head coaching position was in a small college setting. He was only 24 and might have been in a little over his head. Common sense told him he needed to get some direction on how to go about running the program.

The first week on the job he made appointments with the admissions director, the financial aid director, his athletic director, and even the school's maintenance supervisor. His main questions were, "How do I do my job relative to your area?" and "What do I do to make your job easier regarding my program and athletes?" The financial aid director told him it was the first time in her 20 years that any coach had approached her in this manner. Do you think he gained respect and support? Instantly. He's now 12 years on the job, and his relationship in his school's aid department and other departments just keeps getting better.

Keep in mind that your baseball program is not the only show on campus. Respect the positions of authority of those around you. You need to be responsible to your administration. As a coach, *you* are an administrator to your athletes. I don't know about you, but I sure wouldn't like it if my players were constantly fighting me or questioning my actions. Your athletic director is in a similar position.

It's fine to challenge something if you believe your program needs improvement in an area. You need to do what you believe is best for your team, but do so while maintaining respect for your administrator's authority.

Player Support

Players don't support you just because you have the title of head coach. Get rid of that illusion. Gaining players' respect is something most of us must work at diligently.

You must be knowledgeable about the game. As a head coach, you must have knowledge of all areas—pitching, hitting, defense, and offense. You must show that you have a grasp of the game. Be knowledgeable. Discipline yourself. Teach yourself. Work hard to gain as much understanding as possible. This is a lifelong process.

Off-Season Approach

During the off season, try these suggestions to improve your knowledge of the game:

- Study to become an expert in a new aspect of the game.
- Visit with an opposing coach to discuss ideas.
- Go to summer league games to see teams in and out of your area.
- See as many championship games as possible to determine how your team matches up.

Self-education is a lifelong process, yet having knowledge is not the most important factor in gaining your athletes' support. Knowledge without the ability to express it to your team is useless. Often I'm reminded of this truth: It's not *what* you teach but *how* you teach it that makes you successful. There are many theories and approaches in coaching this game, and many of them will work, as long as you can convey them to your team.

Your athletes must be receptive, but you have to make them receptive to *you*. If your approach is to say, "Because I am the head coach you *must* respect me and be receptive," forget it. Get out your resume and find another profession.

The best thing that happened in my career was that I was required to teach classes my first 11 years. I taught freshman Spanish in high school, and I was an associate professor in college. I was forced to understand teaching principles and concepts. I'll be so bold as to suggest that if you're a young coach and you do not understand these concepts, go enroll in an education class. It will be a big help.

Through my schooling and teaching experiences I learned the part-versus-whole concept of teaching. It was also at this point that I became convinced of the value of long-term planning. The discipline of having daily and monthly lesson plans is certainly a valuable skill in planning your program. Having a teaching plan in mind on a daily basis is a principle that I certainly apply to my coaching.

If you are knowledgeable, if you approach athletes with proper teaching concepts, they will respect you. They will be receptive because you've made them receptive. Knowledge of the game alone will not get it done.

HITCHHIKING ON THE HIGHWAY OF LIFE

Most of us work with young athletes, and these athletes are looking for things that have meaning for them. Do not lose sight of this. They're searching for who they are as they hitchhike down the highway of life. They have their thumbs up every day, and one day they may turn to alcohol, one day to women, one day to movies, another day to religion. They're searching.

When they've sorted through it all, we hope they turn to the things that are right. It's up to you to get them to understand the best way to handle life. You accomplish this by teaching a solid set of principles: the importance of academics, the need for self-discipline, the obligation to respect others, the necessity of having a good work ethic, and the need to have a solid value system, to name a few.

Community Support

Believe in something. Stand for something. Be sincere in your beliefs, and share them with the community every chance you get. In other words, if you're fund-raising or have a speaking opportunity, you need to be prepared to represent and communicate your cause. Forget the cliches here. Everybody has heard the coach's promise to turn a program around or to make it to a championship. They're a dime a dozen. To be truthful, I never present to the public our goal of winning a national title. Present this goal to my players? Yes. To the community? No.

What I do share is our goal of having class and dignity. I want our program to stand for class and dignity. We want to be a class act. If your program can live up to a class image, the community support will come quickly and often. They'll back you to the point that you'll feel the blessings.

Stand for truth, integrity, responsibility, and accountability. Stand for all the ideas that people think are corny. The community is usually made up of people raised on these ideals. They love to hear them, and they will love to see them. If they see these principles in you and your program, they will offer their support.

Motivating Your Community

Here are some tangible ways to motivate your community:

- Make yourself available as a speaker (Little League opening day, banquets, father/son breakfasts, service club meetings, and so on).
- Put on free clinics for the youth in your area.
- Create a hospital visitation program for your athletes to visit unfortunate children.
- Organize team blood drives for blood donations.
- Organize cleanup days in the community or on campus with your athletes doing the labor.
- Volunteer to hold advisory positions on local boards (youth league, Boys and Girls Clubs, and so on).

Hiring Your Assistants

One of the most important decisions you'll make is whom to hire as your assistants.

This importance is magnified if you have limited financial resources with which to work. In my first two positions, I did not have a paid assistant. Not until I reached Pepperdine did I have adequate financial support in hiring an assistant.

Regardless of your situation, take the decision very seriously. Do a thorough background check on every assistant you hire. Ask about past positions and relationships. Be diligent. Make some calls. Talk to references and others who may have coached against or worked with the candidates. Some of us have learned the importance of doing this the hard way. Whether assistants are volunteers or are paid well, approach the search diligently.

Assistants' Support

Give your assistants responsibility and then give them the authority to carry it out. Make them accountable over an area that will succeed or fail based on their performance. This is why a thorough background check is necessary. If you give assistants responsibility, you'd better know they have the potential to carry it out.

As a result of your hiring process, your coaches should be as I described earlier in this chapter—ready to be quality where they are. If you hire an individual whose only goal is to move up the ladder quickly or who even covets *your* position, you will have problems. Let's not ignore that. You *will* have problems.

If you have loyal assistants who are supportive, give them all the responsibility they can handle. Challenge them to grow. As they respond to your trust, they will continue to improve as coaches. Of course, doing a quality job in his assistant position might just give him the opportunity to move up in the profession.

Recruiting

At the college level, recruiting is a daily event. The equivalent at the high school level and in summer league programs is working to establish a feeder system that will help your program.

High School Recruiting

In most cases, it's illegal to recruit at the high school level. Recruiting amounts to making sure players from your community do not go elsewhere. If you do a good job with your youth leagues (i.e., make your field available and make your time available) you should be successful in getting athletes that are already exposed to your style and philosophy.

NO SURE BETS IN RECRUITING

Two instances at Mira Costa High School come to mind when I think about encouraging athletes to play baseball for us. In both instances I failed to get who I thought was the best athlete on campus to play baseball. In 1978 the top athlete on campus chose to spend the spring of his senior year learning to master the skills of riding a skateboard instead of playing baseball for us. He was one of the best athletes on campus, but even without him we won the CIF championship. Again, in 1981 we lost who I felt was the school's top athlete. A switch-hitting infielder, he had an outstanding arm with excellent speed, and as early as his sophomore year he was being looked at by such baseball powers as Stanford and the University of South-

ern California. Instead of baseball, he decided to play volleyball during his final two years of high school. Even without this young talent, we were fortunate enough to play in the CIF title game. Once again the lesson that needs to be learned—and learned early—is that you need to find athletes who have heart rather than those who fit into someone's concept of what a recruit should look like. Never overlook a recruit with heart!

Another way to establish a feeder system in high school is to put energy into your lower-level programs. Most high schools have junior varsity or freshman teams. Get involved! In my five years as a varsity coach, I made it a personal rule that I spend one day a week with a lower-level squad. I wanted them to know I cared, that I was aware of what they were doing. They needed to know the varsity level was not so far away.

I often left my varsity team to make these visits, but the effort added continuity to our program from top to bottom, encouraging and motivating the younger athletes to continue playing.

ESTABLISHING PRIDE IN FRESHMEN

One rule I introduced while coaching at the high school level helped develop pride in our younger players. The rule stated that if an upperclassman were ever seen belittling an underclassman, the two would trade places for a day. The freshman would practice with the varsity while the senior went down to the freshman squad. I'd make them trade uniforms. This happened four or five times in my five years.

This concept continues at Florida. We do not want our younger players to be mentally beat up because of the way they're treated. Everyone has value—including freshmen.

College Level Recruiting

The biggest part of recruiting is the educational process. You really do need to educate the player, the coach, and the family on how recruiting works. They need to understand NCAA rules. They need to know about the admission process. They need to understand financial aid sources. Most parents are uninformed about all the aid possibilities (other than athletic) that are available. They need to be aware of all avenues that are available for a young man to obtain his goal of playing college baseball.

Then educate about your program. Sell your program. Present the qualities of your institution that make it attractive; don't point out your competitors' problems, which I call negative recruiting. My top suggestion to any young coach is *never* to get involved with negative recruiting. Sell the virtues of your program and stick with that approach. Be clean and ethical.

1989—A VERY GOOD YEAR

My first real recruiting class at Pepperdine was highly scrutinized by local baseball critics. Due to their physical size, many of the athletes who committed to play baseball in Malibu were questioned. Steve Rodriguez was too small to be a Division I infielder. Scott Vollmer was much too thin to be a big-time catcher. Eric Ekdahl was far too short to be a productive shortstop. Steve Duda did not have the physical size to be a dominating college pitcher. Yet these four athletes made up the bulk of a recruiting class that was to go on and win an NCAA Division I baseball championship. All four went on to play professional baseball. Don't get me wrong; we also had some big-time athletes in that recruiting class. First-round draft pick of the Chicago Cubs, Derek Wallace, and one of our top hitters, first baseman Danny Melendez, were outstanding physical athletes.

The lesson to be learned here is never to overlook the size of a young athlete's heart and the desire he has to excel. This is a lesson I learned early in my career.

Year-Round Process

When scouting for recruits, I think it is important to determine your program's needs not just for the next season, but for the next couple of seasons. I have found it important not to over-recruit; otherwise too many athletes will hope for an outstanding chance to make your ball club. I am convinced that a better approach is to determine your needs and recruit specifically toward those needs. Once those needs have been met, it is important to be up-front with any remaining recruits, letting them know the current status of your potential roster. Organization is the key to having a quality scouting process in recruiting. Acquire the schedules of high schools or junior colleges that have athletes that you believe you must see and map out the necessary times and places in which you can see them.

I doubt that a day goes by that I don't spend some time either recruiting or at least determining how best to handle recruiting responsibilities. It is a continual process and a coach could spend virtually 24 hours a day trying to do a good job. It is often said that you can be a good recruiter but a poor coach and still win, but you can also be a great, knowledgeable coach who lacks the ability to recruit and lose. If you find that recruiting is not a strength, I highly recommend that you hire an assistant coach who can handle this area well. It is not an individual responsibility. Recruiting should be the responsibility of everyone on your staff, as well as every player on your roster.

It is important to establish a rapport and develop relationships with as many junior college and high school coaches as you can. It is important that they know your program and the type of student athletes that you will typically pursue. In time an understanding can be developed between yourself and coaches from whom you recruit; this will enable them to make better recommendations to you.

I like to approach our recruiting not only as a process of acquiring new players but also as an opportunity to expose our program to various people. I see it as an opportunity to expose my beliefs and philosophies to far more people than eventually end up at our institution. I am convinced that by doing a good job of recruiting you gain the respect of even those athletes who decide to go elsewhere. Keep this in mind. The more exposure you can give your program through the recruiting process, the better chance you have of developing a solid image of yourself and your team throughout the baseball community.

Know your institution and its goals and philosophies. Sell your institution in your program as you recruit. If you believe in your institution, then it's easy to sell and be considered a good recruiter. Avoid making comparisons with the competition, yet do a good job providing recruits with information about your program. Then encourage them to do their homework so that they have enough information to make a good decision about their futures.

Do a good job with your local talent. Do not overlook this area. Making yourself known in your local community can only help your program's standing. Do not assume you will get local talent just because they live in the area. Pursue them as you would pursue a blue-chip athlete on the other side of the country.

We will generally send out letters to coaches of high schools and junior colleges, asking for recommendations on student athletes who might fit into our institution. Upon receiving these recommendations we will send a questionnaire to the athlete. Much can be discovered from reading an individual's questionnaire. Not only the obvious general information but also the interest the athlete may have in our institution—much can often be determined about the academic ability of athletes just by evaluating their ability to fill out the questionnaire. At this point, if we believe that he may be an athlete who can help us, we feel strongly that we must see the athlete play to evaluate how he might fit into our plans.

As a high school or a junior college coach responding to recruiters, it is very important that you be as helpful as possible. Once again, honesty is the key. Keep in mind your reputation for the long run. Over-selling your athletes will hurt the opportunities for future athletes in various programs. You must learn to gain the trust of those coaches at higher levels so they may depend on your evaluation of your athletes. Making information available about your athletes, such as complete rosters, statistics, phone numbers, addresses, and social security numbers will make the recruiter's job easier.

Today, scholarships are a major issue for parents, athletes, and coaches alike. Yet it is probably good common sense to save the scholarship discussion with parents for a later time if at all possible. We have a rule in my programs that we will never offer athletic aid to a student athlete we have not seen play. Other general ideas are to know your

financial aid rules and the recruiting regulations at your level of coaching. Above all else, be ethical and honest in all that is said and done in the area of recruiting.

Your best source to any type of feeder system at the college level is your players. My best recruiters are my players. If I've done a great job with my athletes, they will be a great sales resource for me. They know of athletcs to follow up with, and when an athlete does visit, your players can share their personal experiences.

It's been said before, but it's worth repeating: Recruiting is like shaving. You need to do it daily or you look bad. Recruiting is the lifeblood of your program. That does not mean I need to sacrifice my relationships with my wife and kids, though. I would *never* do that. Don't forfeit quality time with your family. It's not worth it. Still, a day does not go by that I do not think of some type of recruiting— a phone call, a note, checking on a recruit's playing schedule. It's a daily process—like shaving.

Raising Funds

What programs do not need more funding? In this age of budget cutbacks, it's rare to find programs adequately funded. In high school, I remember vividly selling coupon books and pizzas, running phone-a-thons and jog-a-thons, and washing cars until my hands wrinkled to help fund our programs.

When I reached the college level, I thought those days were gone. Yet in my first college job I not only had to raise money for operations, but for scholarships as well. My mother even made tamales and sold them at Christmas to raise money for scholarships.

Without getting too deep on this subject, I want to share two thoughts. First, if you don't want to raise money, find another profession because coaches have to raise funds. The second idea is even more important. Be wise. Learn how to be successful with the essentials. Don't feel you need to raise money for two sets of new uniforms. Don't go out and raise money so your team can have batting practice tops. I learned early in my career that if I had the essentials—uniforms, balls, and bats—then I had enough to be successful. What many coaches do is spend their time raising money for non-essentials when they should be spending that time teaching the game.

It's our job as coaches to motivate our athletes so they don't need all the frills. It's an image-versus-substance concept. In short, image is what you appear to be, what others perceive you to be. It can be faked. Substance is what you actually are, what's inside, what you stand for. It's your character. Image will lead you to spend too many hours raising money on non-essentials and not enough on coaching. Substance will lead you to raise funds for the essentials and coach during the remainder of your time.

If you have an amazing budget and you can acquire some luxuries, more power to you. But my advice to young coaches is to avoid getting caught up in images. Get caught up in the substance of the game, and get your club ready to play.

One final warning. When you do raise money for non-essentials, they soon become essentials. It becomes a yearly project. If you have home and away hats one year, your athletes will expect them every year.

Establishing Rules and Directions

Here's a very simple statement: As the head coach, you set the direction of your program. If you continue to demand punctuality, you'd better be on time. If you continue to emphasize, "We're a class act," then don't show up in sandals. If you are always on your players about paying attention to detail, you'd better be highly organized. In its pure sense, you're the lead dog of the sled, and you are the rules and the direction of your baseball program.

Again, if you come to my program, you'll see I treat people ethically, with courtesy and manners. I stress being on time. Athletes know that if I say I'm going to meet you at a certain time, I'm going to be there. If I set the rules and directions for the program, I have to live by them and serve as a model of the standards. Don't be a hypocrite.

Developing Team Pride

Team pride begins on day one. In high school it's your first meeting. In college, it's the first recruiting contact. Once again, it all comes from you, the head coach. You set the standard. You set the tempo. I'm not big on cliches, motivational signs, or special T-shirts. If I don't believe we can reach the goal of a championship, it simply won't happen. I tried all the motivational gimmicks at Cal State Dominguez Hills. But it wasn't until I firmly believed we could win that we reached the Division II World Series. It has to come from the head coach.

I'm convinced the head coach develops team pride by leading, so I'm big on establishing personal class, dignity, and integrity. I'm big on a high standard and a passion for excellence. Establish these factors, and the result will be team pride. But to solidify your team pride, you have to live a life that exhibits this pride. You must be an example. You must be professional in your actions—dressing well, keeping shaved, having your hair cut, keeping your shoes shined, and being polite and courteous to others. Word travels quickly if you treat others with professional courtesy. Word will get back to your players. If you're out spending time at a local bar, word will also get back to your players. Be a solid example.

OMAHA ON MY MIND

My wife Linda did something for me when I was first hired at Pepperdine. She bought me a set of pencils, each of which included the word *Omaha* on its side. Nothing fancy or expensive, but I left those pencils everywhere my players might see them—in the clubhouse, on clipboards, in the office, everywhere. I've stated that gimmicks don't work for me. However, in this case I wanted to expose my athletes to the fact that Omaha (and the College World Series) was on my mind!

Pride and expectations come from the example and leadership of the head coach. By the way, I still have one of those pencils in my briefcase. It's a little worn, but Omaha is still on my mind.

Summary

This chapter covered areas which are often overlooked, but which are essential in the development of your program:

- Work diligently to do a great job where you are. Prepare yourself professionally by acquiring the necessary degrees. Together these will help you move up in the profession of coaching.
- Seek counsel from your administrators. You will gain their support.
- Knowledge is useless without teaching skills. Combining the two will gain you the respect of your athletes.
- Stand for something! Project a sincere image of class to your community.
- Thoroughly interview your assistants before hiring them. Once hired, give them responsibility and the authority to carry it out.
- Be involved in the youth leagues of your area. Make yourself available. Recruiting is educating. Educate all parties involved. Avoid negative recruiting at all times.
- Fund-raising is a way of life for coaches. Raise funds for the essentials. Seek substance rather than image.
- The head coach is a main source of pride in any program. The development of pride starts with you.

Part II

Coaching Plans

Chapter 5

Planning for the Season

To fans at the ballpark, it may seem that baseball coaches only make out lineups, give a few simple signs, encourage their teams, and react to a win or a loss. Most outsiders would be very surprised to learn about all the planning and preparation that takes place.

In this chapter we'll take a look behind the scenes at those aspects of coaching of which most people are unaware. This will include medical and insurance screening for your players, conditioning programs, medical staff, scouting your opponent, scheduling, equipment, putting it together with the coaching staff, and overall season planning. These are often thankless areas. However, they only go unnoticed because you are diligent in han-

dling these areas daily. Neglect them and they will rapidly become major problems for your program.

Medical Screening and Insurance

Just as it's hard to be an expert in every facet of baseball, you may find it difficult to acquire an expertise in the area of medical screening and insurance. First and most important is to be aware of your institution's policies. Become fully knowledgeable about the medical screening process that your institution requires. Go directly to your athletic director for this information. If you are a Little League coach, be sure to secure this information from the league president or officer in charge of this area.

Second, learn to rely on your medical training staff. Staff roles vary from institution to institution and from the college level to the Little League level. Learn to take full advantage of the expertise of the individuals on your staff. At the university level we have an outstanding team of athletic trainers that I go to often and rely on heavily. Our team physician takes care of preseason physicals, as well as any major injury problems we might incur over the course of the season. We also have a team trainer with a staff of several student trainers who oversee the day-to-day practices and games. Finally, we are fortunate to have a strength and conditioning coach who oversees our weight training and conditioning programs, as well as nutrition concerns. I rely on each member of my medical staff to keep me abreast of any and all situations that I need to be aware of regarding my athletes.

At the high school level, and sometimes at smaller colleges, access to such staff is not available. Whether you have medical staff or not, I strongly recommend that all coaches take some type of general first aid course to be prepared to handle both minor and major emergency situations. Many institutions make this a requirement of their coaches. Even if this is not true in your case, get the training on your own. You will find this time well spent and very beneficial to your confidence and abilities as a coach.

At all levels of baseball, some type of preseason medical screening of players should take place. At our university, our athletes are given physicals by the university's medical staff. In high school it was a requirement of our athletes to get physicals from their own private doctors before they would be allowed to participate in extracurricular sports activities. Even in Little League, parents must sign a release stating that their son or daughter is physically able to participate in the sport. Again, it is up to you as head coach to become fully aware of the policies and methods of your particular institution.

This approach applies to insurance procedures as well. Be familiar with what takes place following an injury—who pays for what and which insurance company is liable. Don't wait until after an injury happens.

It's important to let parents know well in advance how the insurance procedure works so there are no secrets when it comes time to go through the claims process. Typically, an athlete's primary insurance coverage comes from existing insurance policies of the parents or the athlete. The institution's insurance is generally secondary and will normally cover whatever the primary insurance carrier does not cover. This may vary from institution to institution, so become familiar with how the insurance system works for your particular institution.

Most institutions will have a short pamphlet designed to explain insurance procedures to the athlete, as well as the parents of the athlete. We send this out prior to our season. Keep this information on file along with other pertinent information on each athlete. Although my training staff handles these things now, I recall that in my earlier days as a coach I kept a small file of index cards on each of my athletes. Each card would contain the athlete's name, the parents' names, addresses, and phone numbers, a person to contact in case of an emergency, insurance company and policy numbers, and any unique medical information that would be specific to the individual athlete. I had these cards in my briefcase at all times—at practices, at games, and on road trips.

Conditioning Program

I believe the foundation for success of any conditioning program is to strive for good overall conditioning and nutrition. We want our athletes to form good habits that will last a lifetime. A good overall program will consist of flexibility, strength training, conditioning, and nutritional considerations. If there is a member on your staff who is a professional in this area, go to him or her for guidance. Again, use the experts to whom you have access.

Our overall plan for the year is broken up into fall practice, off-season, and in-season segments. Figure 5.1 is an overview of our year-round conditioning plan at Florida.

Year-Round Conditioning Program

Month	Emphasis	Description
August and September	Training for fall practice	8 weeks of muscle endurance to muscle strengthening. Also, aerobic and anaerobic conditioning.
October	Fall practice	4 weeks of practice and intra-squad games. Work to maintain overall conditioning level while focusing on strength development.
November and early December	Off-season training	Major strength-building period of 6 weeks. Also work on cardiovascular training during the first 3 weeks and speed development during the last 3 weeks.
Mid-December through early January	Home training	Holiday break—4 weeks at home. Maintain emphasis of previous 6-week training program.
Mid-January through June	In-season training	20-22 week maintenance program—strength and conditioning.
Mid-June through late July	Off-season training and summer play	6-8 weeks of off-season training (as outlined above) for players not in summer leagues. Maintenance program for those playing over the summer.

Figure 5.1   A year-round conditioning program.

Flexibility

Flexibility is an important part of your exercise routine and should be done prior to any exercise to enable an athlete to properly warm-up and to help prevent injuries. Appendix A offers a complete baseball flexibility routine.

Strength Training

Generally speaking, our off-season expectations are such that we may ask our players to strive to increase their overall strength. Sometimes it can be more specific—as in the areas of arm or leg strength—but most often we want our players to work hard to increase their overall strength. During the season we use a weight program designed to maintain the strength that we have developed during the off season. In-season workouts are designed as a maintenance program rather than a strength-building program. Common sense tells us that we would like our players to be fresh during the season and not to be worn out by strenuous weight training. At the same time, we don't want them to lose the strength that they developed earlier in the year.

BEFORE AND AFTER

In 1990 Steve Montgomery was in his freshman year at Pepperdine. He had a tall, lanky body and any athletic movement would be considered gangling at best. He saw very little action, and upon completion of his freshman season we had no expectation of his participation increasing as a sophomore. During the summer, Steve became quite diligent with his weight training program. Upon returning for his sophomore year, the coaching staff noticed a difference in his physical size and strength that was like night and day compared to his freshman year. He became a second-team All-American as a sophomore. As a junior, he closed every game in relief during our stay in Omaha on his way to becoming a first-team All-American. The best part of Steve's physical improvement was that his teammates saw his success and responded by improving their work ethics in the weight training program. Steve Montgomery is now a highly successful professional pitcher. The physical transition Steve went through during his stay at Pepperdine would make a great before-and-after poster.

Figure 5.2 is an example of a basic weight training program for baseball, including areas of concentration, rationale, exercises, as well as an explanation of frequency and other general notes. This is a solid guideline that you might distribute to your athletes to help them develop their own program or for you to follow in developing a program for your athletes.

Rotator Cuff

One area that we focus specifically on is the rotator cuff, part of the throwing shoulder. This is particularly important for your pitchers, although it is good to have all your athletes emphasize this area. The small muscles surrounding the shoulder girdle are often neglected and are susceptible to injury. A consistent exercise program specific to this area is essential for the care of your athletes' throwing arms. A good strengthening program for the shoulder consists of exercises in Appendix B. These exercises can be done with any light weight or resistance. For instance, filling a tennis ball can with sand and securing the open end can be an ideal weight for these exercises. Using an elastic material as resistance is also very good. Your athletes should work up to doing three sets of 10 for each exercise, three to five times a week. Your athletes may initially do less depending on the condition and strength of their shoulders.

Baseball Weight Training Program

I. Areas of concentration:

Leg power, speed

Abdominal strength

Hamstring and hip flexor, flexibility

Posterior shoulder strength and rotator cuff strength

Tricep and bicep strength

Anterior shoulder flexibility and strength

Wrist/forearm strength

II. Rationale

1. Leg power, speed: improves field and baserunning quickness
2. Abdominal strength: improves power for throwing
3. Flexibility: decreases injury potential and increases speed (running and throwing)
4. Posterior shoulder strength and rotator cuff strength: decreases risk rate of shoulder pain; increases batting power; provides greater control while throwing
5. Tricep and bicep strength: provides control while throwing; decreases rate of elbow injury
6. Anterior shoulder flexibility: decreases injury rate in shoulders; increases speed and distance of throws
7. Anterior shoulder strength: important for batting and throwing, but overemphasis leads to shoulder and arm injuries, as well as neck pain

III. Exercises (2-3 from each group)

1. Off-season: August - December—strength emphasis and cardiovascular training
2. Preseason: December - beginning of season—sport-specific strength and drills; cardiovascular training
3. Lower body: leg curls, press, lunges, squats (heels flat, flexion only to 70°)
4. Abdominals: sitting rotation, curls, lower abdominals, crunches (important to mix the types)
5. Back: hyperextensions, seated rows, bent-over rows, bent legs dead lifts, lateral pull-downs, upright rows, prone abduction at 90°, 135°, and 180°
6. Shoulders: military press, lateral flies (raises), front flies (raises), rotator cuff exercise, shrugs, pull-ups
7. Chest: flat bench, incline bench, decline bench, butterflies
8. Arms: bicep curls, preacher curls, tricep pull-overs, chain saws (triceps), wrist curls/rolls, rotations

IV. Methods

1. Sets: 1 set of 12 reps; rest; 1 set of 12 reps; rest; etc.
2. Supersets: (a) opposing groups: 1 set of 12-rep tricep; 1 set of 12-rep bicep; rest; repeat; (b) within group: (exercise 1) 1 set of 12-rep tricep; (exercise 2) 1 set of 12-rep tricep; rest; repeat

(continued)

Figure 5.2 A baseball weight training program.

3. Trisets: (exercise 1) 1 set of 12-rep tricep; (exercise 2) 1 set of 12-rep tricep; (exercise 3) 1 set of 12-rep tricep; rest; repeat 3 separate exercises for same muscle; repeat

4. Circuits: usual type

5. Pyramids: (a) increase weight over 3-4 sets; keep reps constant; (b) increase reps over 3-4 sets, amount of weight the same; (c) increase number of reps and amount of weight

V. Frequency

1. 3x a week if performing all exercises during one session

2. 4x a week if performing a split program; divide program in half and perform each half thoroughly 2x a week

3. 6x a week if breaking program into thirds; perform each group 2x a week

VI. Sets, reps

1. Strength: 3-5 sets, 3-8 reps

2. Size (hypertrophy): 3-6 sets, 8-12 reps

3. Endurance: 2 sets, 15-20 reps

4. Power (quick lifts): 3-6 sets, 1-3 reps

VII. General notes

1. Always lift core groups (larger muscles, 2-joint muscles) first and then secondary muscles.

2. Always perform lower back exercises before abdominal exercises.

3. Vary the order of lifts and methods (avoid plateaus and increases in rate of performance changes).

Basic Weight Training Program

Exercise	Hypertrophy	Basic strength
Bench	12 - 10 - 8	10 - 8 - 6
Flys	12 - 12	12 - 12 - 12
Lat pull	12 - 10 - 8	10 - 8 - 6
Upright rows	12 - 10 - 8	10 - 8 - 6
Curls	12 - 12	10 - 8 - 6
Tricep extension	12 - 12	12 - 12 - 12
Shrugs	12 - 12	12 - 12 - 12
Wrist curls	12 - 12	12 - 12 - 12
Leg extension	12 - 10 - 8	10 - 8 - 6
Leg curl	12 - 10 - 8	10 - 8 - 6
Squats	12 - 10 - 8	10 - 8 - 6
Lunge	12 - 10 - 8	10 - 8 - 6

Figure 5.2   *(continued)*

Anaerobic and Aerobic Conditioning

Our off-season programs are designed to be more aerobic (i.e., distance running, biking, swimming), while our in-season conditioning programs combine both aerobic and anaerobic exercise with a heavy bias toward anaerobic conditioning. Baseball requires bursts of energy and quick, solid bursts of running. Anaerobic exercise conditions for this type of performance and helps develop more explosive leg muscles, as opposed to muscles designed for endurance.

We find it advantageous for our position players to do the majority of their conditioning on the bases during the season. This way we accomplish working on technique as we improve the condition of our players. Even if we are not running on the bases, most of our running conditioning also focuses on the technique of the baserunner. We seldom run sprints or distance just for the sake of conditioning. We emphasize technique throughout the season, and we always try to include technique as we condition. You will find more details on this approach in chapter 7.

WORLD-CLASS JOGGER

It is a rule of mine that our athletes wear only apparel that represents our institution. In 1992 at Pepperdine, right-hander Pat Ahearne showed up for practice one day wearing the wrong T-shirt. Not coincidentally, I decided that this was a good day for staff to report to the track above our baseball facility for a little extra aerobic conditioning. The pitchers, including Ahearne, approached this workout with little enthusiasm, which was reflected in their effort.

While they were training their cardiovascular system, an afternoon jogger was also working out on the track. Her efforts were far superior to the efforts of my athletes, and I pointed this out to my players. I told them they were going to continue to run as long as the mysterious jogger continued to run. Only after considerable time had elapsed did I discover that the jogger was Olympic runner Suzy Hamilton! It seemed that we ran forever, and I feel fortunate that I did not kill off any of my pitching staff.

Figure 5.3 is an exceptional off-season conditioning workout that our athletes are required to do eight weeks prior to the start of our fall practice. As you can see, it follows our philosophy that we initially begin with aerobic conditioning and then proceed to anaerobic exercise, emphasizing speed more than long endurance.

Nutrition

Nutrition is an important component of the overall strength and conditioning program. Nutritional intake has an enormous impact on performance, recovery, and the general well-being of athletes, but many times it is neglected. Although enhancement of athletic performance through weight training, conditioning, and flexibility seems to be the rule in many programs, nutrition is the exception. Failure to address proper nutritional intake can limit your whole program.

Even for a non-athlete, sound nutritional habits are important to remain healthy and functional throughout the day. For athletes, the emphasis on sound nutrition should be even more significant. Above other daily concerns, the physical and mental stress incurred in competition, training, and practice places more of a demand on athletes. From this perspective proper nutrition is even more critical.

Proper nutritional habits must be taught. Athletes must be educated on what constitutes a sound diet and why it is important to their performance and well-being. Of course, controlling what athletes eat on a daily basis may be difficult or even impossible, but a concerted effort to educate athletes must be put forth.

In general, proper nutrition enhances performance by assisting in delaying the onset of fatigue, which will minimize the risk of injury and extend the length of participation time for each of your athletes.

Putting It Together With the Coaching Staff

Knowing that it is difficult not only to maintain expertise in all areas required by the game of baseball, but also to commit the time to properly supervise an organization, you need to establish well in advance of the season the responsibilities of each of your staff members. To take the load off any one

8-Week Off-Season Conditioning Program

	Monday	Wednesday	Friday
Week 1	1.5 miles Abdominals	1.5 miles Abdominals	2.0 miles Abdominals
Week 2	2.0 miles Abdominals	10 yards full speed :35 recovery, 10 reps 5:00 recovery 10 x 100 :17,:15 :50 recovery Abdominals	2.5 miles Abdominals
Week 3	2.5 miles Abdominals	20 yards full speed :20 recovery, 10 reps 5:00 recovery 15 x 100 :17, :15 :50 recovery 2:00 recovery after 10 Abdominals	3.0 miles Abdominals
Week 4	30 yards full speed :45 recovery, 8 reps 5:00 recovery 8 x 200 :36,:32 1:15 recovery Abdominals	400 yards on football field. 4 reps 1:30, 1:25 3:00 recovery Abdominals	30 yards full speed :45 recovery, 8 reps 3 sets 3:00 recovery Abdominals
Week 5	40 yards full speed :50 recovery, 8 reps 3 sets 3:30 recovery Abdominals	400 yards on football field. 5 reps 1:30, 1:25 2:40 recovery Abdominals	50 yards full speed :50 recovery, 8 reps 3 sets 4:00 recovery Abdominals
Week 6	30 yards full speed :40 recovery, 8 reps 3 sets 3:00 recovery Abdominals	2.0 miles Abdominals	60 yards full speed :55 recovery, 8 reps 3 sets 4:30 recovery Abdominals
Week 7	20 yards full speed :35 recovery, 10 reps 3 sets, 2:30 recovery Abdominals	800 yards on football field. 3 sets 2:30, 4:00 recovery Abdominals	40 yards full speed :45 recovery, 8 reps 3 sets, 3:30 recovery Abdominals
Week 8	40 yards full speed :50 recovery, 5 reps 3:30 recovery 60 yards full speed 3 reps, 1:00 recovery Abdominals	2.0 miles Abdominals	40 yards full speed :50 recovery, 5 reps 3:30 recovery 60 yards full speed 3 reps, 1:00 recovery Abdominals

Figure 5.3 An eight-week off-season conditioning program.

individual, it is in the best interests of the program that you delegate responsibilities, particularly in the areas mentioned in this chapter.

At the University of Florida I am fortunate to have a complete and competent staff. Our responsibilities are delegated throughout this staff to enable the baseball coaches to focus primarily on the game of baseball. The following is a partial list of the support staff that I rely on as the head coach:

- Full-time assistant coach
- Full-time restricted earnings coach
- Volunteer assistant coach
- Two full-time secretaries
- Equipment manager
- Student assistant equipment personnel
- Field maintenance crew
- Academic counselor
- Team physician
- Team trainer
- Student athletic trainers
- Strength and conditioning coach
- Public relations director
- Media relations director
- Promotion director
- NCAA Compliance Committee
- Fully staffed booster club

Obviously, I lack for few resources at the University of Florida. I share this list to give other coaches an understanding of the many responsibilities that a head baseball coach at a major university must address. If they lack a support staff, head coaches must assume these duties to the best of their abilities.

It is always wise to delegate responsibilities among your staff. For example, earlier in my career I would allow an assistant coach to oversee our conditioning programs. I would receive input from that coach, as well as observe occasional workouts. It might be in your best interest to allow an assistant to monitor the preseason physicals, ensuring that athletes take care of their responsibilities. It also might help to appoint an assistant as the expert on your staff for handling injuries and insurance. Other areas that can often be given to assistant coaches include scouting, scheduling, and recruiting.

SEPTEMBER 3RD—AN IMPORTANT DATE

I remember scheduling my first staff meeting after receiving my head coaching position at Cal State Dominguez Hills. It was Sunday evening, September 3rd. The staff met in my home in Long Beach. It was a productive meeting, which was enhanced by the hospitality of my wife Linda. She continually made snacks and sandwiches, which helped keep the meeting going, but she seemed a bit quiet throughout the day. After my staff left, I thanked my wife for her hospitality and asked her how she thought the meeting had gone. She graciously replied that she thought it was productive and went well and suggested that future staff meetings not be scheduled on our anniversary. The point was well taken, and I have never forgotten our anniversary since!

Scouting

Scouting takes place for two major reasons: to recruit potential student athletes and to obtain knowledge of your opponents. In both

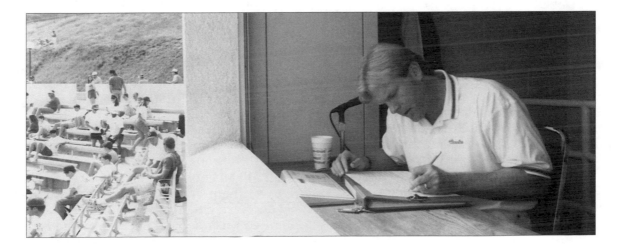

instances it is important to determine what your needs are early and then to be diligent in organizing a schedule that helps you meet those needs.

In the case of seeing your opponents, acquire the schedules of each opponent that you will face during the upcoming season and put together a schedule that allows someone on your staff or on your roster to see these opponents prior to your first meeting. If you lack sufficient personnel with assistant coaches, this duty may sometimes be handled by individuals on your pitching staff who may need an off-day between starts. Organization is the obvious key.

Approach your recruiting in much the same way. Know your list of potential recruits, and then develop an overall schedule of games that enables you to see potential recruits play. At this point there is no magic solution to scouting other than to get out and see as many games as possible. Once again, using your staff as well as athletes on your roster will help spread the responsibility and make it possible to do a more complete scouting job. See chapter 12 for specific information on scouting your opponents and chapter 4 for more details on recruiting.

Scheduling

Scheduling appears to be taking place earlier and earlier every year. It seems that coaches are now scheduling almost two years in advance at the university level in baseball. I think that it's important in organizing your schedule to play the toughest opponents you can find early. This will allow you to discover the character of your ball club and to prepare them for possible playoffs at the end of the season. I don't believe in playing a soft schedule to create a solid win-loss record.

One's self-esteem shouldn't come from how many wins you have as a head coach. A general rule in scheduling is to keep it balanced. You should schedule games that you think you should win, and you should schedule some games that you may lose. The remainder should be games that could go either way. This provides you a good opportunity to be successful, but also challenges your ball club during the non-conference

season to prepare for the upcoming conference schedule.

Often athletic directors will handle the scheduling of your particular program. It is important to give input to this individual on your philosophy and how you would like the schedule handled. Again, balance is a good rule of thumb. Unfortunately, rules dictating strengths of schedules often tie your hands as to which teams you can actually play. I believe all rules have some underlying merit, and it's important to be aware of the rules of your particular conference or institution relative to the scheduling of opponents. For example, the University of Florida has a rule that prohibits us from scheduling non-NCAA Division I opponents. The Southeastern Conference has a strict rule of allowing a maximum of only four opponents outside Division I.

Equipment

A recurring theme in this chapter is to determine your needs and plan to meet those needs. The same is true in your equipment inventory. Well in advance of your first practice you must determine your program's equipment needs. Keeping a simple inventory throughout the year makes this job a little easier.

Once your needs have been determined, it is important to do some shopping for a sporting goods representative who can provide you with the necessary products. I will always select an honest sales representative who is up-front on costs and delivery dates. Up-front costs and delivery dates help you avoid unpleasant surprises somewhere down the road. Unfortunately, in the competitive sales rep business there is the temptation to promise something which cannot be delivered in order to gain the sale. Typically, only experience will teach you which sales rep you should trust with your equipment needs. Be a good steward in this area to use your budget to its fullest potential.

Although this can be a time-consuming, frustrating aspect of any head coach's job, soliciting the help of your assistants in establishing a good, yet simple, inventory system will help you manage your equipment needs more effectively. Some needs can be planned on a seasonal basis, while others, such as large purchases (i.e., new uniforms, batting cages, and so on), can be scheduled on a multi-year basis, depending on your particular situation and budget. Let common sense be your guide.

Season Planning

Now it's time to get down to business, actually planning the on-field activities. As mentioned, most people think this is 95 percent of a head coach's job. The unfortunate reality is that it is a much smaller percentage than meets the eye of the outsider.

In preparing my overall season plan, I first take into account what I felt our strengths and weaknesses were during the previous year. It is my goal to plan with the idea that we must strengthen our previous weaknesses and improve on our strengths. If, for example, our offense was poor in the area of stolen bases, my practices will be designed to spend more time on this skill. If pitching was a shortcoming in the previous year, then we will try to incorporate more time for intra-squads to create game-like pitching situations. Quite honestly, we strive every year to win it all. We certainly don't always accomplish this goal, but I believe with all my heart that you must attack your season with the highest standards and goals possible.

Once again, you must sit down and determine your needs or goals for your particular ball club. Plan to meet those needs or goals over the course of the following weeks. I like to develop weekly plans every Sunday evening, listing my goals and then planning each day's practice trying to reach those goals. I try to begin the season by developing a plan for the first two weeks; then each Sunday evening I plan for the week ahead. The weekly plans become monthly plans, and before I know it I have a plan for the entire season. At the NCAA level the fall program has become limited over the years. Our fall program now allows basically one month to get ready for the spring season.

Early-Season Goals

See the chart at the bottom of the page for a specific example from the fall season of 1993 for an idea of the types of goals I set for my ball club early in the season.

Big Picture

Once we have established the general goals for the upcoming season, we then must create our practices to achieve these goals in the very short time period that the NCAA allows us. At our level we are limited to 22 total weeks of on-field workouts, which includes our spring schedule of games. Each week we are limited to a maximum of 20 hours of practice time, and we must also offer our athletes a mandatory off-day. That means we have about three hours a day to get all our work in. At Florida this breaks down generally as follows:

- September (upon arrival on campus) until first day of practice in October. Our athletes are under the supervision of

Defensive Goals	Offensive Goals	Pitching Goals	Team Goals
Develop infield routine	Develop baserunning techniques and skills	Develop pick moves	Compete
Establish bunt defenses	Establish positive count theory	Establish three levels of pitching	Compete
Establish first and third defenses	Develop offensive skills	Improve time to the plate	Compete
Perfect run-down procedures	Emphasize the important play	Become familiar with verbal signs	Have poise at all times
Develop outfield routine		Establish mental approach to the game	

our strength and conditioning coach and are going through their weight training programs.

- Second, third, and fourth weeks of October. We have scheduled mandatory on-field workouts under the NCAA guideline of 20 hours per week.
- November through first Monday in January. Athletes are under the supervision of the strength and conditioning coach, continuing their weight training programs.
- First Monday in January through first weekend in February. We use on-field workouts to prepare for our season opener, again under the guidelines set down by the NCAA.
- First weekend in February and following. We follow our regular season schedule of practices and games.

- June. Hopefully we take a scheduled trip to Omaha!

Practice limitations vary from organization to organization and from level to level. Junior college limitations are not that similar to those which exist at the NCAA level, and the NAIA has its own set of rules. High school rules vary from state to state as well. Become familiar with the guidelines that are set forth in your particular situation.

The preparation periods in the fall and for the month of January do not allow much time to organize and prepare a ball club to begin a season in a sport which is as elaborate and technical as baseball. However, it can be done if you are efficient in your organization. In chapter 6 I will take you through the step-by-step process that I use to prepare my ball club for the upcoming season.

Summary

Planning for the upcoming season requires far more than just your practice schedules. On-field activities are really just a small portion of a coach's responsibility. Follow this advice to plan efficiently:
- Know what your resources are. Rely heavily on experts around you in the areas of medical screening, insurance, and so on.
- Evaluate the needs of your program, and plan to meet those needs. This is true for all areas.
- In conditioning, build strength in the off-season. Maintain strength during the season.
- Use your assistants wisely in such areas as recruiting, scouting, scheduling, equipment inventory, and so on.
- Establish goals for team development each week. Each day strive to reach these goals.

## Chapter 6

Preparing for Practices

As I've mentioned, I am strongly convinced that game day belongs to the athletes. It is their day to shine in front of their families and friends and to enjoy the benefits of their many hours of preparation. Practice days, then, belong to the coaching staff. The practice session is the time when the coaching staff has full reign in developing the ball club.

In this chapter I will give you examples of our master practice plan and our basic practice schedule. You'll also learn how to emphasize game-like conditions combining several practice components at once and how to keep your practices intense and efficient.

Practice Emphasis

It is important that you have high expectations. You must demand a solid effort from start to finish from all your athletes. It is a mind-set. It is the approach that allows no small mistake to go uncorrected. It is the mind-set that we will never just go through the motions. It is an approach that we hope to establish in practice and carry over into game situations.

Make practices as game-like as possible. The higher intensity level will prepare athletes to face an opponent. Practice plans should serve to create game-like conditions. Be organized. Have specific drills scheduled. Then conduct each practice component at full speed.

Here are a few examples of how to maintain intensity and a competitive environment with your athletes in practice:

• Use a stopwatch whenever possible. When working on pickoffs, time your pitchers to home plate. When working on baserunning, time the drill. Put standards on your athletes that they must live up to or strive for.

• Create competitive situations in defensive drills. For instance, when working on first and third defense, create a competition between the runners and the defense. At Florida we will typically challenge the runners to score five runs before the defense completes five outs.

• Use live pitchers whenever possible. When bunting, make your hitters execute off of good pitching.

• Create a perform-or-get-out mentality. Require your hitters to perform a skill, and if they fail, remove them from the cage momentarily, rotating to the next hitter. This applies pressure and promotes concentration and effort.

• When working on bunt defenses, require your pitchers to throw a strike before you roll the simulated bunt.

 PERSISTENCE

In 1991 our Pepperdine ball club was having trouble handling certain game situations. Our coaching staff decided that our practice format would be changed to include a three-to-four inning intra-squad contest each day to help gain more game-like experience. It was a year in which the last couple of spots on our travel roster were filled by two of four or five pitchers on our staff. Pitchers earned their spots by performing well in the intense intra-squad sessions. One freshman pitcher got hammered every time he went to the mound in these practice games. As a result he never made the travel roster that year. To his credit he never once complained and always took responsibility for his performances. In 1992 that same athlete was an integral part of our championship. In 1993 he was drafted and went on to become a professional ball player. He claims to this day that the toughness of the intra-squads back in 1991 did more to help him mature and to make him a better pitcher than anything else in his career.

Simplicity and Consistency

My practice format has been basically the same throughout my career. I use the same approach in organizing my practice plan at Florida today that I used many years ago at the high school level. My daily practices look something like this:

1:30 p.m.	Stretch and warm-up
1:50 p.m.	Small game/live two strike bunts
2:00 p.m.	Live baserunning versus pitchers and catchers—5 minutes Street Monkey Drill—10 minutes Run-downs—5 minutes Defensive emphasis—10 minutes
2:30 p.m.	Offensive stations
4:00 p.m.	Conditioning/field maintenance

Within the context of this general practice plan, I can make daily adjustments to help us meet our goals. Appendix C of this book also offers a sample three-week practice schedule. Our athletes understand our routine, and they become familiar with it. I'm convinced that familiarity breeds confidence. Because our daily plan is somewhat repetitious, it's up to the coaching staff to maintain an edge throughout the daily activities. But with minor adjustments and fine-tuning, you can alter this practice plan to meet your goals and to keep it somewhat fresh to your players.

As you can see, the plan is designed to allow the players to get loose on their own. We have a brief 10-minute station where we simulate a live game situation and work on particular skills. We then spend time daily with our runners competing against our pitchers and catchers. The next time period is used to cover our defensive skills, and the final 90 minutes allows us to work on offensive skills. We typically finish the day by conditioning.

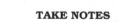 **TAKE NOTES**

One way I monitor the performance of my athletes in practice is to take constant notes during the session. I refer to those notes when I address the ball club. I take note of positive performances, as well as performances that are not meeting our expectations. Either way, the athletes are quite aware that I take the notes during our practice. I have found over the years that players will respond in an interesting way when I pull my 3 x 5 notecards from my back pocket. More times than not, the level of effort increases, sometimes in a dramatic way. Knowing that I am aware and have decided to take note of something puts a little edge on practice that results in athletes working harder. This is a lesson I discovered through experience; I highly recommend the process to you.

Master Plan

We will use the daily practice format to implement the skills and strategies that we have decided to teach our ball club. Although the specific techniques and tactics may vary slightly from year to year, they generally consist of the following:

- team offense
- hitting
- team defense
- bunt defense
- outfielders
- pitchers
- catchers

The chart below lists specific areas af concentration within each of these categories.

Team Offense	Hitting	Team Defense	Outfielders	Pitchers	Catchers
First and third offense	Execution of skills	Pregame infield	Throwing at relay man's knee	First pitch strikes	Signs
Delay steal	Positive count theory	Street Monkey Drill	Drop step	Prepractice picks one through six	Blocking pitches
Fake steal	Hit and run philosophy	Run-downs	Running through the fly ball	Intensity bullpens	Throwing
Steal jumps versus RHP	Bases loaded approach (keep batted ball off the ground)	Cutoffs and double relays	Sun fly ball	LHP moves	Bunt footwork
Steal jumps versus LHP	Quick hands	Bunt defense	Decoy Drill	Concealing pitches	Force at home
Reading the down angle	Six-Out Drill	First and third defense	Batting practice— work up/in, and so on		1.9 seconds to second base
Timed steal	Carry the Guy Drill	Pickoff			Bullpens
Reading the pitchout		Defending the squeeze			Establishing three stages of pitching
The checklist (get sign, read defense, know outs)		Defending the safety squeeze			
Leads at first base		Coordinating pitcher's looks at second with middle infielders and catchers			
Leads at second base		Double play footwork			
Leads at third base		Circle Drill			
Steal of third		Four-Corner Drill			
Home to first					
First to third					
Second to home					
Tagging up					
Staying with the ball					

No Practice Plan

As important as my practice plan is, I will, at least twice each year, not post a practice plan prior to the practice session. The purpose of this is to see how the athletes react without having a specific plan to follow. It is always interesting to note who on the ball club takes a leadership role in the practice. It's also good to observe what they work on that day. It also builds self-esteem and a sense of awareness in my athletes. Doing this on a few occasions each season actually strengthens the practice plan concept in the minds of our athletes. Do this only after regular practice plans have been used for a considerable length of time.

Defense

After stretching and perhaps a team drill or small game, we work on certain defensive drills on a daily basis. We have our pitchers and catchers compete against our baserunners daily for 5 to 10 minutes. We do our Street Monkey Drill for 10 minutes daily. Street Monkey (see chapter 10) is a drill that works bunt defenses and also helps pitchers to field come-backers and to cover first base on ground balls to the right side of the infield. We also work run-downs for at least 5 minutes every day.

Following this 20-minute period, we will switch the defensive emphasis to such aspects as cutoffs and relays, bunt defenses, first and third defenses, or maybe team pick-offs. This is the part of practice that I will vary to keep practices fresh.

I determined early in my career that I never wanted to drive home following a loss due to a blown run-down, poor bunt coverage, or a mishandled ground ball between the mound or third base. At least I want the peace of mind to know that we have spent considerable time fine-tuning the simple but important aspects of defense. That is why we never vary that segment of our practice.

Offense

The offensive station might be the most elaborate part of our practice. If well-organized, this section of practice should keep each of your athletes working, including your pitching staff.

Put the athletes into groups and rotate them through stations on a timed basis. The size and number of these groups can change in accordance with the emphasis of the day's practice. The length of time for each round may also vary. Typically, a round will last somewhere between 10 and 30 minutes, depending on the number of rounds for that particular day. Figure 6.1 depicts a batting practice plan that's a good example of an offensive station practice.

The schedule may initially look very complicated, but it is designed to organize your entire ball club into an 80-minute practice session. It is designed to improve offensive skills. For evaluation purposes, we will break the schedule into four segments.

The top section of the batting practice plan is designed to organize your hitters. In this example I have broken down a roster of 20 position players into four groups (i.e., Groups A, B, C, and D). Below the list of groups I organize the 20-minute stations or rounds. This particular day we will have a live station, a station in the batting cage, a group working on baserunning, and a group working on defense. I also list in what order each group

Batting Practice Plan

Date: _____

Groups	A	B	C	D	E
	Rose	Fullerton	Schniepp	Trujillo	
	Kimmel	Foster	Harrell	Day	
	Heldoorn	Viohl	Pfund	Madsen	
	Red	Ascanio	Glenn	Redick	
	Yakel	Ainley	Adams	Loewen	
Rounds (20 min.)	**1**	**2**	**3**	**4**	**5**
Live	A	B	C	D	
Cage	D	A	B	C	
Baserunning	C	D	A	B	
Defense	B	C	D	A	
Pitcher	Gemberling	Stroud	Biegert	Stephens	
Catcher	Fullerton	Schniepp	Trujillo	Rose	
Bullpen					
Bucket	Martony	Ochs	Cumella	Ashworth	
Condition	Ashworth	Martony	Ochs	Cumella	
	Tubbs	Speshyock	Priem	Ludwig	
	Overfelt	Arviso			
Shag	Cumella	Ashworth	Martony	Ochs	
	Ludwig	Tubbs	Speshyock	Priem	
		Overfelt	Arviso		
Fungo	Speshyock	Priem	Ludwig	Tubbs	
	Arviso			Overfelt	
First base					
Other	Ochs	Cumella	Ashworth	Martony	
drills	Priem	Ludwig	Tubbs	Speshyock	
			Overfelt	Arviso	

Notes   Live: Execution
Cage: CBs off machine; tees
Baserunning: 1st to 3rd
Defense: Infielders—fungos at positions
       Outfielders—live going back on ball (play shallow)

Pitching mechanics:
Good move/great move—to be done during shag round
Conditioning—12 poles
Drills—picks in RF bullpen

Figure 6.1   A batting practice plan.

will go through the four stations. For instance, Group A of Rose, Kimmel, Heldorn, Reed, and Yakel will spend the first 20 minutes hitting live. During the second round or 20-minute segment they will be in the batting cages. In the third round Group A will be working on baserunning. Finally, in the final round of this practice they will be working on defense. Group D begins the offensive station workout in the batting cage, proceeds to baserunning and defense, and then finishes by hitting live batting practice. I believe this small grid organizes the small groups rather simply. Note that there's room for another group, Group E, as well as room to add another station or two. We try to vary the stations regularly. Other ideas for offensive stations might include bunting, conditioning, an additional batting cage round, or possibly a round for pepper. This is where the coach can be creative and keep practices from becoming too mundane for the athletes.

The next two lines, labeled "Pitcher" and "Catcher," allow you to schedule which particular pitchers will be throwing batting practice during what round. In this example, Gemberling, Stroud, Biegert, and Stephens will be throwing rounds one through four, respectively. The catchers listed here are those catchers on your roster who will actually catch the live round. We find it expedites batting practice to have a catcher during this station.

Please understand that we will define each station more specifically in the section titled "Notes." For example, on this day we worked execution in live batting practice. We worked on hitting curveballs off our pitching machine, as well as tee work in the batting cage. Our baserunning station emphasized advancing from first to third on a base hit. On defense our infielders took ground balls—with the pitchers hitting them—while our outfielders worked on going back on the ball by playing shallow against the live hitters.

Pitchers During Practice

As I mentioned earlier, it is our goal to keep our pitchers active throughout the practice session. In figure 6.1, I have organized a 10-man pitching staff to be active and productive throughout the scheduled offensive sta-

tions. Using this plan, you can schedule your pitching staff to throw bullpens, man the shag bucket, condition, shag, hit fungos, play first base, or participate in other drills. At the bottom of the schedule is a portion titled "Pitching Mechanics." Here we help define the pitchers' responsibilities more clearly. Even during their shag round our pitchers are required to be working on a particular mechanic. On this day they are to be working on their good move/great move pickoff approach. We also clarify that conditioning is running 12 poles, and we inform them that they are to do their drills in the right field bullpen.

You can alter your pitchers' responsibilities on a daily basis. Emphasis on certain mechanics can change, conditioning can change, and you can alter the drills you are asking them to do. Combining their throwing schedule with their offensive station responsibilities, as well as their daily warm-up and defensive emphasis, keeps your pitching staff as productive as possible.

Pitchers' Throwing Schedule

As you can see, I place a large emphasis on our pitching staff during practice. Typically it is easy to neglect your pitching staff during the practice session. Not only must you keep your pitchers productive each day, but I will also take my pitching schedule a step further by effectively organizing their throwing schedule. Our emphasis is to monitor the number of pitches our pitchers will throw on a daily basis. We will then strive to develop arm strength over a period of time without allowing our pitchers to over-throw. Figure 6.2 is a daily Pitching Schedule that I use to help develop arm strength for our staff.

I will usually split my pitchers and catchers into two groups to help organize the schedule. Beginning in week one I will allow my pitchers to throw between 30 and 45 pitches at approximately 70 to 80 percent velocity on two occasions, with two days rest in between. I allow them to incorporate their off-speed pitches without trying to break off sharp breaking pitches. As you can see from the schedule, Group A will throw their bullpens on Monday and Thursday, while Group B will throw their bullpens Tuesday

Rest on Sunday	Monday	Tuesday	Wednesday	Thursday	Friday	Saturday
First week 30-45 pitches 70-80% velocity twice this week with 2 days of rest. Incorporate your off-speed pitches without trying to break off a sharp curve or slider.	January 10 **Group A** Throw & condition **Group B** Condition	11 **Group B** Throw & condition **Group A** Condition	12 Change-up Long-toss mechanics	13 **Group A** Throw & condition **Group B** Condition	14 **Group B** Throw & condition **Group A** Condition	15 Optional day of long-toss & conditioning
16 **Second week** 40-55 pitches 70-80% velocity twice in the week with 2 days of rest in between.	17 **Group A** Throw & condition **Group B** Condition	18 **Group B** Throw & condition **Group A** Condition	19 Change-up Long-toss mechanics	20 **Group A** Throw & condition **Group B** Condition	21 **Group B** Throw & condition **Group A** Condition	22 Optional day of long-toss & conditioning
Third week 23 55-70 pitches Follow the same plan as week #2. From this week on, for short periods of time (25 pitches), throw at max.	24 **Group A** Throw & condition **Group B** Condition	25 **Group B** Throw & condition **Group A** Condition	26 Change-up Long-toss mechanics	27 **Group A** Throw & condition **Group B** Condition	28 **Group B** Throw & condition **Group A** Condition	29 Optional day of long-toss & conditioning
30	31	February 1 Opening game	2	3	4 Three-game series—home	5

Fourth week through November: A rotation will be posted every Monday in the stadium.

Figure 6.2 Three-week pitching preparation for first week of competition.

and Friday (see figure 6.2). Wednesday is a day dedicated to emphasizing our long-toss mechanics and throwing the change-up. In fact, each time a pitcher picks up a ball during practice on Wednesday, outside of throwing long-toss, we want him to use his change-up grip. Saturday is also a long-toss day for the staff.

The conditioning aspect of this schedule is very important from the beginning. During the first week I will require our pitching staff to report first thing in the morning to take part in a three-mile run. In the afternoon during our team workouts we will also ask the pitchers to run the traditional *poles*. For those not familiar with the term *poles*, it refers to a conditioning run in which the pitchers run the length of the outfield from foul pole to foul pole. We will typically start with six and work our way up over the course of the season to 15 or 20. We often will interchange poles with intervals around a running track. If a track is not available, a similar interval type workout can be done around the entire baseball diamond.

During the second week we will increase our pitchers' pitch counts from 30 to 45 pitches up to 40 to 55 pitches, again only going 70 to 80 percent of top velocity. Each pitcher will throw twice with two days rest in between. We will build from 55 to 70 pitches during week three, following the same plan as the previous week, but we will allow them to throw 25 of their pitches at maximum effort. I also believe that at this point in their development they can begin to face hitters in an intra-squad format.

At this point the pitching rotation for the remaining weeks will be posted each Monday. Starters maintain a similar work schedule, pitching twice weekly, while relievers get on the mound every other day while lowering their pitch counts to between 20 and 30. The purpose of this is to develop a routine for our relief pitchers of throwing virtually every other day as they will potentially do during the season.

It is important to realize that the pitching coach should be mindful of the exact pitch counts. We will eventually use the individual pitcher's past histories of pitch counts to make decisions during games. Also, depending on an individual pitcher's degree of condition or health of his arm, a pitching coach can also make adjustments.

 **PART OF THE PLAN**

In order to plan quality practices, a great deal of time must be invested in your effort. The more time that you put into planning, the better your practices will turn out. Unfortunately, this planning has the potential to affect your relationship with your wife or significant other. As I mentioned before, without my wife Linda I could never have pursued my career in baseball. Every Sunday night prior to our practice week, I spend at least two hours alone planning for the general practices of the upcoming week. I spend two hours every Sunday, not only during the course of the regular season, but during our fall practices as well. I could not do this without an understanding wife, and I share this brief story to let you know the sacrifices that must be made in order to yield productive practices. Be prepared to put in the time to get things organized.

Posting Your Plan

I am a firm believer in posting my practice schedules. Not only on a daily basis, but also each Monday, I will post a general plan for the week. I post these schedules near my office, in the dugout, and in the clubhouse.

I am convinced that my athletes are far better prepared mentally and physically if they know their responsibilities in advance. I require the ball players to have checked the daily schedule and to know when and where they must be at each moment of practice. This requirement also saves organization time during the actual practice session. Less explaining and directing is needed when you do your organization in advance and require your athletes to be familiar with it.

It's not as important to post the practice plan as it is to post an understandable practice plan. I have now taken over three programs in my career, and it is common-place to see confusion in my athletes as they first look at the posted plan. Initially, they react to the plans as if they were printed in a foreign language. This was a distinct and consistent reaction in all three collegiate programs that I took over. Learn the lesson that the practice plan must be simple and clear enough for your athletes to understand. Also realize that it will take most athletes some time to grow accustomed to any new procedure.

Practicing in Bad Weather

I have been fortunate to have coached in good-weather areas my entire career. The climate of southern California is ideal for year-round baseball. My transition to the University of Florida was smooth due to the fine weather conditions of Gainesville. Yet there have been days even in the Sunshine State and in southern California where rain-storms have forced us into an indoor facility. In California that meant using the basketball gymnasium, as field houses were nowhere to be found. As a result, I developed the following method for conducting indoor workouts so that inclement weather would not hold us back:

1. Reserve the gymnasium when bad weather threatens.
2. Keep workouts short and to the point. To keep players more alert, do not work out any longer than an hour.
3. Get in your warm-up progression and do some throwing.
4. Use the rest of the first half hour to present team concepts and walk through bunt defenses and first and third situations.
5. Dedicate the second half hour to developing offensive skills, again discussing team concepts and working on dry swings. More attention would be spent on our mechanics, both offensively and as pitchers, almost in a classroom setting.

The key to these workouts is in handling them as if they were library sessions. In fact, I referred to these workouts as *library sessions*, which means we were to have no talking during the workout. This approach enhanced our concentration level and kept noise to a minimum, which is no small feat in an old gymnasium. The coaching staff takes this opportunity to teach and refine.

A PLAN FOR RAIN

During practice I always carry a separate practice plan copied onto a 3 x 5 card that I carry in my back pocket, allowing me to refer to the schedule quickly and make proper adjustments. I have done this all my career. My first practice day at Florida changed that habit. As I was referring to my 3 x 5 card around mid-practice one day, it suddenly began to rain. In Gainesville, the weather changes quickly, and storms develop much faster than I was accustomed to in California. The next thing I knew, the ink on my practice plan had smeared completely, making my 3 x 5 card worthless. Now I have the 3 x 5 card laminated prior to practice. Sometimes you need to make adjustments!

Conditioning in Practice

Although much of our preseason conditioning workout has already been presented in this chapter and in chapter 5, I would like to express a few thoughts about conditioning in practice. I believe it's important to keep your athletes looking forward to the concept of running during your practice sessions. If at all possible, avoid using running as a manner of punishment. Doing so will cause some athletes to look upon it as something negative. Conditioning should be kept varied within the practice format to keep your athletes interested.

Typically in the early season, I will have my athletes alternate daily between distance running and long sprints. For instance, Monday, Wednesday, and Friday would be set aside to run distance or interval work between one and three miles. Tuesday, Thursday, and Saturday we will have our athletes work up to 20 long sprints 75 to 100 yards in length. As the season continues, we will cut back on the distance work but maintain a stronger emphasis on sprint work. We feel this will allow the athletes' legs to become fresher as the season goes on. We like to use our baserunning drills as a conditioner as well. Doing conditioning on the bases is a wonderful way to keep your athletes excited, motivated, and interested in the conditioning process. An alternative is to have your athletes condition in the context of the batting practice schedule. Often I will have the athletes do their conditioning immediately prior to their live hitting stations. The idea is to have them try to perform when they are extremely fatigued. An athlete who can perform with fatigue is likely to perform at any time.

Our pitchers will typically condition separately from the rest of the ball club. Their responsibilities in practice allow them the opportunity to condition while other aspects of practice go on. But at times I like the ball club to finish a practice by conditioning together. I believe this is good for building team spirit and drawing the ball club closer together. This may be even more important at the younger levels of baseball.

⚾ QUICK DISMISSAL GETS RESULTS

Following our philosophy of game-like practices, it is important to have athletes in the proper mental state before practice begins. Sometimes you can sense immediately when your athletes are not mentally prepared for their approach to practice. One day at Cal State Dominguez Hills, I noticed the ball club did not have the proper mental framework to have a successful game-like session. Given the way the players showed up at the ballpark, I felt that it would be a waste of two hours to even try to run a practice, so I sent them home. I told them they were going through the motions mentally

and that on this particular day, it was best for them to, "Pack up your gear and go home!" They were shocked. Many wanted to stay around and work out on their own, but I insisted that the privilege had been taken away and they were to report the following day with more enthusiasm for practice.

It was a risk, but it worked. After spending an afternoon without practicing, the players realized how enjoyable practice is and how much they missed it when it was gone. The next day, they were enthusiastic and excited to be there. They went about their work responsibilities with a much improved attitude. It should be noted that some athletes mentioned to me that they learned more about the value of time and realized just how much time they were spending each day at practice. Use this tactic as a last resort for teaching your ball club to not mistake activity for achievement.

Summary

Designing and overseeing practices is certainly a tremendously important responsibility for the head coach. An unlimited amount of time could be spent on producing a highly detailed and organized practice session. I highly recommend that before you step onto the field during practice, you have thoroughly reviewed and meticulously prepared the practice schedule. Keep in mind some of the following ideas as you prepare for practice:

- Game day is for the athletes. Practice belongs to the coaches.
- Have high expectations during practice. Make your practice sessions as game-like as possible. Have your athletes compete on a consistent basis against the stopwatch, against each other, and against high standards.
- Practice schedules should be kept simple. Familiarity breeds confidence.
- Make it a goal to keep your athletes active and productive at all times.
- Develop a master practice plan that entails everything that you, emphasis on *you*, want to teach over the course of the year.
- Post the practice plan for the day as well as for the entire week so your athletes may be better prepared mentally for practice.
- Have a detailed plan for the arm strength development of your pitching staff. Implement the pitchers' throwing schedule within the context of the overall practice plan.
- Keep your conditioning process varied to maintain your athletes' interest.
- Never mistake activity in practice for achievement.

## Part III

Coaching Offense

Chapter 7

Teaching Offensive Skills

Before we begin, we all need to agree that offense is not hitting. Early in my coaching career, I was convinced that our offense was going well if we were hitting. But offense is definitely not hitting! I don't know how many times as a coach I've come off the field and looked at a box score that read, "My team: 2 runs, 8 hits, no errors and my opponent: 3 runs, 4 hits, no errors." It happens so often that you out-hit an opponent, yet don't generate any offense that day and end up on the short end of a ball game.

Offense is the ability to score runs when your team is *not* hitting. How do you do that? Focus your offense first around your bunting game (sacrifice bunt, drag bunt, push bunt, squeeze, and slash variations); second, on bat control (ability to hit and run and to hit to the right side, advancing a runner); third, on baserunning (ability and knowledge of the running game); and fourth and last, on what most people think of first, hitting.

I liked what I heard Whitey Herzog say once: "Speed never slumps." I agree with that statement. To go a step further, I would state that the ability to execute also helps you avoid slumps. Mastering the skills of bat control and bunting will greatly enhance your club's ability to hit.

Sacrifice Bunt

The bunting game is probably the most basic aspect of any team's offensive plan. The bottom-line idea is to advance runners, which is often accomplished by exchanging an out for a base by executing a sacrifice bunt. This bunt is the most fundamental aspect of any offensive game plan.

Batter's Box Position

The most important factor regarding your bunting game is placement in the batter's box. Your athletes need to be up in the front of the box. They need to be as far up in the box as possible for two main reasons: one, to give batters more fair territory with which to work, making it easier to keep the ball in play; and two, to provide a chance for contact with the ball while it's still on one plane. By one plane, we mean a fastball that hasn't moved into a downward plane and an off-speed pitch that a batter might be able to bunt before it breaks. By moving forward, batters enhance their chances to be successful.

Bat Head Position

The bat head should be in fair territory, which helps keep the batted ball in fair territory. If you watch someone bunt successfully, he's usually doing it because his bat head is within the foul lines. If he's a right-handed hitter, the bat is within the first base foul line. If he's a left-handed batter, it's within the third base foul line.

The bat head should also be at the top of the strike zone. As bunters, players want to make contact with the top of the ball. They're focusing on the top of the ball on all bunting executions. Batters want to stay at the top of the strike zone for the simple reason that if the pitch is above the top of the bat head, it's a ball.

Two Techniques

There are two basic techniques that we teach with the sacrifice bunt. First, square around completely to the pitcher. Batters will square up their shoulders, feet, and hips; they will be completely squared to the pitcher as he delivers the ball. The bottom hand is at the knob of the bat with the top hand sliding upward toward the middle of the bat, and the batter is being careful not to expose the top hand to the pitch (see figure 7.1). This technique is normally used when athletes are having a tough time bunting or when it's late in a ball game and we don't want to leave any room for failure. This is when we want to get the sacrifice bunt in play.

The second technique that we like to use is to simply rotate the hips and stay in a ready position (see figure 7.2). We like to do this so that we can set up our slash offense, which I will get into later. This is a more difficult skill and probably shouldn't be taught to younger athletes. From junior high, high school, and on, I think it is important that you teach athletes this skill because they are going into programs that will ask them to execute a slash from this bunting position.

Our goal with the sacrifice bunt is to place the bunt down the first or third base line, never back to the pitcher. Again, we want to make sure that we enhance that goal by the

Figure 7.1   Squared sacrifice bunt.

Figure 7.2 Pivot sacrifice bunt.

techniques that we've already discussed: being in front of the box, having our bat head in fair territory, and making sure that we work on the top half of the ball.

Bunting for a Hit

Often the way your opponent's defense sets up will give you an opportunity to use bunting to try to get on base. Bunting for a base hit can occur when the infield defense is playing deep in their positions. By skillfully bunting the ball down either baseline, or even at a deep-playing second baseman, you may catch the defense by surprise, allowing the hitter to reach base safely. With a highly skilled bunter, this play could also be used in lieu of a sacrifice bunt, enabling the hitter not only to advance a runner, but also to increase his chances of reaching first base safely.

Having a highly skilled team of bunters will also force your opponent to play much more shallow, particularly at the corner positions of first base and third base. This will open up opportunities for routine ground balls to go through the defense for base hits.

Drag Bunt

Once again, we ask our athletes to put themselves in the front area of the box. We want them to be up in front of the box as much as possible when making contact. We want to make sure that our club head again is on the top part of the ball and that it's in fair territory. This doesn't change from the sacrifice bunt.

The technique we like to teach for the drag bunt is one of shuffling the feet toward the mound (see figure 7.3). We like batters to

Figure 7.3 Drag bunt.

shuffle the feet for two specific reasons. The first reason is to enhance movement to the front of the box. In other words, if batters shuffle their feet, they're going to be in the front of the box. This is important! The second reason is to provide some rhythm with the pitch. This is an overlooked technique. We do this extensively now at Florida, asking our athletes to shuffle their feet toward the pitcher so that they have some type of rhythm on the pitch. This should make sense because that's exactly what we're asking for when they're hitting. We ask them to have rhythm on the pitch in a hitting approach, so we don't want to alter it in bunting.

Our goal with the drag bunt is to create an element of surprise. To do that, we want to execute this bunt as late as possible, but we do not want to sacrifice placement for surprise by squaring too late. The ball should be bunted down the third base line for right-handed hitters and the first base line for left-handed hitters. A tip for the drag bunt we like to use is that we ask our athletes to make it a base hit or a foul ball. We can only take one or the other, which keeps the ball from being bunted right back to the pitcher.

Push Bunt

The teaching principles of the push bunt are very similar to the drag bunt, but the goal changes. Our goal for right-handed hitters in the push bunt is to place the ball in a so-called no-man's land, the area between first base, pitcher, and second baseman. There's a triangular area there that is really a no-man's land, and the goal for right-handed hitters is to push the ball toward the right side into this area. For left-handed hitters, that same area exists, although left-handers will try to bring the bunt with them as they begin to run up the first base line. This bunt is a very good offensive weapon versus a left-handed pitcher who falls toward third base in his follow-through, which leaves the no-man's land even more vulnerable.

Spreading the Defense

By having proficient bunters up and down your lineup, you force your opponent to constantly defend against the bunt. As a result, you literally spread the defense out by forcing the corners to play closer to the hitter. Now you have a better opportunity for the ground balls that would not normally be hits to sneak through to the outfield.

Developing a reputation that your club can bunt at any time and at any spot in the order gives you a wonderful advantage because it keeps your opponents on edge. This has been a goal of all my programs: Florida, Pepperdine, Dominguez Hills, and even in high school.

Squeeze Bunt

The squeeze bunt is in many ways the simplest of all bunting skills. Our goal is simply to bunt the ball back toward the pitcher. If we bunt the ball right back toward the pitcher on the squeeze, I think that's the greatest bunt in the world because now you have a pitcher trying to make a difficult play. Once the bunt is down, many positive things can happen, the least of which is a run across the plate.

The key principle in the squeeze bunt is timing. To create an element of surprise, we ask our athletes to delay the execution of the bunt until the pitcher has started to bring his throwing arm forward. The runner delays his break from third to avoid tipping the play to the offense as well. Although the squeeze bunt is the easiest, you must be refined in timing it.

Slash Bunt

The slash bunt, or swinging bunt, is an offensive skill that we like to incorporate quite often. It's used when your opponent has overextended on their bunt defenses. Often the corner positions are very close to home plate in anticipation of the bunt. In addition, the middle infielders may vacate their positions to cover first base or third base. Overextending on defense leaves many holes through which to try to slash the ball. The technique is to have your hitter pivot into the bunting position early. We like to have our hitters pivot even before the pitcher is in a set position of the rubber. We want the hitter to sell the bunt to the defense, getting them to commit defensively as much as possible. That done, the hitter simply rocks back to a shortened hitting position, ready to slap the ball on the ground.

The hitter must hit the pitch on the ground. The ideal slash bunt would be a routine ground ball to the shortstop's or second baseman's position because these players are expecting a sacrifice bunt and have already moved away from their usual positions. But we don't need the ideal situation to be successful here. If we can just get the ball on the ground, we're happy. A ground ball will take advantage of the holes in the infield defense, whereas a fly ball is a much easier play for the defense to handle. Keep in mind that we like to keep the ball away from the second base bag. If we make contact with the ball toward the second base bag, we're probably going to slash ourselves right into a double play.

SLASHING OFFENSE

In a 1993 regional game, we set the tone for our opener by taking advantage of a creeping third baseman. In a bunt situation, we called for the slash bunt and hit a ball that should have been a double play, but it bounced over the head of the drawn-in third baseman. Instead of two outs, we had runners at the corners and no outs.

Try the play with the runner breaking on the pitch from first base, creating havoc and a possible big inning.

Bunting Drills

The drills that we incorporate to develop our bunting game are progressive in technique. Remember how we compared bunting to catching the ball with the barrel of the bat? Well, we begin our bunting drills by asking our players to go to the plate with their fielding gloves on and to catch the thrown pitch as if their gloves were bats. The following is a list of progression drills that we use to develop the skill of bunting. Each drill should be mastered before moving on to the next.

Glove Bunt Drill

Purpose. To emphasize catching the ball with the bat head.

Procedure. Athletes execute bunting fundamentals with glove and without a bat.

Fungo Bunt Drill

Purpose. To intensify difficulty of skill, which forces athletes to have fine concentration.

Procedure. Athletes execute bunting fundamentals with a fungo bat or a bat several sizes smaller than normally used.

Four-Corner Bunt Drill

Purpose. To allow 12 to 16 athletes to work on bunt skills in a short time period.

Procedure. Groups of three to four athletes at each base execute bunts using the respective foul lines. A teammate pitches.

Two-Strike Bunt Drill

Purpose. To develop bunt skills under game-like pressure.

Procedure. Athletes execute the skill off a pitcher with a two-strike count.

The Two-Strike Bunt Drill is the final stage of this sequence that we incorporate in a bunting period each day for 10 to 15 minutes at the completion of our stretching. Not every position player is involved at this point. We choose a select number of athletes who will regularly be called upon to execute bunt plays in a game. Depending upon our roster, it can consist of 8 to 12 players.

The first 10 minutes of our practice plan are designed for those athletes to work on executing all types of bunt plays against a *live* pitcher. The individual throwing might be a pitcher who needs extra work or a coach, but we want it to be as close to game speed as possible.

Each time an athlete steps to the plate in the Two-Strike Bunt Drill, he has to bunt with the count against him. Think about it. Every day at practice, our key bunters are working on executing with two strikes—squeeze bunts, sacrifices, base hit bunts, all with two strikes. If you fail, you're out. Intense, yes. Beneficial, you bet! The concentration level of your athletes as they approach the drill intensifies. If we can execute every day with two strikes, we should be able to do it in the game.

TWO-STRIKE SQUEEZE

Cal State Dominguez Hills versus Cal State Northridge. Big game. First place was at stake. A big right-hander for Northridge named Hernandez had dominated one of our hitters all day. It was late in the game and the hitter was at the plate with the tying run at third. I vividly recall the first two pitches were swung at and missed, not even close. Following ball one we put the squeeze on and executed it perfectly. It stunned our opponent! We won that game and eventually went on to win the conference title.

We ask our athletes to work on two-strike bunting daily. By the way, we do not neglect those players who may not be asked to bunt so often. They will work on their bunting game in their normal offensive practice. In other words, if the number five hitter in our lineup is not going to be asked to sacrifice very often, we just ask him to make sure he works on that part of the game during his normal offensive routine. But our leadoff hitter has to be in this drill every single day and, in addition, work on his bunting game during our offensive stations as well.

Bat Control

Keep in mind our definition of offense. Offense is the ability to score runs when we are not hitting. Bat control allows us to score runs when the hitters are slumping. Bat control involves the ability to hit and run, hit and run drive, and hit the ball to the right side. Bat control is one of the most important, if not *the* most important, offensive skills a program must possess to be successful. I will make that statement every day of the week. If your program does not have bat control, your chances of success, if you equate success with being in a championship game, are going to be slim. Without bat control we have no chance at true success. We might have a good year, but we'll have no chance of being at the final game.

Hit and Run

The ability to execute the hit and run usually dictates, more than any other skill, whether we're going to have a good offensive day or not. Early in the ball game I like to hit and run within the first inning or two. If we execute early in the ball game, I would encourage fans in the stands to stick around because they are probably going to see a good offensive club that day. If we don't hit and run, I don't get discouraged. I'll come back and do it again at the next opportunity. But if we don't execute, chances are we are going to have a tough day.

I make this clear so that our athletes understand the importance of the skill. The first athlete to get the hit and run gets a little bit more excited, a little more juiced, and takes more responsibility. There's a sense of personal ownership on the athlete's part because of his understanding of the importance of executing the first hit and run of the game. We want him to set the tone for us that day.

The goal for the hit and run is to spread the defense out by starting the runner. You then ask your hitter to protect him by putting the ball in play on the ground.

You can approach teaching this skill by breaking it down into the following three priorities:

- With the runner(s) breaking, the hitter must make contact on the next pitch.
- The hitter must put the ball on the ground.
- The hitter must keep the ball out of the middle.

We do not want the ball hit around the second base bag because it is easily turned into an unassisted double play.

HIT AND RUN TO OMAHA

The 1982 Arizona State University ball club was probably the best hit and run team I've ever seen at the college level. That club made contact consistently. They weren't very fast as baserunners so they didn't straight steal a lot, but it seemed as though they would start all their runners on every pitch. Their hitters did a tremendous job of protecting the plate and the baserunners, and that skill helped them get into the World Series. That ASU team showed what an extremely important skill the hit and run is, especially if you don't have tremendous team speed.

In a hit and run situation, hitters often get anxious and jump early at the pitch. This can sometimes result in a missed swing. A teaching tip for this skill is to remind your players to jam themselves on the pitch. Verbally remind them to jam themselves. Tell players that it's okay simply to jam themselves and put the ball in play because in this case they've done the job even without getting the ball out of the infield. The ideal situation, obviously, is that you would make *good* contact on the ground, out of the middle, allowing the baserunner to advance from first to third. But the jam concept will keep your hitter back, resulting in a better chance for success.

We like to say that a big inning for us at Florida is an execution of the hit and run with nobody out. Following a successful hit and run, we will have runners at first and third with no outs. First and third with nobody out in our program is a big inning for the following reason: We will now probably go hit and run two more times in this inning. If we go hit and run two more times this inning, we're going to end up with another first and third with a run scored and another first and third with a run scored. You might be facing us two runs down with runners at first and third and still nobody out. The hit and run can be the foundation of our offense.

Hit and Run Drive

This skill is similar to the hit and run only in three priorities: making contact, keeping the ball on the ground, and staying out of the middle. The beauty of the hit and run drive after those priorities is that we really want to see players *drive* the ball. If the ball doesn't leave the infield on the hit and run, we will commend players and applaud them for their execution. On the hit and run *drive* we're asking our athletes to go ahead and drive it and to hit the hardest ball they've ever hit in their lives on the ground. The irony is that most players will turn their attempt into a line drive in the gap.

Whereas a hit and run is signaled typically either on a no count or when we are protecting a runner on a 1-0 count, the hit and run drive is executed on 2-0 counts and 3-1 counts. We're anticipating a great pitch to hit, and we want the ball driven hard. Everybody in our lineup is obligated to swing (except for ball four on a 3-1 count). We're going to be aggressive and go after our opponent.

In the national championship playoffs against the University of Texas, Danny Melendez hit a 3-1 count hit-and-run-drive home run. Look at that video, and you'll see the ball was at about shoulder height. He got up on the pitch and took it right out of right center field on a hit and run drive. This is the classic hit and run drive that we teach our players.

Hitting Behind the Runner

This skill is another trademark of successful programs. Once again, if we're not executing this particular skill, our chances of success at our level are going to be limited. I believe it's true at all levels—this skill is not stressed enough. We all discuss it, but I'm not sure how many head coaches truly understand how crucial this particular skill is, especially at the end of the season when we're sitting around saying, "We should have won five or six more games!" I will go out on a limb and say that the years I have been diligent in stressing the bat control concept of hitting behind the runner were our greatest years by far.

The ability to hit the ball to the right side of the field with runners on second or third is invaluable. In its purest sense, by hitting the ball behind the runner you actually trade an out for a run, but you are doing it aggressively with a great opportunity for an RBI single or at least runners at first and third. That is a trade that I think any coach would take.

There are three essential components to the technique we like to teach: Batters should fight to keep their hands inside the pitch; they should delay contact or delay the swing to enhance their chances of maintaining bat control and making contact on the right side; and they want to be absolutely sure that the club head is above the flight of the pitch (see figure 7.4).

Figure 7.4 Hitting to the opposite field.

Bat Control Practice

We ask our athletes to work on bat control skills (bat, slash, hit and run, hit and run drive) for at least 20 minutes per day. Everyone on the roster must spend at least 20 minutes a day on those three skills.

If you're fortunate enough to have a cage with two hitting tunnels (we are fortunate enough to have that), set up one side of your hitting tunnel for simply slash, hit and run, and hit and run drive. If you don't have that luxury, and I didn't have that luxury as a high school coach, then you should make sure that in the live station you give them at least 20 minutes per day.

I do not have any special drills for teaching bat control. As you may recall, my philosophy is to teach skills in a whole concept as opposed to a part concept. It is my goal to give players ample time to execute every one of these skills daily in practice.

It's an injustice and poor coaching if you don't give your athletes concentrated time on bat control skills and then get upset when they fail to execute in the 12th inning of a game. If you've given them concentrated time daily and they can't execute it, that's just life. But if you haven't given them enough time, it's a poor job of coaching on your part.

Baserunning

I firmly believe that your players' ability to run the bases at the younger levels will separate your team from the pack. I know as a high school baseball coach our ability to run the bases made our ball club special. We weren't blessed with the best athletes, but we really did a thorough job running the bases. We worked daily to develop knowledge and understanding on creating good angles as we ran the bases. As a result, we created many easy runs at the high school level.

I'll support that statement by saying that in my five years as a high school coach, sometimes we had good hitters, and sometimes we didn't. Sometimes we had people who could execute, and sometimes we didn't. But one thing that we kept constant for five years was that we could run the bases. That should be a constant.

Start by explaining to your athletes that when they are on base they must have an aggressive plan on each pitch. Make them understand that they are literally fighting for inches. If they are stealing, insist on rhythm or movement in their lead to enhance their jump. If there is no steal, then they must be prepared to fight for extra inches in the secondary lead so they can advance on a short passed ball. Players should fight for inches on every turn or angle they take when they're circling the bases.

Keep in mind that these concepts apply to all your athletes. Do not neglect the slower players. Just because they may not get the steal sign doesn't mean they won't win a game by fighting for inches somewhere on the bases.

Movement and Straight Lines

Most baserunning concepts can be included within the ideas of movement (or rhythm) and straight lines. Obviously, the baserunning topic can be as detailed as you want to make it, but if you and your players can be confident in these two areas, your ball club is well on its way to being a threat on the bases.

Most of us realize that the shortest distance between two points is a straight line. This is not brain surgery, right? Then it should make sense that we need to train our athletes to run the bases in the straightest lines possible.

Think how this is applicable to running from home to first. Watch any young hitter's path to first after a swing, and it won't take you long to see the dramatic importance of the straight-line concept. Most athletes can pick up one to three feet in distance just by being drilled on getting out of the box properly. Think how often hitters are thrown out by a step or two. Fight for those inches.

I'm not suggesting that players make 90-degree turns at the base to create a straight line, which is obviously not practical. Still, the runner must create the tightest angle possible without losing momentum or speed. This route will be different for each player. It is important that the player discover what is comfortable for him relative to his athletic ability and speed so he can master this particular skill.

We prefer our runners to make the necessary turn prior to the base to create a straighter line to the next base. We want them to be in a straight line to the next base and to be in a straight line when we are making the decision to advance another 90 feet. For instance, we do not want to make our decision to stretch a single into a double as we approach second following a sloppy turn at first. On the contrary, we want to make that decision while traveling the shortest possible distance between first and second. The same is true when players are advancing from first to third or second to home. The straight line idea can be used in teaching running technique and taking leads.

Keep your runners moving. Have them develop rhythm in all that they do. It can be subtle, as in their primary lead at first, or obvious, as they explode into their secondary lead on the pitch.

Leads From First

Keep it simple here. It's more important that your athletes feel confident in the length of their leads than it is to get large leads. Although leads can vary with circumstances, have your runners memorize the lengths of their leads. We do not want athletes wondering how far off they are in the middle of a game. They memorize it by practicing it. They should be able to consistently produce the same lead, even with their eyes closed (see figure 7.5).

Once the length is established, we need to maintain movement in our lead. By doing so,

we are fighting for those inches that will give us an edge. You do not want stationary runners. Thinking back to physics class, we remember that a body in motion tends to stay in motion. At first base, this movement is a subtle inward turn of the right knee, almost dropping an inch or two (see figure 7.6). Remember, it needs only to be a slight movement. In our program we focus on the right knee.

In a steal situation most programs will teach an initial short jab step with the right foot or an initial crossover step with the left foot (see figure 7.7). Predominant contemporary thought is that the jab step gets a runner going a little quicker. Regardless of the technique used, it should be executed in such a manner that your runner explodes into a straight line to second! One method to determine which is better for each particular runner would be to actually time the athlete using both techniques.

Secondary Leads

The secondary lead allows the runner to extend farther off the base as the pitch is thrown. We ask our athletes to maintain their movement with two or three shuffle steps toward second, while always maintaining balance and eye contact with the ball. Seeing the flight of the pitch enables the runner to anticipate pitches that may be in

Figure 7.5 Lead from first base.

Figure 7.6   Lead from first base with subtle inward turn of the right knee.

Figure 7.7   Crossover from first base in a straight line.

the dirt and to react before the ball gets to the ground. A good, solid secondary lead can provide those extra inches we are fighting for.

Leads at Second

Maintaining movement in leads at second is less subtle. The runner typically has more time and room with which to work. Once again, we want our athletes to be confident in the length of their leads. Remember your straight lines! A runner from second must eventually be in a straight line between second and third, regardless of where he begins his lead. Secondary leads are typically more aggressive as well because of the extra distance between the base and the catcher.

There might be an exception when there are two outs and the possibility of a stolen base is decreased. At this point you would want your runner to begin deeper (two to three feet toward the outfield) for a better angle to create a straight line between third and home as he scores.

Leads at Third

Ninety feet from a run. The runner must maintain his aggressive plan on every pitch here! The secondary lead is all important. Runners should be aggressive, but not over-extend. The best technique is to have a controlled walking lead toward home plate and to stay balanced. Movement toward home as the ball crosses the plate is essential for good jumps. Runners should always antici-pate a wild pitch, passed ball, or the hitter putting the ball in play. The runner takes his lead in foul ground so as not to be called out if hit by a batted ball (see figure 7.8). Follow-ing the pitch, he returns in fair territory, reducing the lane into which a pickoff throw from the catcher may travel.

WHY FIGHT FOR INCHES?

Let's do a little math. Let's say your athlete can go from home to first in 4.5 seconds. It's 90 feet from home to first. Simple division tells us he is traveling 20 feet per second. More simple divi-sion says he is traveling two feet every 10th of a second!

If a runner can pick up a 10th of a second in his baserunning technique, he picks up 24 inches! Small improvement results in a great advantage: Teach athletes to fight for those inches!

Baserunning Drills

I like to work on the finished product as much as possible, again the *whole* concept of teaching. The following two drills are my favorite drills to use when focusing on baserunning skills.

Live Baseball Drill

Purpose. To work on baserunning skills against a pitcher in a game-like setting.

Procedure. Each day following warm-ups, runners compete against pitchers and catchers. Add two portable bases near first base so three runners at a time can work on jumps while a pitcher, catcher, and defensive player at second try to stop them.

Figure 7.8 Lead from third base in foul ground.

Coaching Points. Emphasize game-like intensity. Alter your lines to the needs of your club. Each line of runners can emphasize a different skill.

Three-Spots Drill

Purpose. To work on turns at each base and to improve the cardiovascular system.

Procedure. Split the team into three groups, beginning at home, first base, and second base. The hitter at the plate triggers movement by swinging. Each runner works on advancing 180 feet (two bases). Upon execution, runners from home and first return to the previous base. The runner scoring from second stays at home plate.

Coaching Points. Monitor running of straight lines and emphasize conditioning.

Hitting

Notice where this topic is in the order of this chapter: last. It's not unimportant, it's just not as important as bunting, bat control, and baserunning. Remember: Offense is not hitting.

In our program we hope that with our offensive skills in place (i.e., the ability to drag, push, slash, hit and run, squeeze, and hit behind the runner), our ability to hit becomes an added skill as opposed to the only skill on which we're trying to survive.

I would stress that everyone who works with hitters should be encouraging and positive about each hitter's potential. Simply put, praise the hitter and don't be critical. Hitting has to be the most difficult skill in athletics, and we get far too critical with our hitters. I think that most hitters have some serious doubt to begin with, and if we continue to criticize them, we only create more doubt.

We teach hitting as a four-step progression: vision, stride, staying closed, and balance.

Vision

Vision is first, which for us is the ability to see the ball with both eyes while batters are in the stance. We ask our hitters to rotate their heads to use both eyes (see figure 7.9). We'd like our hitters to see the pitcher as much as a catcher does.

Vision Drills

Number Drill

Procedure. Place numbers or letters on several baseballs. The coach moves the ball around, rotating a baseball in the hand. Athletes attempt to identify the number or letter without moving the head.

Dot Drill

Procedure. Place a colored dot on several baseballs and include them in batting practice drills. Hitters are only allowed to hit balls with certain colored dots.

Another simple but effective practice activity to improve hitters' vision can be performed anytime one of your pitchers is throwing. Hitters stand watching a pitcher's bullpen workout and grade themselves on how well they see each pitch. The benefits of this self-

Figure 7.9   Striding with good vision.

testing will only be as good as the degree to which hitters really concentrate and score themselves on each pitch.

Stride

The second step in the hitting progression is stride. Stride is a timing device for our hitters; we believe that good hitters complete the stride long before bad hitters do.

Stride Drill

Procedure. Use a stride box built to the size of an appropriate stride length. Have hitters swing from inside the box, forcing them to have a short stride.

Variation. Put an object such as a glove or hat on the ground at a spot where the stride length should be. Both the drill and its variation keep batters aware of maintaining a short stride.

Staying Closed

Staying closed or staying back is the third step in the hitting progression. Players need to keep their shoulders turned and hands back while they're still moving forward.

Cord Drill

Procedure. The coach controls a harness placed around the hitter's waist. A bungee cord attached to a belt works well. The coach tugs on the cord to remind the athlete to stay back.

Balance

The fourth and final step in the hitting progression is balance. Teach hitters to maintain stability from the beginning of the swing to its completion (see figure 7.10).

Figure 7.10 A hitter maintaining balance throughout the swing.

Balance Drill

Check Point Drill

Procedure. Constantly check each hitter's balance. This drill forces hitters to check their balance at the end of each swing.

I once heard the statement that there is a time to practice swinging, and there is a time to practice hitting. We like to practice our swing off tees, off a short toss, and in the cage. Then we like to practice hitting on the main diamond during batting practice. We hope that our drills do not just consume time, but that they are progressive steps in practicing the swing that will develop muscle memory. When we practice hitting, we don't have to think mechanics and can go into more performance work.

Hit in Order

A concept that we have found successful in our program is that during live batting practice we always hit in our batting order and we always hit with a count. We like to hit with a 2-1 count and then proceed through an at-bat. We put a strong emphasis on game-like situations. Remember now, we're practicing hitting, not swings. In other words, we'll put our hitters in bases loaded at-bats, hit and run at-bats, hit and run drive at-bats, sacrifice at-bats, advancing the runner, in whatever area we feel we need to work. But the emphasis in this drill is that we spend our time in a batting order so that from a psychological standpoint players are working with the athletes that they're probably going to be working with in a game. In other words, if Steve Rodriguez is working every day on hit and run and his teammate is encouraging him, it's kind of a nice feeling because he's the same guy who's going to be encouraging him in the on-deck circle in the 14th inning with the game on the line.

Our goal is to have our players experience game-like situations in batting practice while hitting in our batting order so that we meet game pressures daily. In essence, we'd like our players to go to the plate with the game on the line and realize they have been in this situation every day of practice. It's going to be a challenge because normal pulse rate is around 80 at practice. In a game situation with the winning run on third base, in the ninth inning of a ball game with people yelling and screaming, the pulse is going to be about 120 to 125. But your goal as a coach is to create game-like situations in batting practice so that when your player gets to that situation in the ninth inning, subconsciously he feels, "I've been here before." I think you enhance his chance of being successful by implanting that thought process in him.

Right Side Hitting

Daily drills we use to practice our swing include taking batting practice from the right side of the infield. This is a drill that we got from Ben Hines, the hitting instructor at Arizona State in the early '80s, who was also with the Dodgers for several years. We place our batting practice screen on the right side of the infield and have our hitter stand as if he's facing a pitcher on the mound. Our pitcher then throws from this different angle. We find this drill is very valuable in helping

our players who are a little bit overeager to hit with power or to muscle up and are continually pulling the ball. This helps our hitters stay back, stay closed, and drive the ball up the middle with authority.

Hitting Drills

I have picked up the following drills over the course of my career. Each one has a distinct purpose and emphasis. We try to use these drills when appropriate for each particular athlete.

Rhythm Tee Drill

Purpose. To practice the muscle memory of rhythm and weight shift.

Procedure. Standing next to a batting tee, the hitter works on going back and forth, shifting weight from front to back foot. About every two or three strokes, a partner places a ball on the tee and the hitter makes contact with the ball. When there's not a ball on the tee, he continues to go through the same actions, shifting weight from front to back foot (see figures 7.11, a-b).

a   b

Figure 7.11   Rhythm Tee Drill. Shifting weight from back foot to front foot (a) and making contact with the ball (b).

Bat Throwing Drill

Purpose. To emphasize the importance of throwing the barrel of the bat.

Purpose. The hitter in a spacious area actually throws the bat. The hitter throws the barrel of the bat in the direction from which the visualized pitch is coming. We include going to the opposite field, going to the middle, and pulling the ball. We typically do this in our outfield or any spacious area.

Belly Button Drill

Purpose. To improve hip action quickness.

Procedure. The athlete locks the bat in his arms behind his back and works on swinging, emphasizing the quickness of the hips through the entire swing.

Summary

I am convinced that offense is much more than just hitting. It includes the following concepts and philosophies:

- Offense is not hitting. Offense is your team's ability to score runs when it is *not* hitting.
- Your offense can be described in four concepts: bunting, bat control, baserunning, and hitting.
- The bunting, bat control, and baserunning aspects of your offense will help spread the opponent's defense.
- The ability to hit behind the runner consistently when needed is necessary to play at the championship level.
- Teach your offensive skills, such as bunting, in a step-by-step, progressive manner.
- *Never* do drills to fill time. Game-like, intense drills are most appropriate.
- Take batting practice in the order of your lineup, creating a familiarity between your players.
- Practice bunting and bat control *daily*.
- Straight lines and movement are two standards of baserunning. Fight for inches! Have an aggressive plan on every pitch.
- Vision, stride, staying back, and balance are our four most important concepts in hitting. Be positive and encourage as you teach.

## Chapter 8

Teaching
Offensive Strategies

What does the ideal offense consist of? Speed? Power? Bat control? When you see a lineup like the Big Red Machine led by Rose, Morgan, Griffey, Perez, and Bench in the early '70s, you appreciate that the ideal lineup has a combination of these qualities. In this chapter we'll look at each attribute of an ideal offense, position by position. At the end I'll share a few thoughts on special plays and suggest some signs to use to run your offense.

Ideal Offense

Take a moment to think about the ingredients and makeup of the perfect offense. What's the finished product you're striving to create? The ideal offense is a matter of coaches' opinions and can be debated endlessly.

In my book the ideal offense consists of:

1. team speed,
2. power,
3. bat control, and
4. offensive spontaneity.

These four ingredients make up the ideal offense because I've seen them work in both my high school and my college programs. An evaluation of my best clubs shows that these are the offensive team characteristics that made us champions.

Team Speed

Subscribing to Herzog's "speed never slumps," we are diligent in our recruiting efforts to add speed to our program. Even as a high school coach I made a specific effort to locate fast athletes on campus. I pursued wide receivers and tailbacks from our football teams, as well as sprinters from our track program.

Each of our athletes is taught baserunning, and each will fight for inches on the bases. All of our athletes should be fundamentally sound in their running techniques. After evaluating our ball club, we identify those players who possess good speed and equip them with the additional knowledge of base stealing techniques and strategies. Please note that I differentiate between baserunning and base stealing. Evaluation of your personnel is the key.

Our better runners will be taught how to read pitchers in steal attempts. They will be well versed in their abilities to read pitchouts. They will be taught when to run and when

not to run. They will know how to steal third and when to do it.

Chapter 7 describes some of our baserunning drills, but it should be noted here that during our batting practice rotation we will often have a baserunning station that enables our runners to react to hitters.

Power

We all know power when we see it. We know when an athlete has the ability to hit the ball out of the park. But how do we develop this natural ability? If it's part of our ideal offense, how do we enhance our athletes' abilities to drive the ball deep?

We have a concept in our program for *all* our hitters that encourages them to get to a *positive count* in their at-bats. Another name for a positive count is a *hitter's count*, a ball-strike count that is conducive to success as a hitter (i.e., 3-1, 2-0, 1-0, and sometimes even 0-0).

During practice sessions we work with our hitters to *anticipate middle* in a positive count situation. We want them to gear up for a fastball in the front middle-half of the hitting zone. By sitting on a fastball in the front middle-half of the plate, hitters will enhance the power of their stroke. The result will be a double in the gap or a home run. By

anticipating middle our power athletes will be more consistent in their ability to drive the ball for extra bases. Even our bat control athletes will begin to sneak a few hits through the outfield gaps by anticipating middle on positive counts.

When a hitter gears his swing to a particular pitch and location, he can eliminate many of the different options he must deal with on each swing. When a hitter receives the pitch and location that he is anticipating, he can drive it with the barrel of the bat.

Does this power hitting approach make us vulnerable to off-speed pitches? The answer is *yes*. We hope to take the good off-speed pitch in a positive count situation. But if we get the fastball, we plan to win more games than we lose over the course of a 200 at-bat season.

Bat Control

Bunting, hit and run, and hitting behind the runner are key elements in most successful offenses.

The ability to execute these skills is synonymous with the phrase *bat control*. Athletes who cannot hit for power consistently should spend much of their offensive practice time developing bat control skills.

Here's the approach we take to batting practice. We differentiate between swing practice and hitting practice. We work on our swings in the batting tunnels. We work on hitting live at home plate.

Each athlete has been evaluated as to the type of hitter he is: power or bat control. We then require each athlete to practice according to his particular role. If we have an established power hitter, we want him to spend at least 60 percent of his time working on reacting to positive counts. The remainder of his time will be spent on other facets of the offensive game. We do not want to detract from his natural power ability by spending all his time working on bat control. On the other hand, your soft hitting middle infielder needs to spend his offensive practice time perfecting his ability to execute.

In our live station of batting practice we ask our hitters to step into the cage and perform in a game-like setting. Typically, each station group will consist of three to five hitters. Each hitter gets *one* chance to perform per round. Our power hitters will work

on delivering in a positive count situation. Our bat control players call out their objective and then attempt to execute it. They have the option to execute any of the bat control skills, such as sacrifice, hit and run, squeeze, and so on. The emphasis on *one* opportunity makes it game-like. You will rarely see us in live batting practice with our players getting multiple opportunities to perform the popular four-sacrifices-and-rotate approach. They step in the cage and *must* deliver. We'll spend the majority of our live batting practice station in this manner.

Not only is it game-like, but asking your athletes to call out in advance their own objective gives you an idea of what they like to do and what they are confident doing. This is great information come game time!

Offensive Spontaneity

The fourth aspect of your ideal offense is spontaneity—the ability to respond immediately and correctly in every possible game situation. It is our belief that by combining team speed, power, and bat control in our daily practice sessions we will develop this valuable team quality.

To achieve spontaneity, your drills must be game-like. They need to be monitored with correction and reward. You want your athletes to feel the pressure during practice so when they face a situation in the game they will have the feeling of having been there before.

Spontaneity should be the result of daily game-like practice settings covering baserunning, bat control, and positive count approaches. Having your athletes emphasize their own strengths in practice will also enhance your program's offensive success.

Offensive Team Drills

Many of our drills designed to improve our baserunning can be found in chapter 7. The drills that follow are three more characteristics of a potent offense: power, bat control, and offensive spontaneity.

Anticipate Middle Drill

Purpose. To develop anticipation skills when ahead in the count.

Procedure. In the context of your live hitting station or off a pitching machine in a batting cage, the hitter assumes he has a 2-0 or 3-1 count on him. He works on anticipating a fastball in the middle of the plate.

Coaching Points. Be aware of each hitter's pitch selection and ability to stay back on a fastball in the middle of the plate. Hitters will tend to want to pull a 3-1 or 2-0 pitch. Do not let your hitters become lazy and develop this bad habit.

Bases Loaded At-bat Drill

Purpose. To develop power and the ability to stay out of double plays.

Procedure. In the context of a live hitting station or against a machine in a batting cage, the hitter assumes that the bases are loaded in this particular at-bat. His goal is to lift the ball in the air in the middle of the yard, avoiding a rally-killing double play ground ball.

Coaching Point. Watch that hitters don't become defensive in trying to avoid the double play.

Hit and Run Drill

Purpose. To help develop bat control skills and to provide live action for your defense.

Procedure. Place nine defenders on the field in their positions. Hitters take turns executing the hit and run. Defenders react to the batted ball appropriately.

Variations. The defense can be set to work on double plays or with no runner on base. Outfielders can react to varying situations as well (i.e., hitting cutoff men to various bases).

Coaching Point. This drill is a good opportunity to move defenders to various positions to see how they will react.

Setting the Lineup

Evaluating your team's individual abilities helps direct your approach to offensive strategy. Part of that strategy is creating the best nine-person batting order possible. If my personnel allowed, I would start my lineup with a right-handed hitter, followed by a left-handed hitter in the two spot, right-hander hitting third, left-hander fourth, alternating through all nine hitters. There are two reasons for this approach: (1) it's difficult for a pitcher to get comfortable; more importantly, (2) it's a difficult lineup for your opponent to match up against with relief pitching in the later innings. I must admit that it's been rare for me to achieve this, but it's nice when it happens.

Another general approach would be to get your best hitters at the top of your order so they will get the extra at-bats at the end of the game. I know when I coached in high school I would often hit my top hitter in the leadoff spot to ensure he would get the most at-bats. This is more crucial in a seven-inning game. In college, with nine innings, your number three, four, and five hitters have a good chance at the extra plate appearance.

Now let's look at the specific things I try to do when developing an offensive lineup. The batting order would ideally consist of the following.

Leadoff

My ideal leadoff man has a solid knowledge of the strike zone and as a result has a good on-base percentage. Patience is involved here. He also has good speed to put pressure on the defense from the very first pitch of the game.

Two Spot

Ideally, this player is left-handed. His chances are good to put the ball through the right side with the first baseman holding a runner. He blocks a catcher's vision to some extent as well. Good patience and selectivity from the number two hitter (i.e., ability to take pitches) enable your leadoff man to steal bases. Bat control is desired to move runners, and foot speed should not be overlooked to avoid possible double plays.

Three Hole

The best overall hitter on our roster will always be put into the third position in the order. He'll have good power with a low strike-out percentage. Hitting in this spot helps assure us that he has a good chance to be at the plate in the late innings with the game on the line.

Cleanup

We want an RBI man here, yet more importantly he must be able to protect our third hitter. We try to have him hit from the opposite side of the plate from the previous hitter. He also must have such ability that our opponent will not pitch around our third hitter. By following these guidelines, we expect the third spot to see good pitches to hit.

Five Through Seven

I like to call these three hitters our *power or miss* guys. We want them to swing aggressively so when they make contact it has an impact. Hopefully, they will produce RBIs. I'd rather have them swing and miss than to be tentative, grounding weakly into a double play. I literally tell them I'll trade a strikeout for a double play any day. When they make contact, it usually produces runs.

Bottom End

Simply, I want my eighth and ninth hitters to mirror the abilities of my first two men in the order. Good foot speed and bat control are essential. As much as possible, I would like to create the same opportunities with these two hitters as we do with the top of the order.

Keep in mind that the first time through the order is the only time that you can actually determine when your players come to the plate. By assessing your individual talent you should be able to coordinate your style of offensive play. Hopefully, you'll never be out of sync with at least one of the three qualities of speed, power, or bat control.

Lineup Drills

Six-Out Drill

Purpose. To create pressure in your live batting practice station and to simulate the final six outs of the game when trying to come from behind.

Procedure. In a 20-minute live batting practice station, allow your hitters to rotate until they have made six outs in a row. The six outs represent the last six outs of a game situation, and the hitters are fighting to get a baserunner on to start a rally. As long as they avoid six consecutive outs, the hitters may stay at this station for the entire 20 minutes. If they make six outs in a row, they rotate to the next station.

Coaching Point. Develop teamwork and confidence in this drill by creating situations in which individuals and groups can come through in the clutch.

Carry the Guy Drill

Purpose. To create live offensive pressure, which helps players learn how to come through in a difficult situation.

Procedure. Allow your live group a certain number of total outs (9 to 12). Hitters stay at the live station until they make the designated number of outs. This approach creates a situation in which one or two hitters in a group can actually *carry* the other guys and extend their time in the batting cage. As soon as the designated number of outs is recorded, the group leaves the live station.

Coaching Point. A great drill for teaching players how to battle a pitcher and be resourceful in reaching base.

Special Plays

We do not have many trick or gimmick plays in our offensive approach. We would hope that our offense would be developed to the point that we have too many other options to consider before we resort to such plays. Yet there are times when you may need something to offset bad days. We all know there are situations when runs are tough to come by. It's these times when a little creativity is in order.

Safety Squeeze

One of my favorites when we try to steal a run is the safety squeeze. When executed, it virtually guarantees a run. With a runner at third base and a good bat control man at the plate, you ask your hitter to square early, executing a bunt at the third baseman. Your baserunner extends down the line, shadowing the third baseman. If the third baseman completes the throw to first, your runner scores easily. If he holds onto the ball, your runner returns to third base with the bunter safe at first. The success ratio is greater with runners at first and third, since the shortstop will break to cover second, leaving no one to cover third base and allowing the runner from third to move farther down the line.

Early Break Versus Left-Hander

Execute this play when runners are at first and third, and there is a left-hander on the mound (the less experienced, the better). Your runner at third should have good baserunning skills. He initiates the play by racing for home as the pitcher comes set. Following his teammate's first move from third base, the runner at first breaks. Your goal is for the left-handed pitcher to react to the runner he sees while the runner scores easily from third.

Again, I don't enjoy being in a situation where I must use these plays, but they are good to have in case you need them!

Signs and Signals

It may be interesting to note that as you go higher in this game, fewer signs are necessary. The talent level in the professional ranks is such that you rely more on raw talent than designed plays. In college, you have a few more signs, and in high school you may have many signs to have better control of what your team does. When I was a high school coach, I had over 20 signs—one for almost everything.

There are so many variations to giving signs that I'll just cover the basics here with a few examples. Particularly for coaches new to giving signs, it's important to stay simple and consistent. A complex system might sound good at a coaching clinic, but is of little practical value. Your players need to be able to easily understand and read your signs.

Indicator

Use an indicator, which is a sign your athlete looks for that tells him the next sign will determine what play is on. For example, I've often used a skin-to-skin indicator. Any two consecutive touches that include skin will be followed by the sign desired. You could use cloth-to-cloth or any single predetermined area of the body as your indicator.

For those of you who have never given signs before, understand that typically each play coincides with a part of your body. For

example, the hat could be bunt, the chest might be steal, and the leg could be the hit and run play. If you had a skin-to-skin indicator, any two consecutive touches to skin followed by a touch of the chest would be the steal sign. You can give several meaningless signs, but your athletes key on the indicator and the subsequent sign.

Wipe-Off Sign

You need to have a wipe-off sign, which gives you the opportunity to correct mistakes you may have made in giving a sign to a hitter. It also gives you the opportunity to change your mind in the middle of a series of signs. A classic wipe-off sign would be to wipe across your chest or down one of the arms. This sign would inform the hitter that you are starting the sign series over.

Repeat Sign

Often I will include a repeat sign. This sign enables me to call the same play on back-to-back pitches without repeating the original signs. Repeating the same sign over and over enables your opponent to try to interpret the sign, anticipating your offensive strategy. By having a simple repeat sign, your offensive players will understand that the strategy on the previous pitch will be repeated on the next pitch. The repeat sign can be as simple as touching a certain part of your body that's considered an automatic sign.

Verbal Signs

You need to have verbal signs, but use them sparingly. Combining visual and verbal signs can be productive. For example, when verbally communicating outs to a runner, anytime I use the word "down," it's the steal sign. So "one down" or "two down" would signal steal to my runner. As with visual signs, verbal signs can be unlimited.

The problem with verbal signs is that if you play in front of a large crowd, they become tough to hear. Since we all want to play in big games and championships, the big crowds may restrict the use of verbal signs. At the high school level, I had a thorough list of verbal signs, but at Dodger Stadium I found those signs neutralized by the large crowd and greater distances from my athletes.

Summary

The ability to evaluate your athletes' talents is essential in directing your offensive approach. Once you are comfortable with your evaluation, the following ideas will help create a productive offense:

- The ideal offense includes team speed, power, bat control, and spontaneity.
- Focus your athlete's practice time toward those skills which he will be asked to produce during the game.
- Offensive spontaneity is the result of disciplined, well-monitored, game-like practices on a daily basis.
- Get your best athletes at the top of your lineup. Ensure they are at the plate in the later innings.
- In general, speed at both the top and bottom of your lineup with power in the middle is a good offensive mix.
- Limit the temptation to spend extended practice time on gimmick plays, yet have a few such plays at your disposal when it becomes necessary.
- Keep signs simple and consistent. Use an indicator, a wipe-off sign, and a repeat sign.
- Use verbal signs, but use them sparingly.

## Part IV

Coaching Defense

## Chapter 9

Teaching Defensive Skills

Offense can win you some games. Defense will win you more games. Defense *and* pitching will win you championships.

In this chapter we will discuss what it takes to play each position on the field. We will also include the desired characteristics of each spot and drills to incorporate into your daily practice routine. Because I believe pitching is so important, we have committed an entire chapter (11) to that skill.

Constants: Pitching and Defense

Making adjustments is a major part of the head coach's job description. It can be changes relative to the roster, coaching staff, offensive approach, or even your practice format. Adjustments are a way of life. To survive, a coach must learn this lesson early.

Amid all this change, one thing remains constant: Pitching and defense are the keys to a long-time successful baseball program. No matter what year it is, no matter who the players are, no matter who my coaches are, no matter what the preseason predictions are, I know that if we get better pitching and defense as the weeks go by, we'll get better as a team. And, we'll probably be playing for a championship before the year ends.

Offensive concerns should be number three on your priority list. You can get by with an average offensive club if you have sound pitching and defense.

Baseball: A Game of Catch

Teaching the simple task of catching and throwing a baseball is probably the most challenging concept we face in our program. In our program we approach every athlete as if he has *never* thrown or caught a baseball before. We're convinced that the teaching approach to throwing must begin at the most simplistic stage and be developed over the course of the season.

Basic Throwing Mechanics

We have our athletes grip the ball across the seams with a loose, controlled grip. We teach our players to dominate the top half of the ball with their grips. Many athletes allow the ball to dominate them by dropping underneath the ball with their hands or arms, but the proper throwing technique is to stay on top of the ball as much as possible. This helps the elbow to be even or above the shoulder through the throwing motion.

Our players *always* throw at a target. They step toward the target with the front foot, close the front or lead shoulder, and point it at the target (see figure 9.1, a-b). Some coaches refer to the lead shoulder as the *gun sight* to be pointed in the direction of the throw.

Twenty Extra Minutes

Playing a high level of catch is the foundation of a good defense. Coaches of all levels should realize this and place greater importance on the first 20-30 minutes of practice (when the players loosen their arms). Don't waste this time at the beginning of practice. These first 20 minutes should be used to teach throwing, catching, and footwork fundamentals that develop a sound foundation. If you have an athlete who is having a difficult time with a defensive skill and you spend 10-15 minutes a day with him during warm-ups, you

a   b

Figure 9.1   Players throw by stepping toward the target (a), closing the front or lead shoulder, and aiming at the target (b).

are spending close to two hours with him over the course of the week. Use this time wisely!

Another way to maximize your warm-up time is to pair up your athletes by position. Pitchers warm up with pitchers, catchers with catchers, middle infielders with middle infielders, and so on. This will enable them to work on fundamentals that are specific to their particular positions. We will expound on this as we discuss each position separately.

Positions

In putting the best defensive athletes on the field, we need to look for specific qualities at each position. Once we determine the qualities each athlete has and where he might fit into our overall defensive scheme, we can approach him with drills that we hope will develop the athlete at his best position.

Outfielders

Ideal characteristics of outfielders include:

- foot speed and quickness,
- arm strength,
- good instincts, and
- the ability to get good jumps on batted balls.

We hope outfielders have the physical attributes of foot speed and arm strength for obvious reasons. They need to be quick because they cover a large area of the diamond. They need strong arms because they are going to be making long throws.

Often overlooked is the ability of an outfielder to get a good jump on the ball. An outfielder with good instincts can compensate for a lack of speed and arm strength. Therefore, having good instincts is the most important characteristic I look for in my outfielders.

Traditionally, your right fielder has the strongest arm of the three outfielders due to the longer throws he must make. Because your center fielder must cover both alleys and does not have a foul line to restrict the field area he must cover, he is typically your quickest outfielder with the best instincts.

Your center fielder should be a leader as well, since he has close proximity to both of the other outfielders and can verbally control things from his position. I like my left fielder to be my next best remaining outfielder with the most offensive potential.

Getting a Good Jump

Getting a good jump on a batted ball is a priority for outfielders, and I am convinced this skill can be taught. To teach an outfielder this skill, we ask him to concentrate on two key principles. The first is to see the pitch through the hitting zone. We want him literally to see the ball travel through the area where contact will be made. This demands a high level of concentration.

The second principle our outfielders follow is to *decleat* on every pitch. We all have seen tennis players waiting on a serve. Their feet are in constant motion, waiting to explode toward the ball. We ask *all* our defensive players to incorporate this technique as they watch the ball through the hitting zone. Their feet must be in constant motion.

Maintaining Mental Toughness

An intangible principle which benefits outfielders is their mental toughness: their ability to stay ready on every pitch. This certainly helps them to get a good jump on the ball, but more importantly it allows them to be ready on the last pitch of the last inning of the game, even if the ball has not found them up until that point. If the outfielder does not have this mental toughness to approach each pitch this way, it could, and usually does, hurt the ball club. Your defensive players have to believe with all their hearts and with every fiber of their bodies that every pitch in every inning is coming their way.

The *one more* concept is designed to develop this mental toughness. This concept can be incorporated into anything that we may be doing. The basic idea is to add one more to everything: one more ground ball, one more fly ball, one more sprint—just one more. When the athlete feels he is finished with a particular drill, we add just one more. This forces the player to reach into his reserve tank within his frame of mind and know he has to be ready for one more—and maybe one more after that!

Fielding Ground Balls in the Outfield

We expect our outfielders to be highly competent in fielding ground balls in three different manners or techniques, depending on the situation. The first situation would be with no runners on base and a routine single. In this situation our emphasis is to keep the single from turning into an extra base hit. We are much more cautious in our approach to the ground ball and ask our outfielders to drop to one knee to keep the ball in front (see figure 9.2).

When runners on base do *not* represent the tying or winning run, we ask our outfielders to field the ground ball using the techniques similar to those used by an infielder. This will allow the outfielder to get the throw off in a much more expedient manner and to have a chance at throwing out the advancing runner.

In a do-or-die situation with runners in scoring position, it becomes much more urgent that the outfielder get off a quick throw to home plate. The quickest possible way for an outfielder to get off a good throw is by fielding the ground ball off to the side with one hand (see figure 9.3). Moving quickly through the ball, the outfielder immediately gets into throwing position to get off a good

Figure 9.3 An outfielder fielding a ground ball off to the side.

throw. Keep in mind this technique should only be used with the tying or winning run at second base in the late innings, as it is highly vulnerable to a bad hop passing by the outfielder. This is a risk you should only take in situations when the game is on the line.

Outfield Drills

Long Catch Drill

Purpose. To develop arm strength and incorporate the technique of running through a fly ball or ground ball to get maximum possible into the throw.

Procedure. Once the outfielders' arms are loose, ask them to play catch from approximately 200 to 300 feet, depending on the athletes. The coach should distinguish between *long catch* and *rainbow catch*. For long catch, players are to throw a long distance, but also to keep the throw low to the ground as if a cutoff man might need to cut the throw off. By contrast, rainbow catch is a lazy, looping manner of catch, and it's quite ineffective. Mastering the long catch is essential for outfielders.

Coaching Point. Check throwing form and accuracy. If players are using poor mechanics

Figure 9.2 An outfielder dropping to one knee to keep the ball in front.

and are wild in their throws, shorten the distance and correct the flaws before building up to longer throws.

Short Toss Drill

Purpose. To provide numerous controlled repetitions in order to develop defensive techniques for outfielders (i.e., going back on balls, playing balls in the sun, playing balls off the wall, and so on).

Procedure. From a short distance the coach tosses the ball in a manner similar to desired defensive situations. Having several baseballs enhances the repetitive aspect. The numerous repetitions enhance footwork, movement toward the ball, and the player's jump.

Coaching Points. Be mindful to incorporate three concepts. One is proper technique. Two is mental toughness—remember "just one more, just one more!" Three, you're working on decleating, so prior to throwing the ball tell the athlete, "Windup . . . pitch . . . hitting zone." On the "hitting zone" command, athletes should decleat and then proceed with the technique that the drill calls for.

Live Batting Practice Drill

Purpose. To exaggerate defensive situations that an outfielder has problems with.

Procedure. During batting practice place your outfielders in exaggerated defensive positioning to create numerous specific defensive situations.

Coaching Points. This is one of our most prominent drills to develop outfielders. Stress the importance of approaching the drill as if it were a game situation. We are very specific about where we play the outfielder in order to exaggerate a particular weakness on which we need to work. For instance, if an athlete has trouble going back on the ball, we force him to play shallow during batting practice. This creates more opportunities for him to play balls over his head. As a coach, you dictate the situation on which he should work. Take every opportunity to emphasize mental toughness ("one more"), getting jumps, decleating, and so on.

We spend a tremendous amount of time with all our defensive players during batting practice, but particularly with our outfielders. They are the easiest defenders to neglect

as a coach. The sad part is they can be exposed at the worst possible time: ninth inning, no fly balls. Then, when all of a sudden a fly ball goes out you'll have miscommunication or improper technique, which will cost your ball club. The outfield is one position that I constantly remind myself to monitor diligently so that we can prevent such breakdowns.

Catchers

Ideal characteristics for catchers include:

- quick feet,
- arm strength,
- good, quick hands,
- intelligence, decisiveness, and aggressiveness,
- leadership qualities, and
- physical toughness.

Most Important Position

The catching position is probably the most important from a defensive standpoint. The catcher must possess just about every physical trait that you would ask of all your defensive players. You're looking for quick feet. You're looking for arm strength. You're looking for leadership. You're looking for all these traits for one simple reason. In my opinion it is the most demanding position on the field. In many respects, I treat my catchers as if they are assistant coaches.

The catcher must be demanding because he will have to go out to the mound and occasionally, in place of a coach, get on one of the pitchers. The old saying is that you can take a good pitching staff, put them with an average catcher, and your staff will quickly become average; this is very true. Yet if you take an average pitching staff and combine it with a solid catcher, your staff will improve!

Physical Tools for Catching

A catcher must have good, quick feet to come out of his crouch position and throw to first, second, or third base on all steal attempts. Without quick feet he will not be as successful as desired from that defensive position. Arm strength is a key attribute in that he will be asked to help shut down an opponent's running game, which can only be done with quick feet and arm strength. Needless to say, he'll need good, quick hands to be an outstanding receiver for his pitching staff.

Intelligence comes into play when the catcher takes note of opposing hitters. He has to communicate to the pitchers, to the infielders, and to the coaches about how we're going to attack every hitter. He has to be physically tough. Anyone who's going to put his body in front of balls going 80-90 miles an hour day-in and day-out has to be tough, not only physically, but mentally.

We want the catcher to visualize his body as a giant glove and to shape his body similar to the shape a glove is in as it catches a ball: rounded, shaped, all headed into the middle into a funnel-type action. Many times young catchers hear the word *block* and immediately become too rigid and too squared in body position. The catcher's body should take a cupped or rounded body position (like a glove) rather than the rigid block position.

Catchers in our program are the most appreciated, yet most challenged, of any of our athletes. Daily they go through rigorous drills and long bullpens. Because of the demand we place on our catchers, we allow them the freedom of going anywhere they desire during offensive stations to get their offensive work completed.

Catchers' Drills

Exchanges Drill

Purpose. To achieve numerous repetitions of a catcher's throwing position and release.

Procedure. Each day, once your catchers are loose, they should approach every ball as if it were a steal attempt. Monitor your catcher's foot movement toward the ball and the exchange of the ball from glove to throwing hand.

Coaching Point. The key in this drill is being sure the catcher's hands do not drop below the letters of the uniform as he takes the ball back to his release point (see figure 9.4).

Variation. Long catch can also be incorporated daily to develop arm strength, quick feet toward the ball, and the exchange of the ball from glove to throwing hand.

Blocking Pitches Drill

Purpose. To work on pitched balls that are low in the dirt.

Procedure. Using a softer, cloth-type ball, the

Figure 9.4 Catcher taking the ball back to his release point without allowing his hands to fall below the letters of the uniform.

coach stands 10 feet from the catcher and throws short hops in the dirt to simulate pitches.

Coaching Point. Have catchers *catch* the ball with their body instead of blocking it rigidly and having it bounce far out of reach (see figure 9.5).

Infielders

If I had my choice, I would love to have infielders that I could interchange at all the positions and still be solid defensively. Ideally, my first baseman would always field as well as my shortstop does. It's interesting that my infielders on the 1992 championship club (with the exception of our left-handed first baseman Danny Melendez) were all shortstops in high school. It's not always realistic, but we always pursue this goal in our recruiting and teaching technique. If we can

Figure 9.5 The catcher's body in a cupped or rounded blocking position.

have every one of our infielders perform like a sure-fielding shortstop, we feel extremely confident about our chances.

Playing Catch

This is the most fundamental skill we monitor. In playing catch we ask all our infielders to work from their feet to their hands. Players are only as quick as their feet in this game, so that is where we start.

We want players' feet moving toward the ball with a good wide base. We don't want our infielders to have slow, lazy feet that look like they're stuck together. During the 15-20 minute period of warm-up, we want our infielders to have good, quick feet, moving toward every ball thrown to them. They move their feet quickly, keeping their feet at a wide base, minimum shoulder-width apart. We ask that their knees be bent, providing flexibility and balance. We do not want rigid knees. Regarding players' hands, we ask that their hands be together and that they're extended out in front of their body, above the letters of the uniform. We want their chests to be going toward the ball at all times. By putting it all together, infielders are working from their feet and up to their hands in unison.

If we do this consistently, we feel that we are at least starting a good foundation that will take us to the next step, which is the small intricate plays that take place with each player and his position.

Fielding the Ground Ball

We like all of our defensive athletes to be mentally alert to the point where they actually begin defending the batted ball before it is put into play. By knowing the hitter, his pitcher, and the type and location of the pitch, the infielder may anticipate where the batted ball is likely to go. The defender can then mentally or actually physically lean in the direction of his anticipation.

To help them anticipate, we tell our infielders to decleat as the pitch enters the hitting zone. We want movement in our infielders that will enable them to get quicker jumps. Be careful that your infielders do not exaggerate this movement forward, as it will restrict their range. But prepitch movement for all defenders is of the utmost importance. Do not tolerate flat-footed defensive players.

Once the ball is hit, emphasize to your infielders that they are to be aggressive and charge the batted ball whenever possible. When fielding the ball your athletes should be mindful of the following basics:

• Be balanced and under control.

• Feet should be spread to approximately shoulder-width apart with the weight forward on the balls of the feet.

• Infielders should get as low as possible, bending at both the knees and the waist.

• Both hands should be low and out in front of the infielder. As the ball enters the glove the throwing hand should remain on top and follow the ball into the glove (see figure 9.6a).

• Infielders should maintain eye contact with the ball throughout the entire fielding process. Seeing the ball is of ultimate importance. Lose sight of the ball in this game and a player's chances for success are greatly limited.

• Upon receiving the ground ball, throwing hand and glove hand should separate as soon as possible into a throwing position (see figure 9.6, b-c).

a

b   c

Figure 9.6   Fielding a ground ball. With hand on top, follow the ball into the glove (a). Throwing hand should quickly separate from glove (b) and move into throwing position (c).

Moving Left and Right

Obviously, not all ground balls are hit directly in front of your infielders. The crossover step allows the infielder to make the quickest movement toward ground balls hit in either direction. On a ball hit to your infielder's left, the athlete should crossover with his right foot as he simultaneously pivots on the ball off his left foot. The opposite would be true on balls hit to his right.

Emphasize that your infielders should attempt to get in front of as many ground balls as possible. Quite often, athletes resort to a backhand style of play when they could have placed themselves in front of the ground ball with just a little more effort and hustle.

The Corners

An ideal first baseman should be:

- tall and lanky,
- left-handed,
- quick with agile feet,
- soft-handed, and
- productive offensively.

The perfect first baseman would be tall and lanky with quick, agile feet, coupled with soft hands to handle all throws from the infielders. A left-handed first baseman has an advantage when receiving pickoff throws from the pitcher, as well as when making throws to second base. Wearing his glove on his right hand also gives him more range between himself and the second baseman. All things considered, defensive ability can be sacrificed in lieu of strong offensive production at the first base position.

An ideal third baseman should have:

- quick initial reactions,
- lateral speed,
- arm strength,
- agility, and
- courage.

Because the third baseman is often only 90 feet or less away from the batter, quick initial reactions and lateral speed are far more important than overall foot speed. Range is not nearly as important as quickness. Arm strength comes into play quite often because the third baseman plays a good distance away from first base and often has to make long throws following a backhanded play.

Courage becomes a factor because batted balls often seem to explode upon the third baseman. Once again, a coach needs a third baseman to be productive offensively. Defensive characteristics are important, but you can sacrifice some defense to gain a little offense out of your third base position.

As mentioned earlier, it's a luxury if your first and third basemen are former shortstops who have great fielding skills but lack the necessary foot speed to be as successful at shortstop as your level of competition requires.

Corner Drills

Slow Rollers Drill

Purpose. To work on first baseman's and third baseman's abilities to field slow rollers and bunts.

Procedure. Place five to six baseballs in a straight line from home plate moving out toward third base, beginning about 20 feet from the home plate area. Balls are about three or four steps apart. The third baseman reacts to each ball as if it is a bunted ball. Drill the first baseman by placing balls up the first base line in a similar manner.

Coaching Points. Stress the importance of your third baseman catching the ball off his right foot and throwing in the same manner. For drill purposes we ask our athletes to field the ball with both hands, although quite often when a ball is not moving we allow them to field bare-handed. This could be a variation in this drill. Drill a first baseman in much the same way. Your corner infielders must possess the ability to field bunts, and this drill will enhance these skills.

Cone Drill

Purpose. To establish a sense of lateral range for both your third baseman and first baseman.

Procedure. Place a cone between third base and the shortstop position so that your third baseman knows exactly where the shortstop would be at his deepest in terms of the shortstop's throwing side. Tell the third baseman that the cone represents the shortstop's positioning. Coaches then hit ground balls in the direction of the cone, which emphasizes that the third baseman needs to use his lateral movement. This gives him a better sense of his defensive responsibilities. The same drill can be adapted to the first baseman, with the cone representing the second baseman's position.

Coaching Points. Be diligent in emphasizing the first lateral step of your athletes. One of the faults that you'll see in corner infielders is the tendency to give up on ground balls to their glove side. We would like to see both our corner positions really attack the glove side. This is a play often miscommunicated with the middle infielders, so we work on attacking this play to the point that our athletes know where the middle infielders will be on each and every ground ball hit toward the middle of the field.

Middle Infield

The ideal middle infielder will possess:

- good range,
- overall quickness,
- a quick mind,
- arm strength,
- knowledge, and
- leadership skills.

We like players at these two positions to be interchangeable: Ideally, your shortstop can play second and your second baseman could go to short. The only major difference might be physical arm strength.

In our recruiting plan we look for two shortstops every year and eventually move one of them to second base. The qualities that you would like players at these two positions to acquire are quite similar. The first quality is overall quickness. We mean quickness of the feet, hands, body, and mind. We not only need young men who can cover the range and turn the pivot, but we also need a quick mind in these two positions because they're going to be involved with a lot of plays defensively.

Another quality we would like to see is arm strength. We would especially like to see good arm strength with our second baseman because he's going to make some tough pivots. Arm strength is something we hope we can develop day-in and day-out. Once again, we try to develop arm strength during the 20-minute warm-up period. Knowledge and leadership skills are also important attributes of these two positions. They're going to have to have knowledge of every single pitch that's being delivered, every pitch that's being called by the catcher, and every pick-off attempt. Literally everything that's going on defensively is going to have to either come from or go through the shortstop and second baseman. They're right in the heart of everything that's going on defensively. If they don't

have good leadership abilities, they're going to be exposed and you'll need to move them elsewhere.

Catching the Top of the Ball

To enhance our shortstop's and second baseman's ability to have quick hands, we ask that they concentrate on catching the top of the ball. This emphasis will shorten the arc of the arm as players approach the point of release. The teaching principle here is that the shorter the arc, the quicker the release, which should be the desire of every defensive player.

When players catch the top of the baseball, they shorten up the arc to the point of release and arc in position to more quickly make their defensive plays. You might visualize this as being similar to a catcher who frames a high strike while receiving. His fingers are pointed toward the direction of the throw with the palm facing down. In the case of an infielder, he would be using both hands.

We emphasize this technique each day during our prepractice or our pregame warm-up period. Catching the top half of the ball is a very highly skilled technique, but I will guarantee that any infielder who gets to the point where he can catch the top half of the baseball consistently is going to quicken up the arc of his arm. If his arm is quicker, his throws are going to be out of the glove quicker.

Turning the Pivot

We normally designate a time, either before or after our normal practice, to practice the double play. We will take out a bucket of balls and simply roll balls to both positions, working on starting and completing the double play.

Starting the Double Play. Have your middle infielders understand the first out is the most important in a double play. If players hurry and lose the first out, they've missed a great opportunity. They should be quick, but they shouldn't hurry. Players need to be quick getting to the ball so they can cut down the distance the ground ball must travel.

Teach players to field the ball in a manner that allows them to be open to the throw to second base (see figure 9.7). An early separation of the hands after catching the ball will

Figure 9.7 Throw to second base.

allow the pivot man to see the throw clearly. Both the shortstop and second baseman should stay low and avoid wasted movement.

Second Base Pivot. The key elements of the double play pivot are as follows: First, at second base the player must cheat in toward the hitter a couple of steps to cut down the distance to the bag.

Second, he must be in complete control of himself as he reaches an area approximately three feet before the bag. This approach ensures that he can still catch a bad throw on the feed from the shortstop or the third baseman. We like to call this area a *control zone*. We want our second baseman to move in aggressively, but then come under control to be ready for a bad throw.

Third, a player's hands should be extended in front of him (see figure 9.8). One of the faults that we see in our second basemen is that their hands are too close to their bodies. This makes it more difficult for them to catch the top half of the ball—in essence they will continue to catch the middle part of the ball, which will give them a long arc. Speed and

time are of essence in completing a double play pivot. We really want our athletes to have their hands out in front and to catch the top half of the ball, which results in a short arc.

A player's footwork is going to vary with each and every throw that he receives for the pivot. On any throw going toward the outfield side of the bag, his left foot should be stationary on the outfield side of the bag. He will pivot, plant, and throw off his right foot.

On any throw toward the inside part of the bag, a player's left foot will be stationed on the inside part of the bag, and he will use the bag to push off and complete his pivot to first base.

For those throws that come across the middle part of the bag, the player will step with his right foot on the second base side of the bag and continue into the throw, planting with his right foot and throwing to first when his left foot hits the ground. At the completion of each pivot, we ask that our second baseman decleat or take a small jump to avoid the runner and avoid injury (see figure 9.9, a-d).

Figure 9.8 Player's hands extended in front of him as he prepares for second base pivot.

Figure 9.9   The pivot. As left foot hits the ground (a), the player throws to first (b-c), and then takes a short jump to avoid the runner (d).

Shortstop Pivot.   The shortstop's pivot at second also depends on the location of the throw. On any double play feed coming from the outfield side of the bag, the shortstop will catch the ball and simply kick or drag his foot across the outfield side of the bag.

On any throw from the inside part of the bag, the shortstop will station his left foot on the inside part of the bag, pivot off that foot, and complete the throw to first (see figure 9.10, a-b).

On those throws coming directly over the middle of the bag, we would like to see our shortstop catch the ball just prior to the bag and make contact with the back of the bag with his left foot as he releases his throw to first (see figure 9.11). This technique will help to protect the shortstop from oncoming runners and will put second base between him and the baserunner. This is a difficult technique, a highly skilled technique, but a technique that I think needs to be taught.

Like our second baseman, we ask that our shortstop decleat after every throw. On throws from the pitcher or catcher, the shortstop and second baseman have the option of using any of these pivots.

As mentioned before, we drill these techniques each day by simply rolling simulated ground balls to each of our infielders and having them complete the double play. This is done quite regularly in the early part of our season and then occasionally on certain days as the year winds down. What we hope to do with our infielders is to challenge them daily to quicken their feet, keep their bodies in balance, and quicken up the arc of their throws.

Double Play Drills

Four-Corner Drill

Purpose. To develop the ability to turn the double play pivot.

Procedure. A minimum of four athletes gets in a square formation. Athletes then play a quickened game of catch with each throw simulating a double play feed. After an athlete receives the feed, he turns a simulated double play pivot to the athlete to his immediate left.

Coaching Points. Emphasize catching the top half of the baseball, as well as being quick with the feet and accurate with feeds.

a   b

Figure 9.10   The shortstop positions his left foot on the inside part of the bag (a), pivots, and completes the throw to first (b).

Figure 9.11 Shortstop making contact with the back of the bag with his left foot as he releases his throw to first.

Circle Drill

Purpose. To develop the ability to complete under-handed and back-handed feeds on double plays.

Procedure. Place four or more athletes in a circle approximately 15 feet apart. Athletes then play underhanded toss around the circle, beginning with the partner on their immediate left. After one minute the players reverse direction and perform the drill to their right.

Coaching Points. Emphasize movement following the throw, as well as making good, chest-high feeds.

Keep It Simple!

Defense will win you games, but keep it simple. We constantly stress to our athletes that we *must play catch*. We must play a high level of catch consistently and daily. If we understand this overly simplistic statement (and our athletes hear it 50 times a day), our chances of success are enhanced by the simple truth that the ability to play catch is challenging.

Summary

A good defense will enable you to compete for championships at the end of each of your seasons. Despite the importance of defense, keep your approach as simple as possible while emphasizing the following points:

- Offense will win your share of games. Pitching and defense will win championships.
- Playing a high level of catch is the foundation of your overall defense.
- Outfielders need good speed, strong arms, good instincts, and mental toughness to stay focused on every pitch.
- Your catcher can be the most important player in your defense. Quick feet, a strong arm, good hands, intelligence, leadership, and toughness are all necessary to be a great catcher.
- It would be ideal to have athletes with shortstop abilities at all four infield spots.
- If you must sacrifice defense to earn some offense, it should be done at the corners and not in the middle.
- Most defensive plays come from or go through your middle infielders. They must be intelligent leaders willing to take responsibility.
- Keep your defensive philosophy as simple as *just play catch*.

Chapter 10

Teaching
Defensive Strategies

Once basic defensive skills have been taught and are in place, it's time to fine-tune your defense, working on relay throws and situation-specific strategies. A team needs strategies to defend such plays as the sacrifice bunt, squeeze bunt, and double steals. This chapter covers the strategic defensive plays to teach your athletes. With proper instruction, players' decision making and execution will be (almost) error-free.

Making the Great Play

I can relate our entire defensive philosophy to something that took place throughout our 1992 national championship season. From the very first day we were together to the very last day of the national championship game,

our philosophy was very simple: Make the routine plays; allow the great plays to take care of themselves.

We had a very talented team, obviously, but we wanted to make sure that every player understood that defensing the routine play would lead to a championship situation. Once we took care of the routine play, the great play occurred because of our athletic ability and diligent preparation.

PLAY OF THE SERIES

A perfect example of this philosophy was in the eighth inning of the national championship game. Our second baseman, Steve Rodriguez, made what many will say was one of the great plays in College World Series history. With the tying and winning runs at second and third base, he dived for a hard ground ball to his left in the hole and made a tremendous play, ending the inning. Many would probably agree with me—most likely that play gave us the national championship. I would not disagree that that particular play was a big one, but our defense throughout the entire College World Series was outstanding, not necessarily in the great plays, but in all the routine plays! A side note is that Steve's play did not particularly surprise me. I had seen Steve work diligently on such plays during batting practice every day. His hard work on a daily basis obviously paid off for our Pepperdine ball club.

Our premise is that we work hard and prepare ourselves mentally to make all the routine plays. It's not a new concept and it's easier said than done. By working hard I mean we work hard to concentrate and to be aggressive verbally on defense, resulting in great anticipation. We also ask our athletes to visualize prior to every pitch. By visualizing ground balls before they occur and visualizing where cutoff men will be, we have a better chance to make the routine plays.

Defensive Positioning

Several factors influence our defensive adjustments. As coaches we analyze the following variables before making any defensive decision.

- Pitcher's strengths
- Type of hitter—e.g., power hitter or contact?
- Type of pitch—e.g., hard or off-speed?
- Location of pitch—e.g., can hitter pull this pitch?
- Negative or positive count?
- Number of outs
- Field conditions—e.g., big park or small park?
- Wind conditions
- Inning
- Home team or visiting team?

When we move our players in or out of different positions, we consider these variables very seriously.

Know Your Pitcher

Our defense needs to know our pitcher's strengths and weaknesses. Is he a power

pitcher or a finesse pitcher? Is he a pitcher who likes to attack hitters on the inner-half of the plate, or does he like to work hitters on the outer-half of the plate? We would position our players according to what type of pitcher we have pitching for us that particular inning or day.

To take the thought process further, we consider what a pitcher throws in negative and positive counts. We refer to any count in which the pitcher is behind as a negative count (i.e., 1-0, 2-0, 3-1, and so on). Does he throw fastballs in that count? If he does, then we need to deepen our outfield a few steps. The hitter is probably sitting on a fastball.

If he tends to throw off-speed pitches in a negative count, we may keep our ground because we know that if someone hits that pitch hard, he's probably going to hit it well over our heads and we really have no chance anyway. If he does make a good off-speed pitch in a negative count, the ball's not going to be hit as well, and we need to be at our normal depths so we can come in aggressively and make the play on a ball that is not hit as far.

We also want to know what he throws in positive counts (i.e., ahead in the count: 1-2, 0-2, and so on). We like to think a 2-2 count is a positive count for our pitchers. So we want to know what he's going to throw with two strikes so that we can make the proper adjustment. Most hitters will become more defensive with two strikes as they attempt to protect the plate, so we might play hitters more to the opposite field and a bit more shallow.

Infielders must be mindful of these considerations as well. We ask that our middle infielders know every pitch that's being called and that they know every variable regarding the pitcher's strengths, the hitter's strengths, what the pitch and location is, what the count is, and what the score is. We want our second baseman and shortstop to know exactly what pitch is being called by the catcher, and then we ask that they relay this information to our corner infielders. In essence, our infielders begin their work well before the ball is hit.

First and third basemen must know when off-speed pitches are being called so that they can anticipate something that might be hit hard down the line. If you are throwing change-ups in particular counts (i.e., 1-0, 2-

0, 3-1), opponents will often pull the ball. We want our corner people to know when off-speed pitches are called. This can be communicated by our middle infielders with a simple verbal sign.

We used to have our middle infielders tell our outfielders when particular off-speed pitches were being called so that they could adjust themselves accordingly. But some opponents were picking up our relay system and then relaying that information to their hitters. So we haven't used that system lately; our middle infielders continue to relay information to our corner infielders.

As you can see, much of the information we use to set our defense stems from the mound. There are other considerations, but the pitcher is the most important source.

Know the Score

We want to make sure we keep the score in play at all times. Is this the winning run at second base? Is it the tying run? If it is, then we need to move in and give ourselves a chance for an out at the plate. If we're up by four or five runs, we'll keep the double play in order and play a little deeper. With two outs we'll always play a little bit deeper. A general rule for us is that with two outs our outfielders will always play deeper, not allowing the ball into the gap without it being a legitimate extra base hit.

Defensive Specifics

Before we ever speak to our athletes about executing bunt plays, relays, first and third defenses, or run-downs, we first discuss two fundamental ideas: We are going to (1) stay aggressive, and (2) establish a priority before the play occurs. For example, our bunt defenses are designed for our fielders to make an aggressive attempt to retire the lead runner, with the understanding that the priority is to get at least one out. Once you have established your priority, it is easier to decide on a particular defensive tactic.

Bunt Defenses

Develop a simple bunt defense that your players will execute consistently. Establish which runner should be your priority out, and be aggressive. Don't sit back and let the offense dictate its game to you.

Runner at First Base

The priority for any bunt defense is to get an out. Your opponent's strategy is to trade an out in order to advance their runner(s). So you had better at least get the out that they *want* to give you.

Our basic approach to defending a bunt with a runner on first is to establish responsibilities for each infielder.

• The pitcher must throw a strike. He then covers the area from the mound to the first base line.

• The third baseman charges the hitter and has coverage from the third base line to the mound.

• The first baseman holds the runner at first and reacts to the hard bunt past the pitcher.

• The second baseman and shortstop cover first and second bases respectively, being diligent not to clear their positions until they are sure of the bunt. They do this by taking an *L* route to their bases.

• The catcher has coverage in front of the plate and will cover third base if the third baseman fields the bunt. We also like our catcher to communicate where the play should be made since he has a good view of the whole diamond (see figure 10.1)

There are a few variations to this defense. If the priority is to get the lead runner (i.e.,

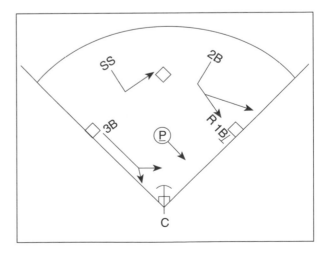

Figure 10.1 Bunt defense with a runner at 1B.

late innings, close game), we will bring our first baseman hard toward the plate earlier. This way we have four defenders (3B, 1B, P, C) all in a position to field the bunt, resulting in a better possibility of getting the lead runner, who is at first base in figure 10.2. To do this, we might include a pick at first base, ensuring that the runner does not leave early as the first baseman leaves the bag to defend the bunt. This will initially hold the runner closer to the bag.

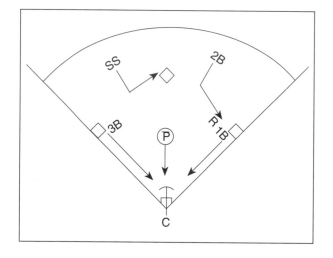

Figure 10.2   Bunt defense with runner at 1B. Lead runner priority.

Runner at Second Base

With a runner at second base or runners at first and second base, the bunt defense responsibilities are somewhat similar, with the corners switching roles.

- The pitcher again must throw a strike. He then has coverage from the mound to the third base line.
- The first baseman charges the hitter and has coverage from the first base line to the mound.
- The third baseman reacts to the hard bunt past the pitcher.
- The shortstop holds the runner close at second base.
- The second baseman makes his *L* route to first base.
- The catcher covers in front of the plate (see figure 10.3).

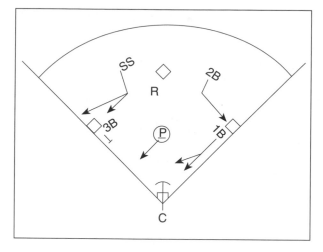

Figure 10.3   Bunt defense with runner at 2B.

Your player's responsibilities can change if you establish the lead runner as your priority. At that point we will bring both corners hard toward the hitter. The shortstop will again keep the runner close at second initially, but then break to cover third base. Once the shortstop has cleared the runner by a sufficient distance (10 or so feet), the third baseman charges, and the pitcher delivers his strike to the plate (see figure 10.4).

You might add a pickoff with this defense by having your second baseman covering second as the shortstop breaks to cover third (see figure 10.5).

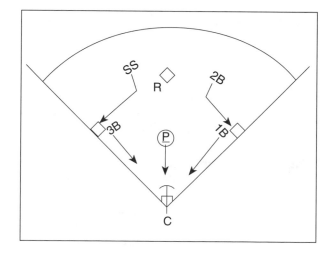

Figure 10.4   Bunt defense with runner at 2B. Lead runner priority.

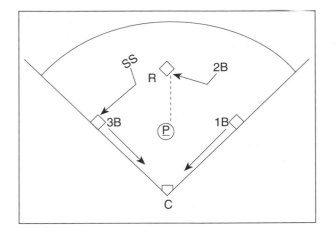

Figure 10.5 Bunt defense with runner at 2B. Pickoff sequence.

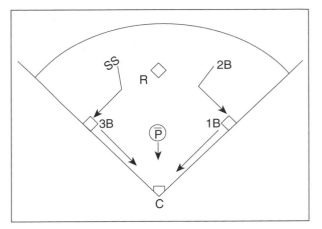

Figure 10.6 Squeeze bunt defense.

Squeeze

The squeeze bunt is designed to be a surprise play by the offense. Some coaches use the play a lot. Others use it only when they have a good bunter at the plate and see the corner infielders on their heels. Anticipation and awareness of the situation is a must in order for your athletes to defense it properly.

- The pitcher's role, once aware of the squeeze, is to throw a fastball up and inside to a right-handed hitter (tough pitch to bunt) or throw a pitchout to a left-handed hitter.
- The corners both charge to field any bunted ball.
- The shortstop breaks to cover third base in case of a rundown.
- The second baseman breaks to cover first base (see figure 10.6).

Being fully aware of the score, inning, hitter tendency, and so on, is a must in all defenses. In all cases, your first priority is to get an out somewhere. As a result, you limit the damage that may occur following a successful sacrifice. Failure to get an out opens the door to a big inning.

First and Third Defenses

We emphasize the idea of playing a high level of catch in our first and third defenses. We want our athletes to have the mental approach that defending first and third situa-

tions is simply a matter of making good decisions while playing catch. This will help our athletes approach these situations with confidence and execute properly, instead of feeling a sense of panic and making errors.

Straight Steal

When your opponents have runners at first and third, their coach will often try to steal the runner from first, hoping to put two runners in scoring position and avoid the double play. Your opponent may also be hoping for a mishandle of the throw to second base, allowing the runner to score from third easily. This can be defended in the following ways.

Option #1: About 90 percent of the time when our opponent attempts to steal second, we will throw straight to second base. We rely on our athletes to play catch between home and second base to record the out. If the runner at third breaks for the plate, we read this and return a throw to home.

We add a few twists to give us an edge. On the initial throw to second, our pitcher will fake a cutoff to attempt to freeze the runner at third base. Any hesitation on the runner's part will be helpful. Also, after the pitch our first baseman will follow the runner toward second. This will expedite a run-down if the runner chooses to stop short of the second base bag. If you have high-caliber athletes in your middle defense, use this option often.

Option #2: I call this a *delay defense play.* This defense will allow you to defend both the straight steal and a delay steal by your opponent. With the runner at first moving, our second baseman comes directly in about a foot off the base line (see figure 10.7). The shortstop covers second base, and now the catcher has an option to throw to either man, depending on the baserunner's action. If he is executing a delay type of steal, it would be better to give the ball up to the second baseman.

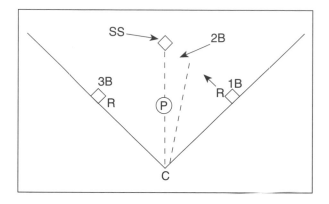

Figure 10.7   Straight steel defense, option #2.

The next two options can be used if you lack confidence in your middle defense or if the runner at third represents the winning run and you don't want to risk a mistake.

Option #3: Your catcher delivers a full arm fake toward second and immediately follows with a throw to third.

Option #4: The catcher delivers a hard throw back to the pitcher, who follows with a throw to third (assuming that the runner's lead has extended on the throw).

More First and Third Defenses

Your opponent may try to create an opportunity in which they can steal a run in a first and third situation. The general idea from the offense's perspective is to create a run-down between first and second, allowing the runner from third to score. This is a high risk play for the offense.

Be aware of this situation in a close game—two outs, runners on the corners, weak hitter at the plate, maybe even a two-strike

count on the hitter. This is not a high-percentage situation to sit back and wait for a base hit! So the opposing coach will often try to manufacture a run. Your solid defensive approach should prepare players to anticipate and respond.

Assuming a close game, your priority needs to be the runner at third base. But if you execute the run-down efficiently (before the runner from third can reach home), you may not have to worry about the run at third.

Early Break Play

One manner in which your opponent might try to create the run-down is by breaking early from first base. You defense this play in the following way:

1. The defense is to yell for the pitcher to "Step off."

2. The pitcher steps off and checks the runner at third base.

3. If there is no play at third, the pitcher throws the ball to a middle infielder, either the shortstop covering second or the second baseman who has broken straight forward from his position in case the runner stops between first and second.

4. The middle infielder checks for a play at third. If there is no play, he executes a quick run-down with the first baseman, who has trailed the runner at first following the pitch.

Intentional Pick Play

Another offensive approach is to allow the runner to be picked off first base, intentionally creating a run-down between first and second and possibly allowing the runner from third to score. Here's how you would defend this play:

1. Your first baseman checks for a play at third base.

2. With no play he begins to work a run-down between first and second.

3. The shortstop closes down the distance to execute the run-down more quickly.

These defensive plays become possible when a runner breaks for home. Your fielders should react accordingly. With two outs, an efficient run-down technique often enables us to record the third out before the run can score from third base.

Run-downs

Remind your players that a runner caught in a run-down is the one who is in trouble. Young athletes too often panic in defending this situation. So reinforce that the defense has the ball in its hands and is in full control.

Our priority in a run-down is to record the out as quickly as possible. Therefore, our first response on defense is to go hard at the runner, getting him to commit himself to a particular base. We want to attack the runner aggressively, under control, and remove any opportunity for him to dictate what we do. Once he is committed to a particular base, we then give the ball up to our teammate to make the tag. With this aggressive approach, the pursuing player often catches the runner before needing to throw to another base.

Many coaches teach *always* to run the player back to the base from which he started, in case a mistake is made defensively. Then, at worst, your opponent is back where he started.

We do not subscribe to this approach. We emphasize a defense that lends itself to fewer throws, fewer opportunities for the runner, and as a result, fewer mistakes.

We use two other run-down tactics. One, we create a throwing line before beginning to get the runner committed. Both defenders immediately involved must get on the same side of the runner in case a throw is necessary. We do not want our athletes to throw into the path of the runner.

Tactic two is if the pitcher begins the run-down process, as a result of a pickoff, for example, he'll always follow his throw to that particular base. This will help you avoid leaving open the base from which the runner started, closing one more loophole in your run-down defense.

Cutoffs and Double Relays

Cutoff plays are used defensively following balls hit into the outfield. Cutoff responsibilities for your infielders are relatively basic and are shown in figures 10.8-10.10. Communication is generally the responsibility of the man covering the base as the throw approaches. We keep our communication simple by loudly repeating the command three times directing the cutoff man to throw the ball to the proper base. For instance, with a runner at first base and a base hit to right field, the third baseman will communicate to the shortstop where the throw should go. If he wants the throw to come to third base and be relayed he will yell, "Three, three, three." If he wants the ball to be cut off and thrown to first base to catch the runner rounding the bag, he will yell, "One, one, one." If the throw from right field is of good strength and he wants the ball to go untouched into third base, he will yell, "Go, go, go." Loud and clear communication is essential.

Double relays extend the defense somewhat and are used in case of a sure double or possible triple by the hitter. A double relay helps get the ball to the appropriate base as quickly as possible. In executing a double relay, both middle infielders go out toward the point where the ball was hit, lining themselves up to the base where the ball needs to go.

The priorities of your double relay must be established in advance. Determine who has the stronger arms between the outfielder and your middle infielder. With this information you establish who makes the longer throw. Take advantage of your athletes' strengths. If your infielders have adequate arms, then it is best to make the first throw (i.e., from the outfielder) the shortest throw. The first throw must be executed to successfully complete the double relay. The shorter the first throw, the better the chances of success.

The second priority is to determine what base to line up toward. We have a simple rule here. With first base unoccupied, we line up to third base (possible triple). With first base occupied, we line up the relay toward home, hoping for an opportunity to throw out the runner attempting to score. However, we can always consider the option of throwing to another base if a play develops elsewhere with the batter/runner.

Both middle infielders are involved for communication and backup purposes. The trail (or second) infielder in the tandem helps communicate where the ball is to be thrown on the relay. He is also approximately 10 yards behind the relay man to handle an

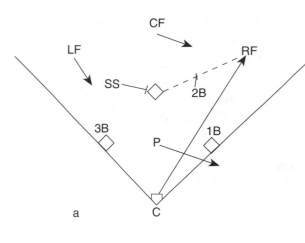

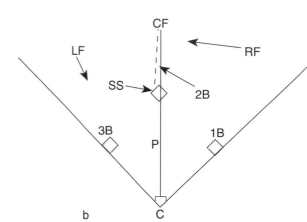

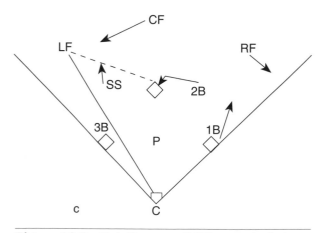

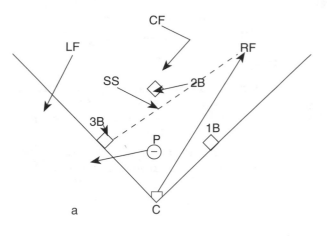

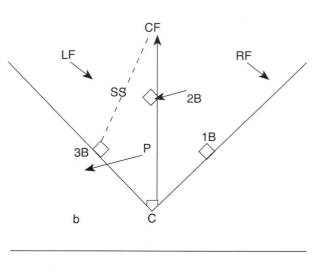

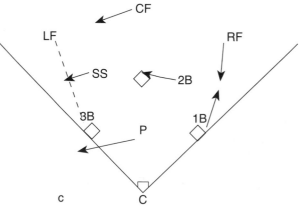

Figure 10.8 *Cutoff responsibilities on single to outfield with no one on base.* a. Single to right. 2B is cutoff. LF is back-up at 2B. P backs up possible throw to 1B. b. Single to center. 2B or SS can be cutoff with other covering 2B. P backs up throw. c. Single to left. SS is cutoff. RF and 1B back up throw.

Figure 10.9 *Cutoff responsibilities on single to outfield with runner on first.* a. Single to right. SS is cutoff on throw to 3B. 2B covers bag. LF and P back-up 3B. OF anticipates overthrows. b. Single to center. SS is cutoff on throw to 3B. 2B covers bag. P backs up 3B. OF anticipates overthrows. c. Single to left. SS is cutoff to 3B. 2B covers bag. P backs up 3B. 1B backs up 2B. OF anticipates overthrows.

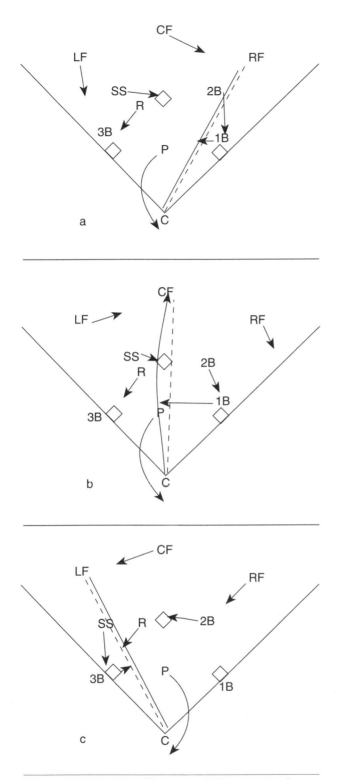

Figure 10.10 *Cutoff responsibilities on single to outfield with runner on second.* a. Single to right. 1B is cutoff to home. 2B covers first. SS covers second. P backs up home. b. Single to center. 1B is cutoff to home. 2B covers first. SS covers second. P backs up home. c. Single to left. 3B is cutoff to home. 2B covers second. SS covers 3B. P backs up home.

errant throw by the outfielder. Whether second or third base is occupied is not an issue. These runners will score on the extra base hit anyway.

The first baseman trails the batter to second base. Once the batter reaches second base, the first baseman retreats to a good cutoff position in the infield to prepare for a possible throw to home.

Relay Technique

Communication is an important aspect of any cutoff or relay. Often the outfielder is hurrying to get the ball and make the initial throw toward the infield. The infielder has to communicate to the outfielder where the throw should go. The communication should be visual and verbal. The relay man who is to receive the ball should have his arms extended into the air and at the same time be shouting, "Hit me, hit me, hit me" to the outfielder fielding the ball. Both the raised arms and the communicated command of "hit me" will tell the outfielder where to deliver the ball. Combined with his own anticipation prior to the play, this technique will ensure that the ball is thrown to the proper base or cutoff man.

In receiving the throw we like our cutoff man to make an initial step toward the outfielder, anticipating the difficult low throw. As he receives the throw, we like him to move his momentum back toward the base he will be relaying the ball to. As he receives the ball, his body should be opened up in a position to throw toward the target base, which will enable him to relay the ball as quickly as possible.

Pickoff Plays

Let's play smart here! The percentages for picking people off are not very good. Maybe it's a lost art, or maybe umpires won't call the out even when you do pick someone off because it's a difficult call to make. Our philosophy is not so much to pick runners off as it is to keep them close (see figure 10.11). This will help our outfielders get more assists or set up the double play in the infield.

Too many times I've seen a pitcher try to make a fantastic pickoff throw. He hurries, throwing the ball into right field, and a run scores. That's something we want to make

Figure 10.11   Pickoff attempt at first base.

sure that we never do. We're not interested in picking people off. If we pick someone off, that's their mistake. We're interested in keeping the runner close enough that if a base hit occurs on the next pitch, our outfielders have a chance of throwing him out at the plate.

Pickoff Basics

At first base we have a basic pickoff that we call a *trail pick*, with which we are trying to pick off the runner at first when he's the trail runner. With bases loaded or runners at first and second, we have our first baseman come in behind at first and, through a visual cue from our catcher or a verbal cue from our second baseman, our pitcher is signaled when to turn and pick to our first baseman.

At second base we run the same type of concept. If there are runners on second and third and the runner on second is a little lazy or negligent, we run a trail pick at second base. This is simply done by the catcher signaling to the pitcher to pick by making a downward motion with his glove. In essence,

when the catcher's glove drops, the pitcher knows that he must now turn and throw to second base because a position player is waiting for his throw at the bag.

We also have a move that has become very popular throughout all of college baseball— youth baseball as well. I've even seen it in the major leagues occasionally. In a first and third situation our pitchers will fake a throw to third, turn, and pick the runner off at first. It helps if it is a running situation for the runner at first.

Our pickoffs are not intricate by any stretch of the imagination. We have very few picks in addition to what you will read in chapter 11 about how we hold runners. We're just trying to keep runners close so that we can keep the double play alive and get some assists from our outfielders.

Championship Preparation

One teaching technique we use with our situational defenses is to run them without verbal cues. We won't allow them to say a word. This forces every player to use his eyes and his ability to anticipate. And, if the situation ever presents itself, it will help in a championship setting. In the College World Series, with 20,000 people yelling and screaming, sometimes defensive players can't hear one another over the noise of the crowd. Visual information is important if you are heading toward a championship situation.

Early in the season, we like to practice that daily. As the season goes on, we'll do it occasionally, and when we get into postseason, we'll do it pretty regularly as well. But it's a good drill to do all your bunt defenses, your first and third defenses, your double cuts, and your pickoffs without any type of verbal assistance. Make sure that the athletes are all doing it off their own visual information and their abilities to anticipate.

Defensive Strategy Drills

Your defensive drills should create spontaneity and quick reaction. In bunt defense, rundowns, and pickoff drills, it is all the same. Emphasize being spontaneous and having quick feet. Never do drills just to occupy time. Whether you use the drills I suggest or some of your own, by creating a spontaneous reaction, you train your athletes to react to visual information, enhancing their ability to anticipate and make good, quick decisions.

Bunt Defense Drills

Live Infield Defense Drill

Purpose. To perfect the infield's ability to defend the bunt play.

Procedure. Place a defender at each infield position, including one pitcher on the mound. The remainder of the pitching staff will be in foul ground, ready to take their turns on the mound. Use your outfielders to run the bases. Direct the drill from one of the batter's boxes. The drill begins with the pitcher on the mound throwing a strike. The coach responds by rolling a simulated bunt to various parts of the infield and observing the defense accordingly.

Coaching Points. Depending on the location and speed of your "bunts," you can create any situation you desire. Work on the most common situations first and foremost.

Variation. You may use outfielders or extra players to do the actual bunting, depending of course on their abilities and roles as hitters. For best control a coach works just fine.

Street Monkey Drill

Purpose. To provide high repetitions of fielding bunt plays, as well as ground balls, to the right side of the infield between the pitcher and first baseman.

Procedure. Place your infielders, catchers, and pitchers in their positions. Then split your infield in half. The right side of the infield will be working on bunt plays up the first base line, as well as ground balls to the first baseman and second baseman where the pitcher will be forced to cover first (see figure 10.12). Simultaneously, on the left side of the field another group of pitchers will be working bunt plays up the third base line in conjunction with the third baseman. This drill requires two coaches, or a coach and a responsible catcher, and is very productive. This drill works on tough plays. But if you do them daily, these plays become routine plays.

Coaching Point. Keep an eye on your pitchers as they make their approach to first base. Run the drill late in practice when they're

Figure 10.12   Street Monkey Drill.

tired and you'll probably catch them running on a diagonal instead of parallel to the first base line.

Variations. You can vary this drill by adding a first baseman who starts the double play at second with the pitcher covering first. You can also add comebackers to the mound for which the pitcher starts the double play at second base.

WHAT'S IN A NAME?

I decided very early in my career never to drive home upset following a loss that resulted from our inability to handle a bunt play or a ground ball mishandled between our pitcher and first baseman. These routine plays, when not handled, result in big innings. So daily, absolutely every day, we work our Street Monkey Drill. Why the name Street Monkey? On the sandlots of San Pedro, the two teams were known as the Street Monkeys and the Devil's Pups. As fate would have it, I was on the Street Monkeys, and we usually won. The name evolved into the title of this daily drill. Street Monkey continues to be successful today!

First and Third Drills

First and Third Defense Drill

Purpose. To create live defensive situations with runners at first and third.

Procedure. Place your infielders at their respective positions with one pitcher on the mound. Your outfielders will serve as runners at first base and third base. As coach, you create the offensive situation desired, such as straight steal, delay steal, intentional pick, or early break. You also control the particular defensive play that you desire, creating a realistic setting for defending these plays.

Variation. Have one coach run the offense while another coach controls the defense. This should create a little competition between the players and the coaches, creating a more realistic environment.

Run-down Drill

Four-Corner Run-downs Drill

Purpose. To create a high number of run-down repetitions.

Procedure. Your infielders are in their positions, one pitcher is on the mound, baserunners are occupying every base, and a coach stands behind the pitcher's mound. From that position the coach initiates the run-down by throwing to a particular base. The defense executes the run-down between those two bases only. Once completed, the coach can move to another base. We like to have our coach make the throws simply to speed up the process and avoid the carelessness of bad throws.

Pickoff Drill

Three-Corner Pickoff Drill

Purpose. To perfect our pitcher's abilities to pick runners at all three bases.

Procedure. Infielders are in their positions. You need three pitchers and three catchers. Each pitcher/catcher combination will simulate a particular pickoff situation. One pitcher is directly on the rubber, working with second base and shortstop with picks at second. Another pitcher is on the third base side of the mound, working on his picks to third base. Another pitcher is on the first base side of the mound, working on trail picks to first or pickoffs to first base. We have created three pickoff areas working simultaneously—picks at first, second, and third—and they're responding to catchers' commands on our pick plays.

Double Relay Drills

Double Relay Drill

Purpose. To create double relay situations with your defense.

Procedure. A coach will fungo various extra base hits with the defense reacting accordingly. Use your pitchers to run the bases, simulating a live situation.

Variation. We will often begin this drill without using the ball. The coach will describe where the runners are on base and describe where the ball has been hit. Observe that your double relay tandem is lined up to the proper base. Once they are comfortable knowing which base to line up to, implement the drill using a baseball.

TEACHING DEFENSIVE STRATEGIES   121

Relay Line Drill

Purpose. To improve relay technique.

Procedure. Using all your infielders, line them up in a straight line from home plate to a spot in the outfield near the fence, separating them by approximately 90 to 120 feet. This will vary, depending on the number of infielders you have. An outfielder then will start the drill by picking up a ball near the fence and delivering the throw to the first infielder. Each infielder will then complete the relay technique to the next infielder until the ball reaches home plate. It is important that each infielder handles the ball and exhibits both visual and verbal communication, coupled with proper footwork.

Please remember that the goal of your drills is to create spontaneity and quick reaction. It is better to do these drills for a short period of time on a daily basis, as opposed to long periods of time one or two days a week. Despite being a daily routine, the drills can be kept fresh by limiting the length of time spent. Done daily, these drills strengthen our defensive abilities in game situations.

Intangibles

I allude to the concept of anticipation throughout this book. You can play the game of baseball well only if you anticipate well. Nowhere is this more evident than on defense. We train our athletes to anticipate by teaching them to be verbal, to be aware, to visualize, and to keep things simple. You must anticipate to be a great defensive club.

Attacking Verbally

In our program we like to attack a team verbally. I don't mean making fun of opponents—how they dress or what they look like. Lord knows that there is too much ragging in our game, and we don't tolerate that in our program. I mean that we attack a team verbally on defense. If it's a squeeze situation, before the pitch is even delivered, we will make sure that two or three guys have communicated, "Hey, be aware of the squeeze." If it's a first and third situation, or a possible bunt situation, we ask our athletes to communicate the situation, to break down our opponent verbally. Communicating in advance enhances our players' anticipation.

Awareness

We ask our defensive players to be cognizant of many things: the abilities and tendencies of the hitter, the pitching strategy of our pitcher, the hitter's performance in the past couple of at-bats, the speed and aggressiveness of the runner(s), the count (positive or negative), and the score. Our players are constantly quizzed on their awareness of this mental checklist. By constantly quizzing our athletes, we keep them mentally sharp and develop good awareness habits. This will enhance our chances of being a good defensive club.

Visualization

We ask that our players visualize ground balls and that our outfielders visualize where the cutoff people will be in every situation. We ask them to do this before every pitch. We ask our infielders to visualize the routine ground ball, where the hops would be— actually take their eyes to those spots, let their eyes look at the hop three times and where they would probably catch the ball. We ask our outfielders to look in the outfield where the cutoff people will be if a ball is hit to them. By doing their visual work before, they just react when the pitch is made.

Simplicity

The last thought that we have for improving our defensive play with intangibles is that we would like to stay as simple as possible. We don't get so technique-minded that we forget that the basic idea is to catch the round white thing with red stitches on it. We want our guys to understand that there is technique involved, but the most important thing is that we must be able to make the routine play. Remember, that's where this chapter began: Make the routine play and let the great plays take care of themselves.

Summary

It is not enough just to have athletes with good defensive skills. As a coach you must take the skills of your players and combine them with good, reasonable strategies to defend the many situations that come up on a game-by-game basis. A good fundamental philosophy combined with a simple approach to execution will help you be a good defensive ball club.

- Make the routine play. Let the great plays take care of themselves.
- Visualizing, anticipation, and being verbally aggressive are the keys to good defense.
- Defensive positioning is only done after careful consideration of many different aspects of both your team and your opponents.
- Bunt defenses, first and third defenses, run-downs, relays, and pick-offs should be kept relatively simple to ensure consistent execution.
- Defensive intangibles include attacking verbally, awareness, visualization, and simplicity. This will enhance your anticipation.

## Chapter 11

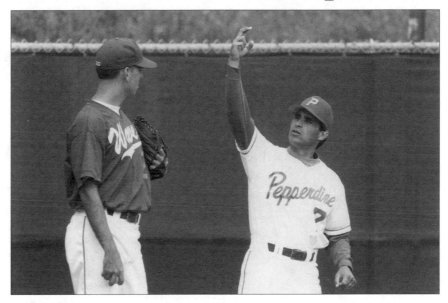

Teaching Pitching

When I began my coaching career I had little or no experience in the area of pitching. I had to decide whether to find a quality pitching coach or to commit myself to learning as much about the subject of pitching as I possibly could. I chose to become my own pitching coach and to discover from other coaches, through books, as well as through my own experiences, what makes a quality pitching staff. You can do this too. Pitching is not as complex as some people make it seem. It is far more important to me that our pitching staff (as well as all our position players) be competitive-strong as opposed to technique-strong. Being competitive is our priority. You may look at our pitching staff and see some minor mechanical flaws with a couple of our pitchers, yet you will also discover that our pitching staff in general is very competitive-strong.

Baseball experts say that, "Pitching is 80 to 90 percent of the game." If that is true, consider the following question: What percentage of your practice time is spent on developing your pitching staff?

Competitive Strength

I place a great deal of importance on the competitive strength of each one of our pitchers. This places a large burden on their performances and work ethic. How our pitching staff performs in any particular season will directly correlate with the success of our ball club.

At our first meeting I will excuse our position players and directly challenge each one of our pitchers as a group with the following statement:

"If we as a pitching staff this year are average in our work habits, location, second pitches, holding runners, developing our fastballs, the way we go about our job responsibilities, and so on, we will be an average club. If we are good at our job responsibilities, then we will be a good club. If we are superb in our work habits, if we dominate our second pitches, our holding runners, our fastballs, and so forth, we will order rings."

Then I go on to clarify that we may not win a championship, but we will have a season that people will want to remember. It is made clear to the pitching staff that they are the biggest factor in determining the success of the program. This can be considered pressure, but that's what a pitcher's job is—facing pressure situations and coming out on top. If the staff does its job, the ball club will almost always have a successful year.

Pitching Plan

Our plan is simple and straightforward. It must be clear so that the pitchers on the staff know what we are trying to emphasize. Our pitching plan consists of the following three specific areas and should give each athlete a specific overview of our approach to pitching:

1. Strive to work pitchers through our three levels of pitching.
2. Dominate the outer half of the plate.
3. Develop the ability to throw the fastball.

Levels

All pitchers fall into any one of three categories or levels:

- At Level 1 are pitchers who throw strikes.
- Level 2 pitchers are those who throw low strikes.
- Level 3 consists of the athletes who have the ability to throw the low strike on both the inside and outside of the plate.

From day one all evaluation and teaching will be relative to the level a pitcher fits into. Our athletes and coaches are always to be aware of the level at which each individual is pitching. And a pitcher's level may change—for better or worse—during the course of the season.

In all evaluation and teaching, I discuss with my pitchers and catchers, as well as my assistant coaches, into what level each individual falls. We obviously want to get as many pitchers to the Level 3 position as possible. I firmly believe that if we have three or four athletes pitching at the third level of our pitching plan, we are going to have a successful year.

In high school some programs can get by with pitchers who are in Level 1. Even at the college level, if pitchers throw low strikes (Level 2), they will have moderate to good success. But to have a championship staff, you need athletes with the ability to throw the low strike on both parts of the plate.

Dominating the Outer Half

The second part of our pitching plan is to emphasize to each one of our pitchers that our goal is to dominate the outer half of the plate. Much is said now in professional baseball about the ability to pitch inside, and I think relative to professional baseball there is an importance to being able to pitch inside consistently. In college programs, we want to dominate the outer half of the plate.

Most hitters avoid this part of the plate, looking for a ball down the middle or one that they can turn on. In addition, when pitchers focus on the outer half of the plate, their mistakes will not hurt so much. If a pitcher is thinking inside and doesn't get the pitch where he wants it, the ball may be driven. If he's focusing outside and misses the middle, chances are the ball will still stay in the ball yard.

Throwing the Fastball

The third part of our overall pitching plan consists of developing pitchers' ability to throw the fastball. As a staff and a program, we spend most of our time working on a two-seam and a four-seam fastball.

The reasons for this approach are quite simple. In my opinion most hitters, at almost any level, have what I call slider bat speeds. If pitchers throw a bad slider, one that hangs over the middle of the plate, most hitters can catch up to that pitch. I do not believe our staff should cater to hitters with slider bat speeds. In order to reach Level 3 of our pitching plan we must have absolute command of a fastball to move it in and out low in the strike zone. It's possible to be successful without a second pitch if your fastball is working. You may enter the game without your curveball or change-up working on a particular day and still manage to have success if you're throwing your fastball for strikes and have complete command of it. The fastball is the only pitch you can place in four different locations—in, out, high, and low. For these reasons we will tone down the emphasis on gimmick pitches and focus on the ability of our staff to master the fastball.

Mental Approach

I want each of my pitchers to go to the mound with a mind-set that gives them a distinct competitive advantage over the opponent. To do that, we ask our pitchers to commit to and firmly believe in these principles when they take the mound:

1. *Pitchers will get hit.* It may sound funny, but this allows a pitcher freedom to fail and maintain better poise on the mound. The average pitcher in the big leagues yields one hit per inning of work. That may seem high, but check the stats in the paper the next time they come out. We ask our pitchers to understand that it's crucial how they pitch both before and after they have given up the hit.
2. *Pitchers need to be offensive.* We want our pitchers to be very aggressive on the mound. Because they are going to get hit, they need to be aggressive and dictate what the individual hitters will hit. In essence we reverse the mind-set and ask our pitchers to understand that they are hitting the bat, not the batter hitting them, which hopefully allows them to be more aggressive on the mound.
3. *Fifty percent of all batters will take the first pitch.* We list this fact because we want the staff to know that the most important pitch in a sequence is strike one. It's been documented that the typical batting average will drop 100 points if the count starts 0-1 as opposed to 1-0. Simply throwing strike one on the first pitch takes a .300 hitter and makes him a .200 hitter.
4. *Sixty-five percent of all balls hit in fair territory go for outs.* We encourage pitchers to forget strikeouts and look for the ground outs. If they can get hitters to put the ball in play, I like our pitcher's chance for success.
5. *It's harder to hit than to pitch.* Some people might argue this point, but I simply ask that you observe the game of baseball. Pitchers who keep the ball down and throw strikes will be successful. Hitters, on the other hand, have much to worry about and analyze: Is my stride too long? Is my weight back? Are my hands in the right spot? Hitters can spend hours, but may never come up with answers.

To convince your pitchers of their advantage, have them observe batting practice a little more closely the next time you're on the field. Have them keep a mental batting average of your hitters as they are taking batting practice. What they'll see are hitters failing even when batting against a practice pitcher who is trying to make them look good.

Unfortunately, most pitchers take the mound worried about mechanics, worried about failing, and they haven't really given much thought to the idea that the odds for success are in their favor. That's something I want our athletes to have, and that is what we call a competitive advantage or being competitive-strong. If I've done my job as pitching coach, following the pitching plan as well as establishing the mental aspect of pitching, our athletes will maintain this attitude of high self-esteem.

Mechanics

Despite the development of our pitching plan and establishment of a sound mental approach, there is no escape from the idea that pitching does have certain mechanical absolutes. The trick is to not allow the mechanics of pitching to become so technical that it interferes with our simple pitching plan or our competitive mental approach to the skill.

The pitching delivery has certain mechanics that are very consistent in successful pitchers. They are as follows:

1. Start with a short rocker step from a short distance behind the rubber (see figure 11.1).

2. Following the short rocker step, plant the pivot foot at 90 degrees to home plate, in contact with the pitching rubber. Reach a solid position of balance—a power position—before exploding to the plate (see figure 11.2).

3. Once at the balance point, get the ball out of the glove as quickly as possible to get the arm position at the proper point upon release (see figure 11.3). Staying in the glove too long will cause the pitcher to rush through the balance point, dragging his arm behind.

4. Use a controlled fall instead of a drop-and-drive delivery to the plate. Stay high on the back leg and then fall toward home plate with a heavy front side and the head toward home (see figure 11.4). The controlled fall allows pitchers to stay as tall as possible, giving them a better opportunity to pitch in a downward plane to the hitter. Dropping and driving tends to lessen this advantage. Also, most top pitchers in the major leagues have a common habit of closing the front foot slightly upon delivering the ball, which allows the pitcher to keep his front side closed as long as possible.

5. Stay on top of the ball. Think in terms of dominating the top half of the ball with the hand (see figure 11.5). From the point of getting the sign to the point of releasing, we want our pitchers to think of throwing the top half of the ball. Pitchers get lazy and will throw the side of the ball or throw from underneath the ball, but by staying on top of the ball they are better able to throw in a downward plane, and get movement on their two-seam fastball.

Much is said about the follow-through in many pitching manuals, but I firmly believe that if you manage to go through the previous five mechanics, the follow-through will take care of itself.

As you can see, we do not spend a great deal of time on mechanics in our program. We stress the ones mentioned here, but we spend much more time on the mental approach of pitching than we spend on the mechanical approach.

Figure 11.1   A short rocker step.

Figure 11.2   Planting the pivot foot and reaching a solid position of balance.

Figure 11.3   Getting the ball out of the glove as quickly as possible.

Figure 11.5   Dominating the top half of the ball.

Figure 11.4   Using a controlled fall.

Pitcher's Daily Routine

I believe pitching is a part of the game that is constant. The distance from the mound to the plate is 60' 6". This will never change. It is constant. It is routine. Therefore, we want our pitchers to see their role as a constant routine on a daily basis.

Each day it is mandatory for our pitchers to bring the following four items to practice: a dry towel, an extra shirt, running shoes, and a jacket or sweatshirt. We do not want our pitchers ever to be without these four items. In fact, if they are to complete their work responsibilities, they will never fail to have this equipment. Each year on day one, one or two pitchers, or maybe a handful, will show up without the mandatory four items. This gives me a great opportunity to verbally discipline the pitching staff as a whole because if one athlete breaks down in this area, it affects the whole pitching staff and thus the entire ball club.

Obviously, the dry towel is to towel off following the workout. We ask our pitchers to change shirts once they are finished conditioning. We do not want them standing around practice in a cold, sweat-filled shirt, so we ask them to bring an extra shirt. Running shoes are much more appropriate for our pitchers to run in to be comfortable and avoid injury. Finally, no pitcher should ever be without a jacket or sweatshirt to put on following a workout.

Getting Loose

Our pitchers will typically throw every day to some extent. We find it important in developing a pitcher's arm, as well as his strength, to have him throw each and every day. Before practice our pitchers will throw down the line. It is during this time that we do most of our mechanical work. We emphasize certain parts of an individual's weak mechanics for him to work on as he gets loose. Also at this time we work on finger pressure and throwing all our different pitches. But since the fastball is the dominant pitch, most of our warm-up time is spent in developing the cut fastball, as well as the sinking fastball.

During the last five minutes of this session, each pitcher works on the following techniques in holding baserunners. This work must be done at game speed and be monitored. There are six particular techniques in holding runners that we work on every single day. They are:

1. Hold 'em—The pitcher comes set and counts three full seconds in a normal pitching pattern. We want our pitchers to become comfortable varying their times to the plate. Getting comfortable in holding for three seconds before pitching enables us to disturb a baserunner's timing.

2. Controlled step-off—We have the pitchers working on a controlled step-off two or three seconds into the normal pitching pattern. Many big league clubs have determined that it is more effective to hold the runner by just stepping off and putting doubt in the runner's mind than it is to actually continue to throw over.

3. Slide step—The slide step is a skill that enables a pitcher to go to the plate from the stretch position without lifting his lead leg. A pitcher must be comfortable in performing the slide step and must be able to throw

strikes. If he can master the slide step, he will go a long way in holding baserunners.

4. Good move/great move—Pitchers, with their partners, work on their pick moves to first base. The first move is a real *good* move to first, but with a *long* arm action of the throwing motion. This move is then coupled with a following *great* move, which uses the same footwork and quickness, but a *short* arm action. Hopefully, the runner will be convinced that the good move was the pitcher's best move. Once the pitcher then delivers his great move, everything looks the same except that the arm angle is much shorter, picking up several inches on the baserunner. Doing this daily will enable your pitchers to master it.

5. Fake to third/pick to first—This has become quite popular at the college level. With runners at first and third, pitchers fake a pickoff move at third to read what the runner at first might be doing. It's self-explanatory, but let me make one very important point. The idea here is to deceive the runner at first; therefore, the pick at third must look as much like a throw to the plate as possible. One small area that is often overlooked is that the pitcher, in his fake to third, should be looking with his head pointed at home plate throughout the entire fake. This small detail will enhance the success of this particular move.

6. Reverse move to second base—There is no excuse why anyone on your staff should not be comfortable on a reverse move with the runner at second base.

By doing each one of these techniques every single day, your pitching staff should become quite adept and comfortable in holding baserunners. Again, this practice needs to be monitored and done at game speed every single day at the end of the pitchers' warm-up period.

Workout or Bullpen

Most of the pitcher's individual work will come within two contexts of our practices, either a bullpen or a workout. Let me distinguish between the two. A workout involves my pitcher and I going to the bullpen and working on a specific pitch, move, or situation. It is not a long exercise. It might be that we want to work on an individual's curve ball; I might take a pitching screen and move it to the 30 to 35 foot mark and work intensely on this pitcher's ability to get the proper curveball rotation. I often won't even use a catcher in a workout scenario. Other workouts might include a highly intensified focus on the cut fastball, trying to get the proper rotation. Again, this is often not a long workout, maybe 20 to 25 pitches at most.

The bullpen is different in the sense that it is a simulated game situation. We never want our pitchers just to play catch with the catcher. We want all our bullpens to be simulated game situations. Fifty percent of the pitches thrown should be out of the stretch. Often we will have a hitter stand in to make it even more game-like. Most bullpens will have a predetermined pitch limit for that individual pitcher, and our catcher will call a simulated game with all the pitches in the pitcher's repertoire.

Mechanics and Conditioning

Probably the biggest killer of a pitcher's enjoyment of the game is how he's handled during practice. More times than not, pitchers will throw their bullpen and then be relegated to shagging in batting practice. I'm convinced that a great deal can be accomplished while a pitcher is participating in the necessary evil of shagging.

During the remainder of batting practice, we assign our pitchers specific parts of the field in which to shag. During that time they will have a specific mechanic on which to be working. For instance, pitcher A may have a little trouble with rushing through the balance point. For at least 20 minutes of that batting practice, we will then require him to be working on his balance point as he is waiting to shag. Never are our pitchers allowed to stand around idle. Another example would be to have an individual working on a particular pickoff move during the time he's shagging. But it should be specific, and it should be expressed to the athlete what the particular weakness is that he is working on that day. This is where most of our mechanical work takes place—on their own while they are either warming up before practice or shagging for our hitters.

Our conditioning is focused on, but not limited to, three types of running:

1. Long runs—two- to six-mile runs that can be done on the track or road.
2. Intervals—usually on a track or around the field, this running consists of alternating sprint work with jogging, usually two to three miles.
3. Poles—a long baseball tradition. Athletes run across the outfield between foul poles, working up to 16 total with up and back counting as one.

These runs are done on an alternating basis over the course of a season.

Following conditioning and typically after practice, we ask our pitchers to ice their arms. We feel this enhances the healing process of throwing and is also good preventive care for future injuries. Understand that we do not make this mandatory. I have had pitchers enter my program whom we forced to ice when they had never iced before in their lives and who later developed arm problems. We encourage our pitchers to ice, but we give them the final say in this area. This is usually done after consulting our trainer. Following the conditioning and icing process, our pitchers are responsible for packing and watering the main mound and all bullpen mounds.

You can see in this list of responsibilities and daily routine that there are many places where you can observe pitchers' desires to complete their responsibilities. It is very important to emphasize early in the season, almost to the point of overemphasizing, the need for them to dominate each one of their responsibilities, from the top man on the staff to the bottom man on the staff.

Pitching Drills

As has been mentioned, I am more concerned about the mental approach of the pitchers than I am about our mechanical approach. You will also notice that most pitchers entering your program have received plenty of physical input, but not so much mental. The fastest way to gain credibility with your pitching staff as a new pitching coach is to emphasize the mental over the physical, simply because they probably haven't heard this before. Yet there are some drills that I would like to include here, or at least some approaches to the concept of drills that might give you some insight on which direction to head.

Throwing From the Outfield

In high school particularly I would often have my pitchers throw from the outfield. This would strengthen their arms, but most importantly it would allow me, as coach, to see their natural point of release. When somebody tries to juice a throw from the outfield, he's naturally going to throw from his correct point of release. Once that point is determined, you can encourage it from the pitcher's mound.

Change-Up Day

Typically, one day a week I will ask all our pitchers to throw the change-up every time they pick up a baseball. For instance, if Wednesday is change-up day, then every time they shag a batted ball, every time they throw in warm-up, every time that they actually touch a baseball, they need to emphasize the change-up grip and release point. You can use this with other pitches that players may be struggling with as well.

Other Considerations

Over the years there have been many subtle ideas that I've added to our pitching approach.

No Home Plate

In the fall workout season, we go about our business as pitchers without any home plate in the bullpen. If we have removable plates, we take them out. If they are painted on astroturf, we will paint them over in green. We do not want our pitchers throwing to home plate early in the year. The only home plate you will find on our diamond during the

fall is the one on the main diamond. This gives the pitcher the opportunity to focus on his target, the catcher, and not be concerned with actually hitting the plate. Hopefully by the time spring rolls around, the plate becomes less important, and hitting the catcher as a target becomes priority.

Pitching Routines

Once starters and relievers have been determined, I like to set up particular routines in their pitching schedules. Your starters may throw on a three-, four-, or five-day rotation. It's easy then to monitor his schedule of work between starts. As for relievers, I am convinced that it is important that they get accustomed to being on the mound every other day, whether they are in a game or not. It is difficult for a reliever to stay sharp by pitching only in games; therefore, we ask our relief pitchers either to be in a game or on a bullpen mound in a game-like setting every other day, pitching 20 to 25 pitches each workout. Doing this will go a long way in allowing your relief pitchers to be accustomed to throwing that amount of pitches on a daily basis, which is their role.

Day Before a Start

Over my years of coaching, I've learned that it's in my best interest to allow the starting pitcher to choose what he wants to do the day before he starts. Whatever routine he wants to develop, whatever routine he believes works for him, he is free to do. If our starting pitcher likes to throw 50 pitches in the bullpen prior to the start, we let him do it. If he wants to take the day completely off and not even show up for practice, we will allow that to happen. Keep in mind they have to be successful in their routine or else we may do some changing as a coaching staff. Yet we like our pitchers to understand that they have the freedom to do as they see fit the day prior to a start.

Summary

Without hesitation, I can say pitching is the most important aspect of the game of baseball. Remember these points for teaching pitching to your staff:

- Pitching must be a priority to you. Establish your expertise in this area or hire a coach who can handle this area well.
- Your ball club is only as good as your pitching staff.
- To effectively teach and evaluate your pitchers, organize them into various, well-defined levels, reflecting their abilities or talent levels.
- Dominate the outer half of the plate.
- Establish the ability to throw the fastball. Make the fastball a priority.
- Make your staff mentally strong, which will give them a competitive edge.
- Keep physical attributes important, yet simple and basic.
- Use warming up and shagging as productive portions of practice for your pitchers.
- Some people believe pitching is 90 percent of the game. It is wise to spend a high percentage of practice time on pitching.

Part V

Coaching Games

## Chapter 12

Preparing for Games

Whether you're preparing for a conference game, a nonconference game, or a championship game, you need to treat it as an important competitive event. As soon as you start placing more importance on one particular opponent than another, you increase your chances of having down days.

Preparing for the Opposition

We share only a portion of our scouting reports with players because we don't want our club so preoccupied with the opponent that they forget their own strengths. Yes, we want our players to possess a general knowledge of their opponent's weaknesses and strengths. Most important, though, we want

our players to feel good about their own abilities. I want them to remember that our most basic concept in preparing for games is the idea that you don't play an opponent; you play the *game*.

You don't worry about an opponent. If anything, you get yourself concerned about the game and execution—the hit and run, throwing strikes, and so on. Once the opponent becomes a bigger factor than the game, you literally have two opponents. No matter who the opponent is, the game of baseball itself is a big enough foe.

Don't be intimidated by the situation, either. When we arrived in Omaha for the 1992 College World Series, the coaching staff had decided that we would approach everything as we had done for the past three years. We wanted to make sure that the players saw our preparation would not differ from what we had done for three years simply because we were playing for a national title.

Remember, in chapter 4 I discussed how the game is designed to beat you. The game is designed to strip you of your confidence, to make you look and feel foolish. Every time you strike out, walk a hitter, or make an error, the game is gaining an upper hand. If we can beat the game day-in and day-out, then we have a chance of winning a lot of games.

Scouting Reports

We keep our scouting reports simple. Sample scouting reports are included in Appendix E of this book. The information we want to gather and share with our club can be broken down into three basic parts:

- Pitching
- Offense
- Defense

Pitching

We want to give our hitters some basic information on the tendencies of each pitcher that we might face through the course of a series, including such information as what types of pitches they throw; what they throw on the first pitch; whether they have a tendency to throw fastballs on the first pitch; whether they throw inner-half, outer-half, or off-speed pitches; what type of pitches they throw when they are ahead in the count or behind to the hitter; whether an individual is mainly a fastball pitcher when he's 3-1, 1-0, and 2-1; and then last of all, what type of pitch he throws in what we call the even count, 2-2 and 3-2. We want to know if he has enough confidence to throw a pitch other than his fastball. Does he have enough confidence in a 2-2 count to throw an off-speed pitch? Does he have enough confidence to throw an off-speed pitch in a 3-1 count? If he doesn't, it makes it easier for us because we're able to sit back and look for fastballs in those situations.

We're looking for tendencies in every pitcher that we face. The average pitcher will throw fastballs when he's behind in the count and off-speed pitches when he's ahead in the count. We want to chart all this information to better prepare our hitters.

Typically, we will have a hitter who is not in the lineup keep our opposing pitcher chart (see figure 12.1). When kept diligently, this chart will give us insights into the habits of a particular pitcher. The main body of the chart gives us ample space to chart each pitch. The bottom part of the chart allows us to summarize the information for future reference.

Something else we look for is how the opposing pitchers control the running game. We want to see what type of pickoff moves this pitcher has. Does he pick to first base on his motion in a down position? In other words, as his hands are coming by his head into the set position, does he have a tendency to pick at that particular time? Or does he only pick when he comes to his belt buckle? Does he look once or twice before he delivers to the plate?

Our baserunning chart will monitor the number of looks a pitcher will give a baserunner at each particular base. It will also allow us to determine any particular habits in his pickoff moves at both first and second base. We will also take the opportunity to time the pitcher's delivery to home plate, as well as the catcher's delivery to

Opposing Pitcher Chart

Pitcher ———————— No. ———————— Throws ———————— Date ————————

Team ———————— Charter ————————

Inning	First pitch	Second pitch		1 - 1 count	Behind in count					Ahead in count					3 - 2 pitch	Strikeout pitch	Total pitches
		1 - 0	0 - 1		2 - 0	2 - 1	3 - 0	3 - 1		0 - 2	1 - 2	2 - 2					
Extra innings																	
Totals																	

Comments ————————————————————————————

Control: ———— FB ———— CB ———— SL ———— CH ———— Other ————

What he throws when: ———— ahead ———— behind ———— Best pitch: ————

How he holds runners ———————————— Tips off any pitches? ————

Key: 1-Fastball 2-Curveball 3-Slider 4-Change-up 5-Other

0-Strike ☐ -Hit hard △-Wild pitch

Figure 12.1 Opposing pitcher chart.

second base (see figure 12.2). This information, coupled with knowledge of our players' speed, should give us advantage in our base stealing attempts.

Pitchers are creatures of habit, and we're trying to determine those tendencies so that we can take advantage of them in our running game. You'll be shocked at how many tendencies there are if you aren't already charting them.

Lastly, we try to determine what type of makeup we have in an opposing pitcher. We want to know if this pitcher is a tough-minded individual. Is he a bulldog-type pitcher? Is he easily rattled if a runner gets on base? Sometimes a pitcher can be very emotional. If a runner gets on base and causes enough movement and commotion,

this pitcher will lose his concentration, enabling you to work yourself into a big inning.

We're also looking for a pitcher who has low self-esteem. In other words, is he the type who looks for something bad to happen? If that's the case, we need to put some pressure on that particular pitcher, make him work a little longer than normal and maybe take a few more pitches than we normally would. We want to know what each pitcher's makeup is to plan our attack from the batter's box and from the base paths.

I won't allow verbal garbage to come from our dugout. But I do believe that you can affect a certain type of pitcher with good, competitive gamesmanship. For example, if we're facing an emotional pitcher, we'll get in and out of the box and try to break his

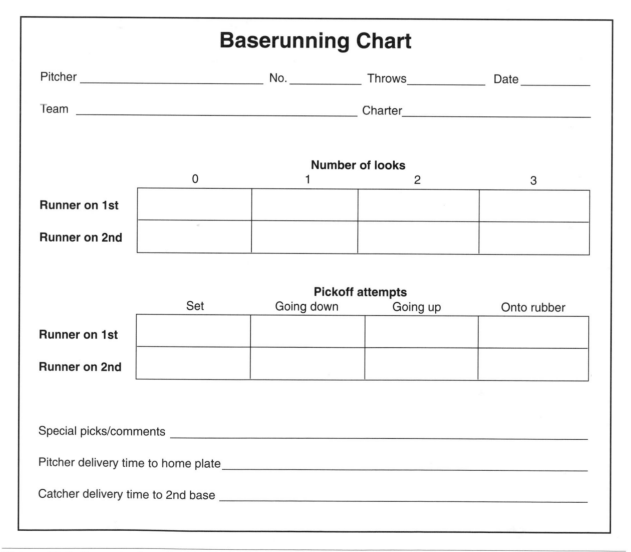

Figure 12.2 Baserunning chart.

rhythm and concentration. We'll have him sit on the mound a little bit longer than a bulldog-type pitcher. On the bases we will act as if we're trying to steal on every pitch, and we try to rattle him so that he loses focus on the hitter.

If we're facing a low confidence or low self-esteem pitcher, we'll try to create a lot of things at the plate—small game skills, drag, push, hit and run. Once we're successful, he'll just be waiting for something even worse to occur. We want to be very aggressive early in the game against a low self-esteem pitcher.

On the contrary, if we're facing a tough-minded, tenacious, bulldog-type of guy, then we need to be tenacious ourselves. And it's probably going to be a real tough day. Against a bulldog-type pitcher we are more inclined to rely on our execution and bat control skills to create runs instead of waiting for the big inning.

STUDENT OF THE GAME

Keeping effective charts on your opponents will benefit you only if your staff and athletes are diligent in applying this knowledge to their advantage. Coaches and players must apply the information to their own personal approach, as well as to the particular game situation. During our championship years at Pepperdine, one of my athletes, Matt Howard, kept his own charts in his own way. In fact, he kept a personal notebook on every opposing pitcher we faced. The notebook was so complete that many of his teammates sought him out on a daily basis to benefit from his well-recorded information.

Offense

Our opposing hitters' reports are shared mainly with our pitchers and catchers. Occasionally, in the case of a certain pull hitter, we will include the rest of our defense. We try to point out to our ball club who on the opposing team has a tendency to steal—the action guy. When does this particular player like to steal second base, or when does he run? Does he run early in the count, or does he run late in the count? When does he drag? When does he sacrifice? When does he hit and run? When does he push?

We identify other strengths and tendencies of the opponent. Which players have power? Who is a guy we cannot make a

mistake on deep in the count because he'll knock it out of the park? What players have solid contact and very rarely strike out? If that's the case, they're very good candidates for hit and run when they're at the plate. Then we want to know who strikes out a lot so that we can possibly pitch around someone to get to that particular hitter in a situation where we need a strikeout.

Our hitter tendency chart helps us track each individual hitter and what his tendencies might be (see figure 12.3). This chart helps us track where he hits the ball and—even more importantly—what kind of action plays were used with this particular hitter. Over time we can see developments in tendencies for certain hitters to be hit and run hitters, candidates to steal a base, or likely to sacrifice bunt in the later innings.

Figure 12.4 is a tendency chart that is similar to the chart in Figure 12.3. In this case the hitters and their tendencies are presented in a card system, rather than having all of the information on one particular sheet. The charts we use vary from year to year. Both charts give the same information, and it's a matter of preference of the particular coach.

We inform our club of who on the opposition we don't want to beat us. In other words, we want to designate a particular hitter we're going to face tomorrow, and if the game is on the line we'll pitch around that hitter simply because either he's on a hot streak or he's just a very legitimate hitter. We make it very plain to our pitchers and catcher so that if the situation arises the following day, they know what to do.

Defense

The information we share about our opponents' defense starts with arm strength of the catcher. We want to know what we're dealing with behind the plate. If he's a catcher who might shut down our running game, we'll have to use more hit and run instead of straight steals.

We also want to know what type of arms we have at first and third bases. If we have poor arms at first and third, we may be dragging and pushing a little more.

We want to know what the infielders look like in terms of shortstop and second base. If their arms aren't very strong, then we're

Hitter Tendency Chart

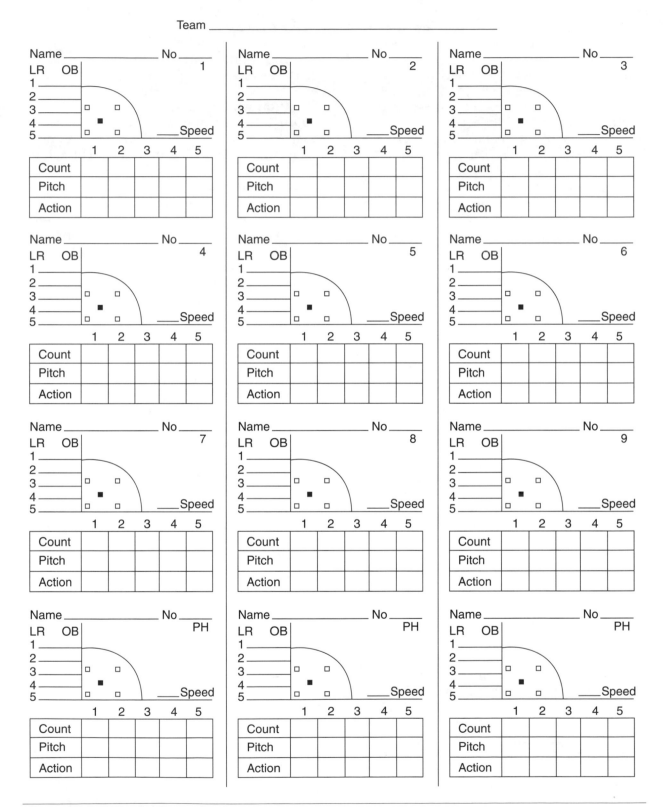

Figure 12.3 Hitter tendency chart.

going to be looking to take the extra base on balls that get into the gap. We're going to take advantage of their inability to make that long throw from the outfielder's relays.

Then we want to look at what type of outfielders' arms are out there. If they're not strong and accurate arms, then we'll notify our club that on any ball into the gap or any ball that looks like it's a base hit and you can go for a double or a triple, take the risk! We'll use this strategy early in the game. As the game goes on, we'll play more percentages, but early in the game we'll test their arms.

We cover all this information in a short meeting with our players after practice the day before a game. We ask that our players keep notebooks and that we go through each opponent relative to the three categories: pitching, offense, and defense. We don't spend so much time on an opponent that our athletes become preoccupied with the team

they are playing; it can affect their self-esteem. We just give them basic information so that nothing will surprise them on game day.

OVERSELLING THE OPPONENT

When I was coaching at the high school level, one of the strongest opponents in our area was El Segundo High School. Before playing them I spent weeks preparing for the game. I produced a highly detailed scouting report on each player in the El Segundo lineup. I felt I knew *everything* there was to know about their strengths and weaknesses.

I then took this information and shared it with my ball club. In sharing the scouting information with the ball club, I left our athletes with the impression that El Segundo was even stronger than they had imagined. The L.A. Dodgers probably seemed more beatable to them at that point.

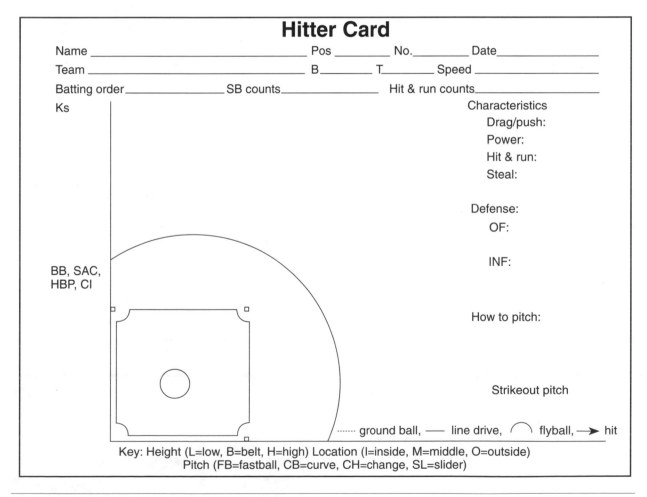

Figure 12.4 Hitter tendency chart—card style.

Because I had oversold our opponent, the scouting information that could have been used to our advantage only made the team more fearful of their opponent. If I recall correctly, we were defeated rather handily.

In sharing scouting reports with our players now, I emphasize our strengths as a team and how they match up with our opponents' weaknesses. This is a much simpler approach and allows our club to focus on the things that we do well without worrying too much about our opponents. There's a lot to be said for using this approach because it also keeps your players concentrating on their true opponent—the game itself.

High School Scouting

Often at the high school or small college level, the coaching staff is not large enough to spend ample time scouting opponents. If this is the case in your situation, I would limit my scouting by determining my opponents' abilities in the following areas:

- Do they have team speed? Are they aggressive baserunners? Will they challenge you?
- Do they have individual speed? How quick are they from home to first?
- How physical are their power hitters?
- Do they have arm strength in the outfield, behind the plate, and in the infield?
- What pitches do their pitchers throw?

Knowing this information will give your ball club a good general idea of its opponent.

More specific information to take advantage of would be the following:

- Does their catcher fall to his knees in a relaxed manner after each pitch? If so, we would run as he starts to drop to his knees.
- Do middle infielders tip off pitches to the outfielders?
- Do middle infielders take a step toward second after each pitch? If not, we might delay steal from first base.
- What are a pitcher's tendencies on specific counts (i.e., first-pitch fastball, 3-1 fastballs, and so on)?
- What is a pitcher's delivery time to home plate?

Although time and manpower may not allow you to chart each opposing pitcher and each hitter that your team will be facing, you can still be prepared. Gather the above information, and you'll have a good feel for how to attack your opponent.

Readying the Team

I like to keep our practices the day before the game very short, very concise. I don't want to leave our best on the practice field. We don't fool around. We keep it very professional, at a good level of intensity—a very quick and crisp workout.

We briefly cover what our opponent might do against us. If it's an action team, we'll run all our bunt coverages, our first and third coverages, and things of that nature. If it's a team with tremendous team speed, we might

spend a little more time controlling the running game the day before we play.

We try to do this without acknowledging that we're really preparing for our opponent. Again, we don't want to spend a lot of time making our opponents bigger than they are. We want to show up at the ballpark the next day for a ball game and know that we've covered our opponent. Then we can go out, be at our best, and be confident to play at our strengths through the course of that day.

Pregame Motivation

The pregame motivation we give our athletes is the anticipation of doing something for the next two-and-a-half to three hours that many people only dream about. I will sometimes remind them, "Fellas, this is a great opportunity. There are thousands of your peers who would love to do what you are about to do, but will never get the chance. So let's make the most of this opportunity! Go out and play as hard as you can."

We want our athletes to play hard every time out. But our pregame motivation isn't based on cliches or long stories that try to touch their hearts. We simply remind our athletes that they're living out the dreams of many young people. We want them to appreciate that, and to show their appreciation through great effort for the next few hours.

WAY UP, WAY DOWN

I'll always remember a game versus Redondo High School during my high school days. It was considered a very big game in the league race, and the players and coaches were very excited. I recall an emotional speech I gave to our athletes before the game that got them really pumped up. I later discovered that their emotions were actually running too high! We were a very good club for four innings, very emotional and excited. But that emotional energy didn't run high for long. In the final three innings we went into a lull that eventually took us completely out of the game. It was a well-learned lesson and is a big reason why I don't use rah-rah speeches anymore as pregame motivation.

Before the game starts, we will go through some basic instructions of what we hope to do offensively. If we want to run early in the count, we'll mention that. If we're going to sit back and let things happen a little bit offensively, then we'll make that point to our players. We'll go over our opponent one more time in basic statements, but we're not going to load players down with so much information that they can't go out and be free to be at their strengths.

Playing Doubleheaders

Throughout my college career I've always been in a conference that has played doubleheaders. They are a challenge, and require some skillfull team management by the coaching staff.

One adjustment we make with doubleheaders is that the starting pitcher for the second game is not allowed to show up for the first game. We tell him to show up during the middle part of the first game. We've found that if we can keep that starting pitcher away from the field, he's going to be fresher and more ready to go when the ump yells "batter up" for game two. Earlier in my career I'd have everybody there from pregame warm-up for the first game through the last pitch of the second game. The starting pitcher for game two would be there for four hours before he even threw a pitch! We found that this waiting period hurt his performance, so now we have him there just in time to get warmed up for the second game.

To prepare our athletes to play doubleheaders, we've found it beneficial to make Saturday workouts extra-long workouts. We are on the field for a long, long time just as we will be for doubleheaders. It's really mental preparation. You'll find that most teams that succeed in doubleheaders are teams that are the toughest mentally.

It's easy to make mistakes in that second game. Players are tired. They're not only physically tired, they're mentally tired, especially if they've had a bad first game and went 0 for 4. If that player is still hitting for the collar when he takes his last at-bat with a chance to win the game, we want him to be at his prime psychologically. It's the athlete who's mentally strong who comes through for you in that situation!

At the end of our Saturday workouts we do some type of mental exercise to see how sharp we are, how mentally strong we are. An easy thing to do is run sitational defenses or go through all our offensive signs. We get our entire team together and go through all our offensive signs, challenging them to be mentally strong at the end of a long day. If they are sharp mentally at the end of a long day of practice, they have a better chance of being successful. The doubleheader is a challenge, and you have to prepare for it.

MID-DOUBLEHEADER MEALS

In my first year at Pepperdine I was amazed at what my players did between games of a doubleheader. Virtually the entire roster was in the stands eating lunch and visiting with family and friends. It was like they were out for a Sunday afternoon picnic! This troubled me as a head coach, as I was already concerned about their mental preparation for the second game of a long doubleheader.

In my research I had noticed that Pepperdine ball clubs traditionally had trouble winning the second game of twin bills. I immediately made it my policy that the team would stay together between games, either in the clubhouse or down a particular foul line, and share lunch together. As a result, our mental preparation was stronger and I had much more control preparing my team for the second game of the doubleheader. Our program's success in doubleheaders improved from that point on.

Keep your players together, keep them focused, keep them united as a team from start to finish of a long, challenging doubleheader.

Summary

Preparing for games can be as detailed or as simple as you choose to make it. My approach is to get the necessary information about your opponent, as well as your own club, and then follow these general ideas in preparing for an upcoming game:

- Be more concerned with your team's abilities than those of your opponents.
- Use charts to accumulate information on your opponent's pitching, defense, and offense.
- If you have limited staff or time, keep your scouting reports general. Include four or five aspects that you can keep track of and use to your advantage.
- In any scouting situation try to match up your strengths with your opponent's weaknesses.
- Keep pregame practices short and precise. It should be intense, but do not leave your best on the field the day before a game.
- Baseball is a game to be played on an even emotional level. Getting your team too high can cause you problems later in a game.
- Keep your pregame instructions short. Cover basic information on what you hope to accomplish that day. Keep your team free mentally to go out and perform to its best level.
- Approach doubleheaders mentally as well as physically. Prepare your players for a long day of baseball through long difficult practices.

## Chapter 13

Handling
Game Situations

If you've coached baseball, you know how complex the game can be. Baseball is an exciting and challenging game that is dull only to those who fail to appreciate the many possibilities that exist on each pitch.

In this chapter we'll review some of the game strategies and management philosophies that really make the game challenging and fun. We'll look at several other game-day considerations: playing at home versus playing on the road, pregame routines, personnel adjustments, game conduct, and reactions to winning and losing. Let's first look at two ways a coach can handle game situations.

Coaching by the Book

Over the years, a mythical book on baseball coaching strategies has developed from the millions of trial-and-error outcomes of coaches' tactical decisions. The "book" tells you what is generally the best move to make in common game situations. Coaching by the book is another way of saying you are going to play the percentages.

The book will recommend using the sacrifice bunt in the later innings and playing for the big inning early in the game, playing for a tie at home and a win on the road, and so on.

This type of strategy is preplanned, well thought out in advance of the game. This strategy can be taught. It's baseball theory and decision making that other coaches have documented in their books, and it is the safest approach to take, because if one of your decisions flops, you can always say something like, "Nine out of 10 coaches would have done the same thing. It just didn't work out in that particular case." Everyone needs to move on.

Coaching by Experience and Instinct

Game coaching would be easy if all the situations you found were predictable. But it would also be boring.

What makes managing a game so interesting and challenging are the situations that are thrown at you, circumstances that you have never dealt with before or even had the opportunity to read about. In that case you're learning by experience. And the next time you face a similar situation, you'll have something on which to base your decision.

Be open to using innovative tactics when the book answer isn't available or seems wrong to you. Coaching is part art, and good art requires using your instincts as well as your training and knowledge. The best coaches have a feel for handling situations as they arise—no matter how unexpected.

CHAMPIONSHIP GAME VERSUS SENIOR PROM

After four years of hard work at Mira Costa High School, we entered our fifth season with a very mature and talented club. We played well from the start, and the season culminated in the 4A CIF championship game under the lights at Dodger Stadium in Los Angeles. It was big time for us! Everything was going in our direction. We were prepared.

Although I was aware that the senior prom was the same night, it did not sink in for me as a coach until I saw my athletes getting on the team bus with their gear bags *and* their tux-

edos. As we unloaded the bus, I noticed several of the players' dates getting out of their rented limousines in the stadium parking lot. To compound the problem, many of my players' dates, dressed to the hilt in their prom dresses, were seated in the first few rows behind our dugout. Talk about distracting!

There is no baseball book on the market that I could have read in advance to help me handle this situation. No clinic was ever held to prepare me. Some situations can be taught, while others simply must be caught and dealt with when thrown at you unexpectedly.

We lost the game. My fault. It was simply my fault. I chose to ignore the distraction and hoped my athletes would do the same. What I should have done was to acknowledge the prom and help my athletes separate the two events. Experiences like this teach you lasting lessons.

Home Versus Away Games

In general, we like to play aggressively early in a game and make the percentage decision in the later innings. Those percentage decisions can change, depending on whether we are at home or on the road.

The idea of having the last at-bat as the home team is crucial. When we are at home, we will go by the book and play for a tie (i.e., sacrifice bunt) in the late innings. On the road you do not have the luxury of the last at-bat. Typically, we'll stay more aggressive as the visiting team by replacing the sacrifice with a hit and run or a straight steal. This is considered playing for the win. A tie on the road gives your opponent a tremendous advantage since just scoring once results in a victory.

Managing a lead is also affected by whether or not we're at home. At home I may sacrifice to pad my lead with one run from the seventh inning on. As the visiting team, I'll again play it more aggressively, anticipating a big inning. Expanding the lead by multiple runs diminishes the home team's advantage of the final at-bat. In essence, we try to take away our opponent's last time at the plate.

The same thinking can be used defensively in terms of positioning your infield defense. At home with a runner at third late in the game, we would be more likely to trade an out for a run by playing the infield back. This would help us avoid a big inning. Yet on the road we would more likely have to stop the run to keep from losing the ball game.

Pregame Routine

Our players are well versed on pregame procedure when visiting another ballpark. Much can be learned in a short period of time that will help players and coaches anticipate game decisions.

Our first and third basemen check both baselines for bunt action by rolling balls down the lines. Our catchers check the backstop to determine how it will play on wild pitches. Our middle infielders work hard to check the background (behind home plate) to get their bearings. The outfielders walk the outfield, particularly around the fence, checking how it plays or looking for holes or other problems that may occur. Our pitchers always go to the mound to try to gain a feel for it. We've actually allowed our relief pitchers to throw pregame batting practice so they can get accustomed to it. All of these field checks by players can be accomplished in a short period of time. It should become a routine.

The actual pregame schedule has varied between my experience in high school and college. Pregame batting practice is seldom allowed prior to high school games, while it is common in preparing for a college game.

The important aspect of pregame schedules is to make them consistent. Consistency breeds familiarity, and familiarity breeds confidence. Whether you are at home or on the road, I believe the pregame schedule should be as consistent as possible.

Table 13.1 depicts sample schedules prior to both high school and college game times. These schedules should be posted in both the home and visiting dugouts to make the athletes aware of their responsibilities.

In addition to posting the pregame schedule, we often post a game administration sheet that will list game responsibilities for athletes and coaches (see figure 13.1). This can be as detailed or as simple as you are comfortable with. It helps athletes, and especially nonstarters, understand their roles for that particular game.

Personnel Adjustments

Some game strategies can be determined prior to game time. A key feature of successful game management is the ability to communicate strategy to your players. Communicating where, when, and why to your players, relative to a game situation, is important in commanding their respect, as well as teaching them the game.

Most strategic decisions involve a combination of influences. Your personnel evaluation, your scouting report, field conditions, particular matchups, and other factors in-

Table 13.1 **Sample pregame schedules**	
High school pregame	**College pregame**
2:00 Stretching routine	12:15 Stretching routine
2:15 Throw	12:30 Throw
2:30 Baserunning: game-like jumps	12:40 Home team batting practice
2:40 Review signs	1:20 Visitor's batting practice
2:45 Pepper or dry swings	Final instructions
2:55 Infield/outfield drill	1:50 Home infield/outfield
3:05 Final instructions/field prep	2:00 Visiting infield/outfield
3:15 Game time	2:10 Field prep
	2:20 Ground rules
	2:30 Game time

Game Administration Sheet

Pregame Practice

Date _____   Opponent _____

_____ Florida batting practice

_____ Opponent batting practice

_____ Florida infield/outfield

_____ Opponent infield/outfield

_____ Field preparation

_____ Game time

Game Assignments

Pitching charts	Score book	Starter
Scouting charts	Stay in box	Middle relief
	Bullpen catchers	Short relief
Foul ball crew	Designated runner	Umpires

Figure 13.1 Sample game administration sheet.

fluence the moves you make, yet there are guidelines I like to follow, particularly in the area of substitutions.

Pitching Changes

Calling this a crucial area of game management is an understatement. Making a pitching change a pitch too late can cost you the ball game. For this reason, I would rather make a pitching change too early than one pitch late. You've lost your chance to make a decision when you allow a struggling pitcher to throw one pitch too many that results in a big hit.

We make our pitching moves based on total pitches thrown and how our pitcher matches up with a particular hitter. Pitch counts are very important to us from day one. We do this to help track the number of pitches thrown daily, weekly, and monthly to insure the health of our pitchers' arms and to monitor their performance history at certain pitch totals.

For instance, I knew that when Pat Ahearne reached the 100-pitch mark he was 10 to 20 pitches away from needing relief. I'd seen it,

monitored it, and knew what was likely to happen when he reached that point. My bullpen was ready. Derek Wallace had a history of struggling early, but if he got to the 45-pitch mark, I could consider taking the day off because he had a history of great success from that point of the game. Diligent monitoring of a pitcher's past history relative to pitch counts makes some decisions easier.

In conjunction with pitch counts, knowing how a pitcher matches up with a particular hitter will also come into play. This comes from knowing the strengths and weaknesses of each athlete and making pitching changes accordingly. There are charts in Appendix D that will help you monitor these areas.

Pinch Hitting

Knowing your bench personnel is essential for effective use of pinch hitters. You must first evaluate the needs of the situation. Then consider what you have to work with on the bench. If the circumstances of the game are such that a reserve player's skills give you the best chance of success at the plate, it's time to make the move. For example, with a breaking ball pitcher on the mound, you would not want a strict fastball hitter at the plate. If you're facing a pitcher who consistently tries to establish the outside part of the plate, make sure you have a good opposite field hitter at the plate. Need a fly ball to score a runner from third late in a game? Get a power guy up there who routinely hits the ball deep into the outfield.

Keep good records of your players' past performances in certain situations. Know their strengths and weaknesses. Combine the information with the game situation. Then make the decision.

Try to explain the move to the player you pull for the pinch hitter. I never let him leave the ballpark without letting him know my thinking. The same is true for other decisions I make during a game.

Pinch Running

If you have a runner on base who represents an important run, make sure he can run. If not, get a runner on first who can score on a double. Make sure you have an athlete who will score from second on a single. Replacing average speed with good speed to avoid an out at the plate late in the game is simply common sense.

Defensive Changes

Here's my simple idea on defensive changes: If we have a lead and cannot get the last nine outs of a ball game with my top defensive players in the game, we don't deserve to win. Therefore, I consistently have my best defense in the game from the seventh inning if we have the lead. If it's a seven-inning game, I'll make my defensive moves in the fifth. It may be a simple concept, but it's based on solid reasoning *and* success.

Conduct During the Game

In addition to the strategic decisions you make during a game, there are other facets to managing your club during a game. I happen to be very particular about the actions and behavior of my players. Setting clear expectations about your conduct, and your players' conduct on the field and in the dugout, will help achieve and maintain the kind of behavior you desire. I may be oversensitive about language, respect toward umpires and opponents, and so on, but I never want to compromise the character of our program or our institution by how we conduct ourselves during a game.

Dugout

Throughout the game, players who aren't on the field should sit down and be students of the game. When you look into our Florida dugout, you will see an organized, highly attentive roster of athletes who are following every part of the game. I insist on this. It's part of their development.

At any point in the game every player in the dugout should know the count on the hitter and how we got there. I will constantly quiz my bench on the game situation to help maintain their attention. For instance, if I ask an athlete the count on a particular hitter, he not only has to answer "two balls, one strike," but he also needs to answer "first pitch fastball in the dirt, ball one; second pitch fastball at the knees, strike one; third pitch, curveball in the dirt, ball two." The athlete needs to be able to answer without hesitation. This is a learned skill, and it may take your athletes most of the season before they can concentrate at this level.

Your Conduct

How you, the coach, conduct yourself in game situations is always noticed. As the team's leader you must always handle yourself in the utmost professional manner.

I must be prepared, and as a result of my preparation I want to portray confidence and poise in every situation. I want to be as organized as possible, having access to any charts I may be using, including the lineup card and scouting reports. A high degree of respect should mark my relationship with umpires throughout the course of the game.

Remember that part of our philosophy states that game day is for the athletes; practice is for the coaches. On game day I hope to remain as positive and encouraging to my athletes as I can be. Any anger or frustration that may develop over the course of the game is held back for another time where the correction can take place in a practice setting. This should free your athletes to relax and concentrate on the task at hand—striving to win the ballgame.

Your Players' Conduct

I would like my players' conduct to be similar to mine throughout the game. In addition to being mentally in the game on every pitch, I want them to show confidence and poise as a result of their preparation.

They should be organized, knowing exactly where their gloves and equipment are at all times. They should be prepared for their role on that particular day. For example, I want my pinch hitters to have a bat in their hands from the third inning on, in anticipation of being called upon to hit. I want my pitching staff to know the opposing hitters from the third inning on, in preparation for their opportunity to pitch later in the game.

As a side note, be assured that there is no room in our dugout for rally caps. In my program we do not rely on gimmicks or a

"rah-rah" mentality to try to win games. We want to be prepared and organized and gain our confidence through those factors. Be clear with your players on your expectations for conduct, and then lead by example through your own conduct. This will result in an imposing force throughout the game.

Life on the Road

Team road trips are important events. If approached properly, much can be accomplished by spending time together on the road as a unit. Play the toughest early-season opponents you can, and schedule some of those contests away from home. You'll soon find out which players will perform in adverse situations. Early road games help you evaluate your personnel. A loud and perhaps hostile crowd also gives your club an early taste of playoff caliber baseball. If you win, you'll feel good about your chances if you see that opponent in the playoffs later. If you lose, you can look at the playoffs as a second chance.

At the Division I level I have always tried to play a tough opponent in a likely regional playoff location. Arizona, Arizona State, Texas, and Stanford were all potential playoff sites on our past schedules.

TOROS VERSUS THE CATS

If you have the right makeup and attitude within your players, playing a tough opponent early is a no-lose situation. Regardless of the result, your club has the opportunity to improve. While at Cal State Dominguez Hills, we had the opportunity to face Coach Jerry Kindall and the Arizona Wildcats each year early in the season. I recall two of these trips in particular. The outcomes of the games were very different, but the benefits to our team were similar.

In 1985, we traveled to Tucson only to get blistered by the Wildcats, absolutely beat up! Our ball club used the experience as a time to regroup and evaluate. The players turned it into a positive, knowing it would not get much worse. We won our next 15. We had the right attitude. The early-season thrashing could have buried us and ended our season, but we kept it in perspective and had a much better year as a result.

Two years later, we again arrived in Tucson. Only this time we were fortunate enough to take two out of three. The early-season confidence boost carried us to a third-place finish in the NCAA Division II World Series!

Road trips can help establish a team's identity. As a coach, you have an opportunity to set the tone for the year both on and off the field. We approach our road trips in a professional manner. We want to be a class program, so we travel in a coat and tie. We stress being responsible adults, loyal to each other. The road setting is also good to be accustomed to since most championship settings are on the road.

Road trips give you the chance to reinforce team expectations. For instance, we ask our players to be on time and do things right. In 1989 prior to leaving our campus in Malibu to catch a flight from LAX, we discovered that one of our players had not shown up for the vans. After being informed by his roommate that the athlete was still sleeping, we loaded up the vans and proceeded without him. It never happened again.

Travel situations magnify the responsibility that each player and each coach has to the team. Mistakes are more glaring because they impact everyone negatively. As coach, you must put the team first.

A coach needs to be strong and courageous in setting the tone for the year. Be quick to discipline or you'll be challenged later. Remember, good news travels fast, bad news faster.

Postgame Conduct

The time immediately following a ball game and your reaction to it will often dictate what kind of practice you have the next day. I have two slightly different approaches to how I handle the ball club on the day that we win, as well as on a day that we lose. It's usually more important how you react to your team following a loss than a win. Whether we win or lose, I'll always address the team.

Following a Loss

Following a loss I normally attempt to stay as positive as possible. I will always be mindful to address a solid team effort, as well as good individual efforts.

My goal is to make players want to come back the next day. It's easy to look forward to tomorrow following a win, but as a coach you must create an environment that makes players want to come back tomorrow following a tough loss. I seldom will confront the athletes on their failures because they are typically aware of them at this point. It is my approach to wait until the next day to point out the more negative aspects of the loss—when emotions are under control.

Following a Win

I address the team following a win in much the same manner, trying to remain positive, trying to leave them with thoughts that will make them look forward to coming back the next day. Following a win I will be more specific in identifying any failures or shortcomings we may have had that day.

My goal following the win is to keep the ball club on an even keel, to have the players keep things in perspective. Sometimes it helps to bring them down to earth a bit by mentioning

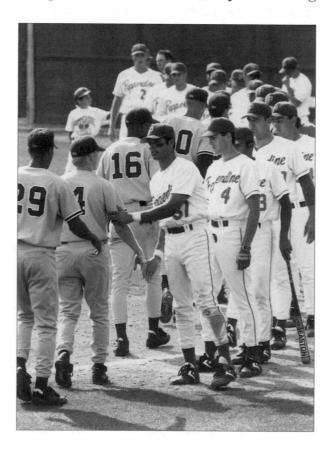

lapses or errors that need to be minimized in future games.

Class and Dignity

It would be my goal to have our program handle winning and losing in a similar way. It should be difficult to determine the day's result by our behavior.

We want to be known as a class program; therefore, we take great strides to make certain our opponent has everything they need on game day in Gainesville. The dugout, clubhouse, bullpens, water, towels, and so on are at the same level that we enjoy as home team. We strive to eliminate any reason, outside our team, for our opponent to have lost. We want our opponent to be treated well, as we would hope to be treated at their ballpark.

Remember, talent without class and dignity is just talent. Talent with class and dignity is an imposing thing!

Winning can become a habit. Unfortunately, so can losing! Always remember the following: A good team that plays hard is tough to beat. A good team that does not play hard definitely can be beat *and* will be beat often. Make sure that playing hard is a habit.

It's been said that a loss only becomes a loss when you fail to learn from it. Our goal is to play hard. If we play hard, there is no shame in a loss. We work hard to learn from both our wins and our losses, which goes a long way in making us a better ball club in June.

Summary

There is more to handling game situations than putting on an occasional sacrifice bunt or hit and run sign. The intricacies of baseball strategy are what make the game unique and exciting, but how you conduct yourself and the way your program represents itself are also important in handling game situations. Keep in mind some of the following ideas:

- Some strategy can be taught; other strategy must be caught.
- The "book" says to play for a tie at home and a win on the road.
- On the road your players should have a set routine to become familiar with the surroundings.
- The key to good decision making is knowing your personnel and your opponent.
- Monitor pitch totals on your pitchers. This helps with the health of their arms as well as knowing when to make changes.
- Get your best defense in the game for the final outs.
- Play tough opponents early.
- React to winning and losing in the same manner—with class.

Part VI

Coaching Evaluation

## Chapter 14

Evaluating Your Players

In matters of evaluation, I find wisdom in a proverb in the Book of Ecclesiastes: "The end of a matter is better than its beginning and patience is better than pride." What I'm saying is that the most important thing to evaluate is player and team improvement. You want your club to be better at the end of the season than at the beginning. And the only way that can happen is if you're patient early in the season. At times during my career, I've lost patience with a club early in the season and we suffered the consequences later in the schedule. When I've been patient and just hung in there through all the errors and frustrations early on, it's always worked out. We've always been a better club at the end of the season than we were at the start.

Knowing your personnel is one of your most important jobs. If you struggle in this area, you can learn and improve. In the meantime get another coach or assistant who can help you. Cal Poly Pomona Head Coach John Scolinos has told me about talented coaches who "couldn't scout sand in the Sahara Desert!" Yet they were successful because they got the help they needed to scout and evaluate successfully.

It's poor coaching to ask your players to do something they're not capable of doing. You need to be aware of their strengths and weaknesses and get the most out of each player without asking too much. Constant evaluation of your club will lead to better coaching decisions regarding your athletes.

In this chapter we'll discuss ways for you to evaluate your ball club. We'll discuss tryout formats, roster decisions, lineup decisions, and suggestions for placing your players in their strongest positions.

Tryouts

Our evaluation of players begins in the preseason. In the NCAA, we have one week before our fall workouts begin. During that period we run a tryout, attempting to evaluate our group of athletes. This tryout consists of testing the player's speed, arm strength, pitcher's control, and athletic instincts.

60-Yard Dash

The first thing we have each position player do is run a 60-yard dash, a distance equivalent to running two bases. We need to know if a player can run, which will affect how we position him defensively and what decisions we make when he's on the bases.

We want infielders to be able to run at least a 7.0-second 60-yard dash. If they don't run at least a 7.0-second 60-yard dash, they need to show some other abilities that might compensate for their lack of foot speed. Outfielders should run the 60 in less than 7.0. They need to run down fly balls, so sub-7.0 is a must!

These times may be too fast for the high school level, and certainly will be for players in their early teens. In high school, if we had one guy run below a 7.0 in the 60 we were excited. Determine the marks that are most appropriate for your level. As for catchers and corner people (first and third basemen), we're not as concerned with their foot speed. It's a bonus if they have it.

Arm Strength

The second area we look at is arm strength. We have the outfielders throw from right field to third base and judge the rotation of the ball. Does the ball die as it comes into the infield, or does it have a little hop when it makes contact with the infield grass? By having all outfielders throw from right field, you present a similar distance and position from which to evaluate each athlete's arm strength.

All the infielders field ground balls from shortstop as we look for the same thing. We look for arm strength and rotation on the ball. Is the ball jumping up at the first baseman? Does it have a little bit of life getting to first? Or is it literally dying on the vine? Is it starting to take a downward plane as it gets to first base?

The catchers will try out by throwing to second base. What we're looking for are athletes who can get the ball to the bag in 2.0 seconds. It is timed from contact with the catcher's glove to contact with the glove at second base. Start the stopwatch when the ball hits the catcher's glove, and stop it when it hits the glove of the middle infielder. Again we're looking for a time of 2.0 or below. Although you can get by with a 2.2 in high school, at the college level they'd run all day against a catcher with that kind of arm.

Pitchers

Pitchers will normally throw a short bullpen for us. We don't want to hurt anyone's arm. But basically what we're looking for there is that they fall into Level 1. Level 1 for us is that they have the ability to throw strikes. If they have the ability to throw strikes, we feel that we can work with them. A Level 1 pitcher has earned the right to show us that he can reach Level 2 or even Level 3 as a pitcher over the course of our fall workouts. If he doesn't show the ability to throw strikes, he's going to pitch himelf into trouble at any level of baseball. Obviously, if he has a tremendous throwing arm and he's not throwing strikes, you're going to be patient and work with him. But if he doesn't throw real hard and he's not throwing strikes, that's a bad combination.

As a pitcher gets through his bullpen, we'll ask him to show us a couple of his off-speed pitches—not too many of them because you don't want to jeopardize a young man's arm. Just enough to judge his off-speed pitch. Does he have a good change-up? Does it have movement or is it a straight change? What's the break on his curve? How fast does he throw his breaking stuff—curve and slider?

We'll also check his fastball. What kind of heat does he have and how well does he control it?

Intra-squad Game

At the end of the week we hold an intra-squad game to evaluate individual game instincts. We're looking for pitchers who can hold runners on. We're looking for infielders who are at the right place at the right time on defense. Outfielders backing up throws—are they moving in when a hitter squares around to bunt? You're looking for the smallest of things: instinctive qualities—a feel for the game, the ability to steal second base, to bunt, to hit behind the runner.

We don't coach during the intra-squad game. We just watch and evaluate. By evaluating a youngster's speed, arm strength, and instincts you will have the necessary information to help you keep the best athletes possible. You'll find this simple tryout format is effective at all levels, from youth leagues all the way to the big leagues.

YOU GOTTA HAVE HEART

An incident with a young athlete early in my career taught me a valuable lesson in player evaluation. The athlete's name was Ken Logan, who played for me at Mira Costa High School in 1978 and 1979. A quick evaluation of Ken was

that he was an athlete with very limited physical skills. He had neither the size nor speed to make a great first impression. But one characteristic he had that impressed me the more I watched him was his desire. Although I didn't project him contributing much on the field, I chose to keep him on the roster. This intangible is tough to describe, but it's easy to recognize. Our successful years at Mira Costa during Logan's career had much to do with his influence on the stars. He helped our ball club improve because of his work ethic and enthusiasm.

Later, at Pepperdine University, a young man named Matt Miller contributed the same qualities to the team. Matt virtually played no innings for us over the course of the year, but we took Matt with us to Omaha because of the heart that he showed day-in and day-out throughout the season. He influenced the Pepperdine club to a higher level. I now make it a point to keep one or two such athletes on my roster to positively influence the everyday players.

Roster Decisions

Decisions regarding your personnel will be some of the most important and difficult decisions you will make over the course of a season. Deciding who to keep on the roster, deciding who to play, and placing your players in their best positions will have a major impact on the success of your season.

Cut List

One of the toughest parts of our jobs is to have to decide who will make the team roster for the season. We don't put up a list during the preseason to identify who did and did not make the club. My policy is to speak privately with each individual player during the course of practice, informing him that he either did or did not make the club.

Breaking the news to players who've made the team is much easier. You really lift the spirits of a young man who thinks he's not made the club or that he's on the fence. It's a pleasure to inform an athlete that he's on the team and just needs to work for playing time. Young guys get excited and may start playing with a little bit more confidence. It's important to share the roster decisions in such a way that it helps motivate and excite the athletes you have chosen for the team.

In telling a young man he did not make the roster, I'll encourage him to apply himself even more in the classroom and to pursue the many other worthy goals outside of base-ball. If he wants to continue to play the game, I might be able to suggest another coach or team he could contact. I thank him for his attempt to make our roster and wish him well in achieving his future goals.

It's a situation where we want to spend some time with each young man who is cut and tell him life doesn't begin or end with baseball, that there are more important things than a white ball with red stitches on it. It's not the end of the world! His self-esteem and self-evaluation as a human being should not be based on whether or not he makes the team.

I also mention the possibility of trying out for the ball club the following year. Frequently, this helps soften the blow to a cut athlete and gives him something to work for or look forward to. Besides, changes can take place over the course of a year both in an athlete's physical abilities and athletic talents. If you doubt it, just consider that Michael Jordan was once cut from a high school basketball team!

TOO SHORT—UNTIL GAME STARTS

One of my finest athletes at Cal State Dominguez Hills was almost overlooked because of his lack of physical size. The 5' 7" shortstop, Craig Grebeck, was not recruited out of high school. In fact when I first saw him I was almost turned off by his lack of physical size, yet in looking further he possessed everything you would look for in a middle infielder: bat speed, arm strength, soft hands, and solid game instincts. We encouraged him to come play at Dominguez Hills. Craig went on to be a two-time All-American for Dominguez. After college, Craig's name was never called in the professional draft. The White Sox gave him an opportunity and signed him as a free agent. Through his work ethic and desire, Craig went on to have a fine major-league career with the White Sox.

Playing Decisions

You can get yourself in trouble by basing player evaluations only on physical attributes. I've recruited athletes with physical abilities second to no one, but with poor character. The result is rarely positive. Never overlook an athlete's character.

After you've selected the right personnel for the team, you need to start and play the right people. Personally, I prefer a set lineup. Again, I like to look for our players' strengths and attempt to put them in the right position so that we have a set lineup day-in and day-out. It's a lot easier at the college level because of recruiting.

We really want to know who our starting players and key reserves are going to be every day, and I think it's important for your players to know that as well. I really believe that when a young man wakes up in the morning or goes to bed the night before a ball game knowing he's going to be in the lineup, he's going to get himself ready. The other side of it is that the players who aren't playing know that they have to work harder in practice and push those athletes who are playing every day to get some playing time.

Finding the Right Spot

Try not to be locked into any one position for a player. Just because an athlete has been a shortstop since he was eight doesn't mean he won't help you elsewhere. There are certain approaches you can take to finding a player's right position.

Look for an outfielder who doesn't hit or run real well, but has a very good arm—right away you make him a pitcher. You tell him, "Hey listen, you're not going to play too much if you stay in the outfield, but here's an opportunity to contribute as a pitcher." Do this early in the season during the tryout period. It's a gamble, but it can pay off big.

We've had outfielders in the past who didn't hit at all in the tryout period and we've given them a week to 10 days in the regular practice to prove themselves. If they still don't show anything at the plate, we ask them to go and start working on the mound, and before you know it you have a pretty good prospect on your hands.

Maybe you have a quick-footed, strong-armed outfielder, a guy who can really run. He has good arm strength, but he doesn't hit real well. Our preference would be to make him a shortstop. We'll ask him just to concentrate on his defense, and look to get more offensive production from the new outfielder who's replacing him.

We look at the strengths of each player and work diligently to put that particular player into the position best suited for his physical abilities. We believe that if a player is at his best physically, then he'll be able to perform the responsibilities of that particular position. As a result, his self-confidence will rise daily. If you have a guy who cannot run, and

you're putting him at short or at center field, he's not going to be able to play those positions physically, and his self-esteem is going to diminish. Make these choices early to allow time for your athletes to develop.

Be patient after making adjustments. When you move an outfielder to pitcher or a second baseman to catcher, be patient. Know that you really have to stay confident in the guy. Let his physical abilities take care of themselves. You never know if you have a dominant player on your hands unless you're patient.

Evaluating Practice

The goal in practice is to come as close as possible to game speed. This helps performance, but it also helps in regard to observation and analysis. If your practice is just a ho-hum routine, it's difficult to see what they're going to do in a tough game situation. If you make it competitive, if you make it crisp, if you make it as close to game speed as possible, your observation and analysis are going to be enhanced tremendously.

Many times certain players can perform in practice, but struggle in games, so you really have to be careful. You have two hours, and in that two hours you need to pick the spots to make game speed. You can't do it for two hours constantly. Even in a regular game there are some lulls. So we pick the spots we want to make game-like. Make your pitchers and baserunners compete against each other. Maybe the first 30 minutes of live batting practice is just one at-bat each, as it is in an inning of a game. Perform or get out of the cage. During run-downs that particular day, you might make it as tough and as challenging as humanly possible. Put something on the line so your athletes are motivated to compete harder. Give the winners the day off from field maintenance, and have the losers do all the field work following practice to let the players know you noticed.

Your bullpens have to be intense as well. Constant coaching encouragement and demands throughout the bullpen can enhance the intensity. Pitching a simulated game can also help. Timing your pitchers to home plate

when throwing from a stretch will help simulate the pressure of baserunners during a bullpen. Make at least a short portion of practice every day as close to game situation as possible for evaluation purposes. Put a little heat on your athletes, and you see who can respond and get the job done for you. Do so with the evaluation goal in mind as you are going to be able to observe, analyze, and keep records on what they do in a close game situation.

Evaluating Games

Baseball is a wonderfully unique game. Each competition presents decision making and evaluating opportunities that will be unequaled for that particular game and circumstances. Being diligent and thorough throughout the evaluation process will enhance your chances for success once the game begins.

Every pitch in a game requires good decision making on your part. Each pitch changes the next decision to be made. Each result will then alter the next situation. Baseball is dynamic in that way. You must rely on all information possible. Past records, past scouting reports, current reports, your assistant coaches, all resources at your disposal should go into your game evaluation process.

Currently at Florida I have an assistant coach in charge of our pitching staff, and I rely heavily on his input to make pitching evaluations during the game. Another assistant is in charge of running our offense from the third base coaching box. As head coach I oversee all decisions that are made, yet rely heavily on the input of my assistants. There is dialogue throughout the game among all staff members regarding developments that occur. I try to use all input from my assistants wisely and will often make my decisions according to their information.

Postgame Evaluation

Pitching is the number one concern in my postgame evaluation. If our pitchers have done well, our ball club will probably have been successful. Certain key stats will often give me the information I need. We look for solid strike-to-ball-ratios, strikeout-to-walk ratios, and first-pitch strike percentage. All are important stats to help evaluate your pitching staff. Three strikes for every ball thrown in a game would be ideal (3:1). Three strikeouts for every batter walked would also be ideal (3:1). Seventy-five percent first-pitch strikes is a lofty but reasonable goal for a talented pitching staff. These are difficult standards, but standards that we shoot for with our staffs.

Over the course of a game I keep brief notes on our offense's productivity. I also have a very simple evaluation method to chart each of my hitters. I keep the chart on a 3 x 5 card. Next to each name, I evaluate them simply with a plus, minus, or zero. For instance, if I was evaluating our athletes' ability to execute in the context of batting practice, a plus would indicate a job well done, a minus would represent a failure to execute, and a zero would be a neutral evaluation, such as a foul ball. A quick total next to each name gives me an idea of how each athlete did. It's simple and effective, and I use the same technique with defensive evaluations.

I also monitor who is giving us maximum effort, who is making good decisions. How well did we run the bases? How well did we execute? I will also note the team's aggressiveness and keep a record of any mental lapses that may have occurred during the game. Although I keep general notes in these areas, some successful coaches keep highly detailed charts to monitor a team's success in these areas. Use what works best within your philosophy and coach's environment. Have in your mind what is important to you as a coach and then keep account of it. A chart need not be elaborate as long as it works for *you*.

Help from Assistants

Everyone on the coaching staff should be providing input over the course of a season. There should be constant dialogue among the staff involving evaluation of all aspects of our program. Frequently our evaluation of athletes is done on an informal basis. Yet we also hold more formal evaluations where we meet in the office to discuss specific players and decisions relating to the ball club. Player evaluation should be a consistent, ongoing process.

What we're hoping for in evaluating our players is to play the right athletes in the right positions and the right situations. This can only be done through daily observations, daily evaluation, and daily analysis of who are the right athletes. Level of intensity and production are two big considerations in these observations. Slowly but surely your analysis and observation starts becoming habit. Before you know it, you're starting to see one particular player rise above the rest and sadly enough another player not be able to get it done when you really put the heat on.

Again, you want to be able to observe, evaluate, and analyze in practice so that you don't have to learn who the right guys are in the course of a game. If you've run your tryouts well prior to the season and are diligent in evaluating practices, chances are good that you'll put the right guys on the field every game.

Summary

Evaluation of your athletes begins the very first day of your tryouts and continues throughout the course of the season. Developing your abilities in judging your players' talents is important to your success as a head coach. Be patient with yourself and your ball club early in this process. The following guidelines will enable you to handle the evaluation process:

- The end of a matter is better than the beginning, and patience is better than pride.
- Use a tryout format to begin the evaluation process for your athletes. Intra-squads are also helpful.
- Determine specific standards relative to positions to help evaluate each athlete.
- Never post cut lists. Communicate openly and honestly with athletes who do not make your squad, as well as with those who do.
- Be prepared to move athletes from one position to another to take better advantage of their skills.
- Game speed workouts help evaluate which athletes will respond better under pressure.
- Keep charts that work for you.

## Chapter 15

Evaluating Your Program

Evaluating your individual athletes is only part of the overall evaluation process. Always keep in mind the big picture. What is the status of the total baseball program? When evaluating a program you try to determine how well you have pursued and achieved the team goals set down at the beginning of the year. While the general philosophy of your program will remain constant, you should evaluate how you need to measure the program against the specific standards you have set.

Evaluation of your players' skills and talents will help you to determine where your teaching will be focused. If you ask an athlete to do something he is not physically able to

do, he'll doubt your ability to coach more than his inability to perform the task! Before any teaching of offensive strategy begins, you must take the time to make a thorough evaluation of each of your athlete's strengths and weaknesses. Once this is accomplished, your ability to strengthen your offensive potential improves.

If you have an athlete who has little or no power, why ask him to drive the ball into the alleys? Instead, this athlete should learn a solid knowledge of his strike zone, focusing on execution of the little game to help the ball club. Enhancing these skills will allow you to get the most from this particular player.

Evaluating With a Plan

When evaluating your program, it's important to keep short accounts. If you wait too long to monitor the evaluation, you'll soon find some areas where you are slipping. As I mentioned in chapter 5, I keep a weekly plan, and from the weekly plan I determine a monthly plan of goals. I make daily summary accounts in which I evaluate the program's progress and I place them in a small folder. At the end of the year, I have a well-documented file of the entire season, which enables me to go back and review our goals whenever I want to check how we're doing. Diligence in developing weekly and monthly plans will pay off in more accurate and effective evaluations.

Evaluating Yourself

In regard to my own performance and goals, I've always felt a bit less successful if our program didn't qualify for postseason play. A big goal is to keep getting better so that we're at our very best at the end of the season, hopefully playing in the postseason.

Postseason play is something you really need to keep in mind as a goal. My goal is that during the very last game we play, we will be better in every respect than in the very first

game we play. If you have that as a goal, your team will get better, and if you have some talent in the club, you're going to get into postseason play. You're also going to be at your best at postseason time. I think all coaches would like to see their teams play well at the end. Our 1992 national championship club was fantastic at the end, winning something like 31 of our last 33 games.

Evaluate your own performance and goals daily. Keep in mind what you're trying to accomplish with your program every single day and what your job is with respect to the coaching staff, players, administrators, the ground crew guys who work on the fields, and the people who do your laundry. You need to keep them in mind and keep them aware of your goal to have the best program possible.

Through self-evaluation and feedback from meetings with players and staff, you can draw some solid conclusions about how you performed during the year. One area in which I evaluate myself is consistency. Have I been consistent in my discipline with the ball club, as well as in my encouragement with the ball club? Have I been fair to all involved, and have I been as honest as possible with the program?

I also evaluate how well I've coached with tough love in mind. It is important for me to love my athletes and be tough at the same time. I want to evaluate whether I've had the courage over the year to stay strong in this aspect of my coaching approach.

I also want to know whether I have communicated well over the year with my staff and players. Have I expressed specific goals for the team and individuals, and have they come across clearly and in an understandable manner? Have I pursued these goals in a consistent fashion? Have I done a good job in preparation and organization throughout the season? As a result, has my confidence and poise improved? Again, these are areas that you can determine not only on self-evaluation, but in using the feedback that you get from your players and coaches.

Finally, and most importantly, I want to know if I have grown both as a coach and as a person. Have I grown or matured in the following areas?

- Patience—with myself, athletes, coaches, and administration

- Knowledge—of myself and the game
- Character—maintaining class and dignity throughout the season
- Courage—growth in the courage of my convictions
- Relationship with the Lord—growth in the strength of my faith over the course of the year

Meeting With Players

I make it a point to meet twice a year with each player in our program: one time in the fall prior to Christmas break and again when our season is completed.

The postseason evaluation process for personnel begins with each player meeting with me in my office. At this point we review his strengths and weaknesses for the season. We go into what we believe he must do during the off-season to improve his game. For example, we may ask a player to work on his foot speed over the summer vacation, to work on his physical strength, or ask a pitcher to work on an off-speed pitch, his slide step, or holding runners on. We'll try to be very specific and tell him what we think he needs to work on. Sometimes we ask the player to work on his attitude, to try to be a more positive contributor to the team's character and motivation.

We try to emphasize an individual's strengths during these meetings. We want to build upon any good qualities the athlete might have. For instance, if we have a young man who is showing good signs of leadership, I would want to point out that it has been noticed. Maybe we can suggest ways that he can become an even stronger leader.

It's important that you be completely honest with your players when it comes to their future in the program. I've never appreciated people who play head games and deceive with statements of grandeur. It is important that you tell athletes exactly where they stand. And these meetings are a two-way street—the athlete should give you feedback on your coaching as well. In the years I've coached I've had to hold tough meetings.

I wish I could say every meeting with my players ended happily, where we all smiled, hugged, and went on to have a great relationship. But those meetings can be very hard. The purposes of those meetings are to be honest with the player, to help him improve

so that he can stay in the program, and to try to get him on the same page with us.

Most of these meetings have ended if not in agreement at least with mutual respect. It's usually clear to both sides that we're headed in different directions and a change is probably healthy.

The rule I use when determining whether to move on is a very simple one: If the individual player or coach is hurting himself or the program, it's necessary to take action. I'll *always* try to communicate and *always* try to point out some weaknesses and strengths in the hope that he can turn it around and become part of the program. But it's detrimental to try to salvage or turn around a situation that you've tried and failed to correct. The rest of the program ends up paying.

Meeting With Staff

After I've met with each player, I meet with coaching staff members and discuss their performances, strengths, and weaknesses. We discuss what I think each staff member should try to do so that our entire staff improves. For example, I might comment that they need to communicate a little bit better with particular players or to be a little bit more aggressive in their teaching mode during practice, a bit more hands-on. They might need to be a little bit more positive, or they might need to toughen up and not try to be so close to some players. Sometimes being too close with an athlete will compromise your position of authority.

It's at this particular time that I ask them to tell me how they feel, how they think they are being used. Are they being used to their strengths as coaches? Do they feel they need more responsibility? I encourage them to be honest and open with me.

This process is a great way to keep the program on its toes and improving. It allows staff members to give input as to how they think the program can stay at a championship level, and it opens up doors of communication, not only from the staff's standpoint, but from the players' standpoint as well. You set the tone by facilitating an open and honest conversation. It's candid, but with a minimum of emotion involved, a businesslike approach in doing what's best for the program.

Evaluating Facilities and Equipment

Regarding equipment and facilities, I will simply state that it is always easier to inventory and assess your facility at the end of the season if you've been very diligent through the course of the year. Keep track of all your minor problems through the course of the season. If you see a little hole in a screen, get it fixed right away. If you see some catching equipment that's starting to get ragged, get it fixed right away, even if it means you have to do it yourself, even if it means you have to sit down and get a screwdriver out. It's important that you do that on the spot. I've been in programs where it was put off, and during the last two weeks of the season we were using the most ragged equipment. If the cages look like they've been through a war, before you know it you'll be sitting there with 10 major repair items, even though they were originally problems that could have been solved in a preventive manner.

Take notice of your equipment. Take notice of your facility. Police these areas daily. If you're talking about pride every day to your players, it's important that you as head coach show this by example. I think that's an area that is really important. If your players feel that you care about the facilities and equipment, they're going to play hard. They're going to know that you really care about them.

Taking Time

The evaluation process is one that can easily be put off simply because it is very time consuming. To sit down with an athlete or with every athlete in your program, sometimes 20 to 30 guys, spending a half hour with each one, you're talking about a two-day event that lasts from 8:00 in the morning until 6:00 at night. I encourage you not to put it off for that reason. Don't let the inconvenient scheduling of meetings stop you from communicating with your players. This process of evaluation is crucial to your program.

You must evaluate to stay ahead of the game, to stay ahead of the pack. You must evaluate to keep your goals always in front of you. You must evaluate so that your program continues on the path of self-discipline and stays as far away as possible from the path of self-indulgence. If you self-evaluate, you're going to see that every year there are some things that you can work on.

Once the season has ended, I know that there are some things that we have done a poor job with and which we need to be better at next year. If you can get it done and evaluate it, police it, correct it, and accomplish it today, tomorrow will take care of itself. Keep short accounts, look at your goals, ask yourself hard questions, study what's going on daily in practice, and ask yourself if you are moving closer to your goal. If the answer is a resounding *yes* and you have a ball game tomorrow, sleep well. You're probably going to play well, and it's probably going to come out just fine. If you continue to evaluate your program in all these areas, your future is going to be bright.

Summary

Evaluating your program is essential for finding success. Keep these points in mind to become an effective evaluator:

- Keep short accounts throughout the year.
- Meet with your players and staff on a regular basis to communicate your evaluation of them.
- Keep a consistent record of inventory and facilities to support your decisions in this area.
- Evaluate your own personal performance and goals daily.
- Be completely honest and open during the evaluation process.
- Evaluation takes time. Be committed to the time it takes to do it right!

Baseball Flexibility Routine

Flexibility exercises are an important part of your exercise routine and should be done prior to any other exercise. This enables an athlete to properly warm-up, which aids in the prevention of injury. The following is a complete baseball flexibility routine.

a   b

Figure A.1 Arms up over head (a). Lean to the left, lean to the right (b).

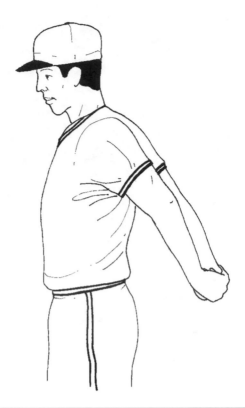

Figure A.2 Arms together behind the back.

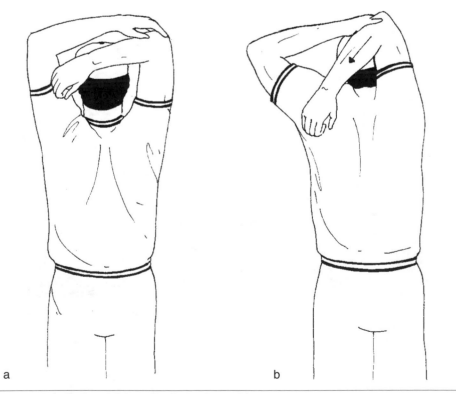

a   b

Figure A.3 Arm behind the head (a). Pull elbow down (b).

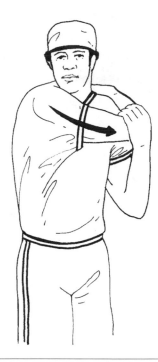

Figure A.4 Arm across the chest.

Figure A.5 Forearm stretch with hand up and down.

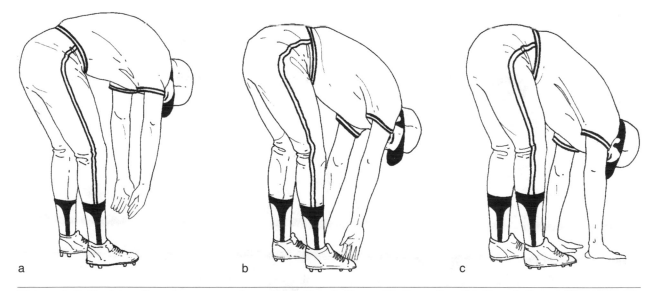

a   b   c

Figure A.6 Feet together, hang arms loosely (a). Touch floor with fingertips (b). Touch floor with palms (c).

Figure A.7 Sitting, cradle the leg (a). Lying back, cradle the leg (b).

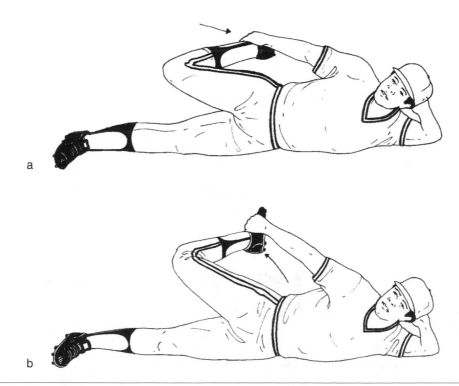

Figure A.8 Lying on side, pull leg back (a) and then forward (b).

Figure A.9 With leg tucked inside, reach out and grab opposite ankle.

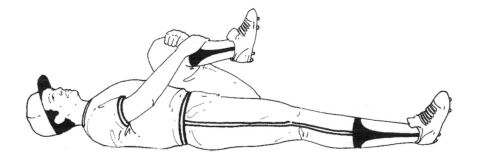

Figure A.10 Bring knee to the chest.

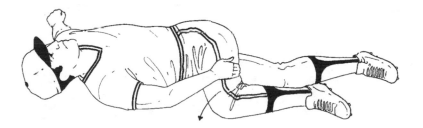

Figure A.11 With shoulders flat, pull leg across.

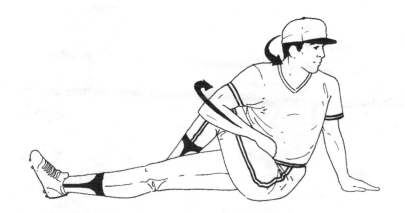

Figure A.12 Stretch lower spine.

Figure A.13 With legs spread out in front, lower yourself down in the middle.

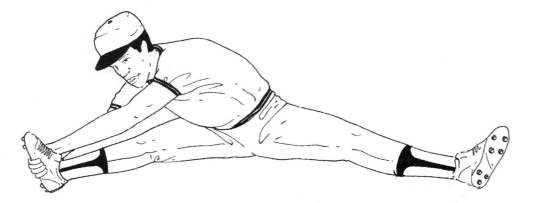

Figure A.14 Reach to each ankle with opposite arm.

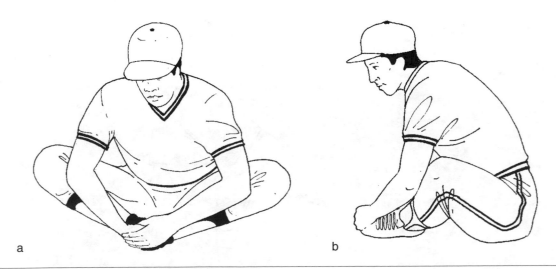

a   b

Figure A.15 Yoga, pause, and yoga again.

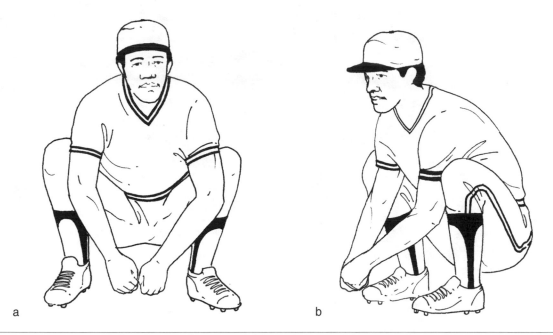

Figure A.16 Squat with feet flat on the ground (a), and then push out on knees (b).

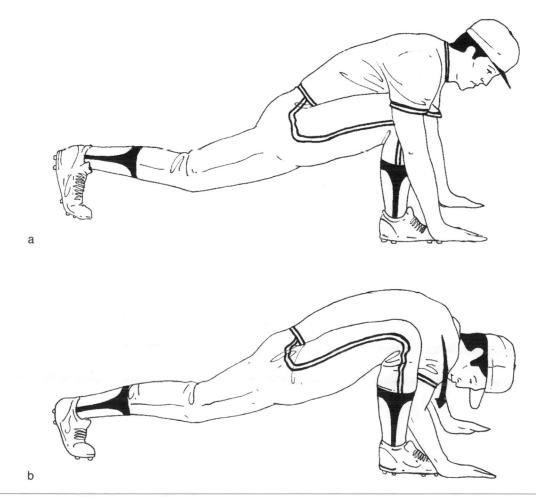

Figure A.17 Lunge with arm outside of knee (a). Lunge farther with arm inside of knee (b).

Shoulder Strengthening Program

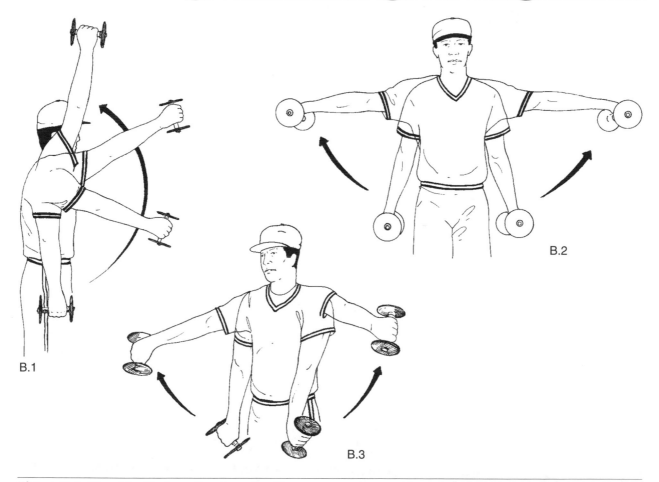

Figure B.1 Shoulder flexion. Stand or sit with your arm at your side, palm toward your thigh. Keeping your elbow straight, raise your arm, leading with the thumb. Continue slowly until your arm is overhead. Return slowly to the starting position and repeat.

Figure B.2 Shoulder abduction. Stand with arms at your sides. Lift arms to shoulder height, keeping elbows straight. Lower arms slowly to starting position and repeat. (To increase efficiency and decrease the risk of injury, work to 90° elevation.)

Figure B.3 Rotator cuff elevation. Stand with arms at your side and weights in hand. Keeping your elbows straight, turn arms in so that the thumbs are pointing downward. Bring your arms forward, slightly in front of your body. Raise your arms to 80°, keeping your elbows extended and thumbs pointed toward the floor. Slowly lower your arms to starting position and repeat.

B.4

B.5

B.6

Figure B.4 Shoulder shrugs. Stand with arms at your side, feet shoulder-width apart. Shrug your shoulders, lifting them toward your ears. Keep the elbows flexed slightly throughout the exercise. Return slowly to the starting position. Begin the next repetition right away to avoid unnecessary traction on your shoulder.

Figure B.5 Military press. Sit with the weight held as illustrated. Raise your arm straight overhead with your palm facing in. Return slowly to the starting position. You may exercise both arms at once or each arm individually.

Figure B.6 Horizontal abduction. Stand next to a table or bench, leaning forward from the hips, with your arm perpendicular to the floor. Lift your arm up and to the side, keeping your elbow straight. Continue lifting until your arm is parallel to the floor. Make sure you don't lift your hand higher than your shoulder. Return slowly to the starting position. Begin the next repetition right away to avoid unnecessary traction on your shoulder. You may also do this exercise while lying on your stomach on the edge of a table or workout bench.

Figure B.7 Shoulder extension. Stand next to a table or bench. Lean from the hips, using the arm closest to the bench for balance. Allow the other arm to hang perpendicular to the floor. Holding a weight, lift the arm backward until it is level with your trunk. Keep your elbow straight and arm close to your trunk. Return slowly to the starting position. Begin the next repetition right away to avoid unnecessary traction on your shoulder. You may also do this exercise on a table while lying on your stomach, with your arm over the edge.

Figure B.8 External rotation. Lie on the side opposite your dominant arm. Bring your arm to your side with the elbow bent 90°. Lift your hand toward the ceiling, keeping your arm and elbow close to your trunk. Return slowly to the starting position and repeat.

Figure B.9 Internal rotation. Lie on the side of your dominant arm. Make sure your elbow is pulled out from underneath your side, slightly in front of your trunk. Bring your dominant arm slightly forward and bend the elbow 90°. Place a pillow or bolster under your chest. Slowly lift your arm toward your chest, keeping the elbow bent 90°. Do not move your trunk. The movement should be confined to your shoulder. Return slowly to the starting position and repeat.

Figure B.10 Horizontal adduction. Lie on the floor or on a bench. Hold your arm out to the side, with the elbow straight and the palm facing the ceiling. Raise your arm slowly, until the hand is pointed at the ceiling. Lower slowly to the starting position, taking care not to lower the arm past the horizontal position.

Three-Week Practice Schedule

Planning is important. The following is a day-by-day, 3-week practice schedule you might use to prepare for the upcoming season.

<u>Monday, January 10</u>

3:00	Stretch and throw
3:20	Live baserunning
	@ 1B (delay, steal vs. LHP, read pitchout)
	@ 2B steal of 3rd
	@ 3B steal of home
	note: clock times to the plate
	Catchers' emphasis on footwork and easy catch
3:30	Defense
	Bunt defense
	1st and 3rd defense
	Run-downs
	Street Monkey Drill (emphasis on verbal between 1B/P)
	Picks
	OFs (base runners)
4:00	Offensive stations—4 groups (15 minutes)
	Live—2-1 count—execution
	Defense—OFs shallow; INF fungos
	Tees
	Cage—60/40
5:15	1st and 3rd offense
	Conditioning—1/2-mile intervals
	4 to 5 60-yard sprints
	Pitchers—8 poles
	note: test on signs throughout the day

<u>Tuesday, January 11</u>

3:00	Stretch and throw
3:15	Small game—2-strike bunts
3:20	Live baserunning
	@ 1B (fake steal)
	@ 2B steal of 3rd
	@ 3B steal of home
3:30	Defense
	Bunt defense
	1st and 3rd defense
	Run-downs
	Street Monkey Drill
	Picks
4:00	Offensive stations—4 groups (15 minutes)
	Live—2-1 count; execution
	Defense—OFs deep; INF fungo
	Tees
	Cages—60/40
5:15	Baserunning—home to first (police turns)
	1st and 3rd offense
	Conditioning—10 60-yard sprints (3-second rest)
	Pitchers—2-mile run

<u>Wednesday, January 12</u>

3:00	Stretch and throw
3:15	Small game—2-strike bunts
3:20	Introduce double relays

3:30   Defense
      Bunt defense
      1st and 3rd defense
      Run-downs
      Street Monkey Drill
      Picks

4:00   Offensive stations
      Live—Six-Out Drill
      Defense—live @ position
      Tees
      Cage—60/40

5:15   Baserunning—reading the down
      angle
      1st and 3rd offense
      Conditioning—1/2-mile intervals
      6 to 7 60-yard sprints
      Pitchers—9 poles

Thursday, January 13

3:00   Stretch

3:15   Small game—2-strike bunts

3:20   1st and 3rd offense with *pitchers
      defending*

3:50   Defense
      Street Monkey Drill
      Picks

4:00   Offensive stations
      Live—Carry the Guy Drill
      Defense—INF fungo; OFs deep
      Tees
      Cage—60/40

5:15   Baserunning—home to 1st
      1st to 3rd
      2nd to home
      Conditioning—8 to 9 60-yard
      sprints (3-second rest)
      Pitchers—2-1/2-mile run

Friday, January 14

3:00   Stretch

3:15   Small game—2-strike bunts

3:20   Pregame infield

3:30   Intra-squad game

5:00   Live baserunning
      @ 1B (fake, delay)
      @ 2B steal of 3rd
      Three-Spot Drill
    Conditioning—3/4-mile intervals,
    review signs
      6 to 7 60-yard sprints
      Pitchers—11 poles

Saturday, January 15

10:00   Stretch and throw

10:20   Double relays

10:30   Defense
      Bunt defense
      1st and 3rd defense
      Run-downs
      Street Monkey Drill
      Picks

11:00   Pregame batting practice

11:50   Pregame infield

12:00   Intra-squad

4:00   1st and 3rd offense vs. pitchers
      Live baserunning
      @ 1B
      @ 2B steal of 3rd
      @ 3B steal of home
    Conditioning—10 to 11 60-yard
    sprints (3-second rest)
      Pitchers—3-mile run

Sunday, January 16—off day

Monday, January 17

3:00   Stretch and throw

3:15   Small game—2-strike bunts

3:20   Live baserunning
      @ 1B

3:30   Review defensive expectations/drills
      Infielders—DP footwork; Circle
        Drill; Four-Corner Drill (Kling)
      OFs—aim for knee; decoy; drop
        step (Lopez)
      Catchers—blocking; signs
        Lopez)
      Pitchers—concealing pitches;
        bunt box; Dead Ball Drill
        (Henderson)

3:45   Defense
      Bunt defense
      1st and 3rd defense
      Run-downs
      Street Monkey Drill
      Picks

4:00   Offensive stations—5 groups (12 min.)
      Live—2-1 count; execution
      Defense—fungos INF; OF
        shallow
      Tees
      Cage—60/40
      Baserunning—1st to 3rd

5:15   Conditioning—1-mile intervals
       6 to 7 60-yard sprints
       Pitchers—13 poles

Tuesday, January 18

3:00   Stretch and throw

3:15   Small game—2-strike bunts

3:20   Infielders—4-spot fungos
       Outfielders—line drives; sun balls;
         run-through fly ball
       Catchers—bunt footwork; force at
         home
       Pitchers—review 3rd to 1st move;
         picks at 2B

3:40   Defense
       Bunt defense
       1st and 3rd defense
       Run-downs
       Street Monkey Drill
       Picks

4:00   Offensive stations—5 groups (12 min.)
       Live—bases loaded; 2-1 counts
       Defense—live at positions
       Cage—60/40
       Baserunning—scoring from
         2B
       Bunts—RF line

5:15   Conditioning—Three-Spot Drill
       12 to 13 60-yard sprints (3-
         second rest)
       Pitchers—3-mile run

Wednesday, January 19

3:00   Stretch and throw

3:15   Small game

3:20   Pregame infield/outfield

3:30   Intra-squad

5:00   Conditioning—1-1/2-mile intervals
       Pitchers—15 poles

Thursday, January 20

3:00   Stretch and throw

3:15   Small game

3:20   Pregame infield/outfield

3:30   Intra-squad

5:00   Conditioning—15 60-yard sprints (3-
         second rest)
       Review signs
       Pitchers—3-mile run

Friday, January 21

3:00   Stretch and throw

3:15   Small game

3:20   Live baserunning
       @ 1B

3:30   Hit and Run Drill

3:50   Defense
       Bunt defense
       1st and 3rd defense
       Run-downs
       Street Monkey Drill
       Picks

4:15   Offensive stations—4 groups
       (15 minutes)
       Live—2-1 count; execution
       Cage—60/40
       Tees
       Conditioning—1-mile
         intervals +

5:30   Baserunning—home to 1st
       1st to 2nd
       2nd to home
       Pitchers—15 poles

Saturday, January 22

10:00   Stretch and throw

10:20   Double relays

10:30   Infielders—drills
        Outfielders—drills
        Catchers—drills
        Pitchers—drills

10:45   Defense
        Bunt defense
        1st and 3rd defense
        Run-downs
        Street Monkey Drill
        Picks

11:00   Pregame batting practice

11:50   Pregame infield/outfield

12:00   Intra-squad

5:00   Conditioning—2-mile intervals
       Pitchers—4-mile run

Sunday, January 23—off day

Monday, January 24

3:00   Stretch and throw

3:15   Small game

3:20   Live baserunning
       @ 1B

3:30   Defense
       Bunt defense
       1st and 3rd defense
       Run-downs

Street Monkey Drill
Picks

4:00   Offensive stations—4 groups
(20 minutes)
Live—bases loaded
Cage—60/40
Defense—INF fungo; OF deep
Baserunning—1st to 3rd

5:30   Conditioning—15 60-yard sprints
Pitchers—16 poles

Tuesday, January 25

3:00   Stretch and throw

3:15   Small game

3:20   Live baserunning
@ 1B
@ 2B

3:30   Defense
Street Monkey Drill
Run-downs

3:45   Offensive stations—4 groups
(20 minutes)
Live—Six-Out Drill
Cage—60/40
Defense—live at positions
Baserunning—1st to 3rd

5:15   Conditioning—2-mile intervals
Pitchers—4-mile run

Wednesday, January 26

3:00   Stretch and throw

3:15   Live baserunning

3:25   Pregame infield/outfield

3:35   Intra-squad

5:00   Conditioning—15 60-yard sprints
Pitchers—16 poles

Thursday, January 27

3:00   Stretch and throw

3:15   Street Monkey Drill

3:25   Pregame infield/outfield

3:35   Intra-squad

5:00   Conditioning—1-1/2-mile intervals
Pitchers—4 miles

Friday, January 28

3:00   Stretch and throw

3:15   Small game

3:20   Live baserunning

@ 1B
@ 2B
@ 3B

3:30   Defensive positions—drills

3:50   Defense
Bunt defense
1st and 3rd defense
Run-downs
Street Monkey Drill

4:15   Offensive stations—4 groups
(15 minutes)
Live—Carry the Guy Drill
Cage—60/40
Defense—INF fungos; OF
shallow
Tees

5:45   Conditioning—15 60-yard sprints
Pitchers—16 poles

Saturday, January 29

10:00   Stretch and throw

10:20   Pregame batting practice

11:10   Pregame infield/outfield

11:30   Intra-squad

4:30   Conditioning—1-mile intervals
Pitchers—4 to 5 miles

Sunday, January 30—off day

Monday, January 31

3:00   Stretch and throw

3:15   Small game

3:20   Live baserunning

3:25   Defense
Street Monkey Drill
Run-downs

3:35   Offensive stations—4 groups
(12 minutes)
Live—2-1 counts
Cage—60/40
Defense—fungos INF; OF
normal depth
Tees

4:45   Conditioning—10 60-yard sprints;
review signs
Pitchers—15 poles
Review game day expectations/
opponent

Tuesday, February 1

Opening day games

Pitching Charts

Standard Pitching Chart

Figure D.1 is our standard pitching chart. Its purpose is to keep pitch totals and to monitor a pitcher's performance. It tracks a pitcher's location, strike/ball ratio for each type of pitch, ground balls, fly balls, hard hit totals, and first-pitch strike totals, as well as some general summary categories. Figure D.2 is a sample of the standard pitching chart after it's been filled out.

Each pitch is charted by (1) writing the number representing the type of pitch in the location thrown; (2) indicating strike or ball in the left-hand column; and (3) marking off the number of pitches thrown in the right-hand column. Following the game, totals can be computed.

Pitch Total Chart

Figure D.3 is a simple pitch total chart that I keep with me at all times. In each column I monitor what every pitcher of the staff has done over a particular week.

Pitcher's Performance Chart

This chart enables me to monitor the pitching staff over an extended period of time. In reality, it is a summary sheet for the standard pitching chart and the pitch total chart (see figures D.4 and D.5).

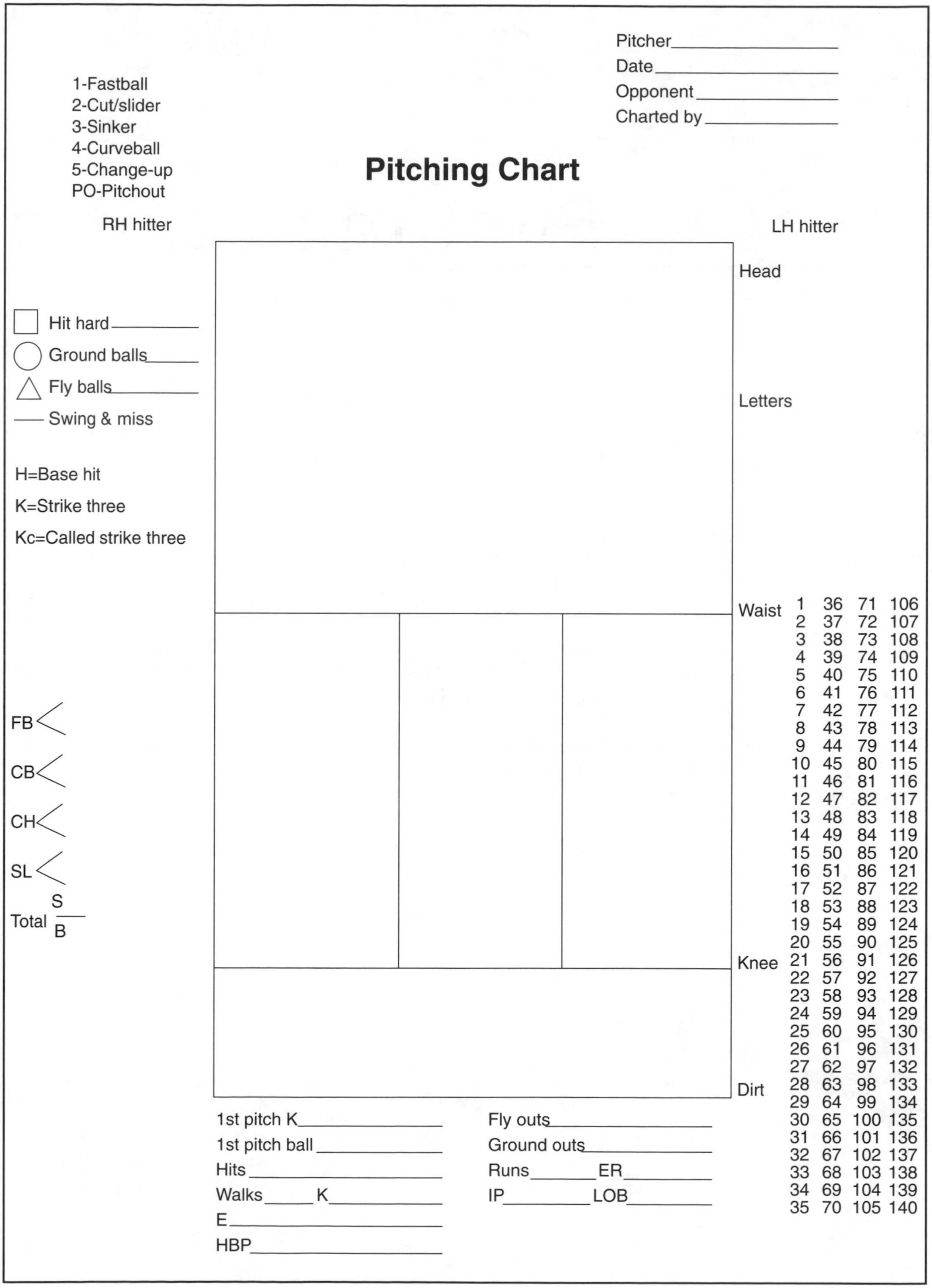

1-Fastball
2-Cut/slider
3-Sinker
4-Curveball
5-Change-up
PO-Pitchout

RH hitter

LH hitter

Pitching Chart

Pitcher_____
Date_____
Opponent_____
Charted by_____

☐ Hit hard_____

○ Ground balls_____

△ Fly balls_____

—— Swing & miss

H=Base hit

K=Strike three

Kc=Called strike three

Head

Letters

FB ⟨

CB ⟨

CH ⟨

SL ⟨

Total $\frac{S}{B}$

Waist

Knee

Dirt

1	36	71	106
2	37	72	107
3	38	73	108
4	39	74	109
5	40	75	110
6	41	76	111
7	42	77	112
8	43	78	113
9	44	79	114
10	45	80	115
11	46	81	116
12	47	82	117
13	48	83	118
14	49	84	119
15	50	85	120
16	51	86	121
17	52	87	122
18	53	88	123
19	54	89	124
20	55	90	125
21	56	91	126
22	57	92	127
23	58	93	128
24	59	94	129
25	60	95	130
26	61	96	131
27	62	97	132
28	63	98	133
29	64	99	134
30	65	100	135
31	66	101	136
32	67	102	137
33	68	103	138
34	69	104	139
35	70	105	140

1st pitch K_____

1st pitch ball_____

Hits_____

Walks_____K_____

E_____

HBP_____

Fly outs_____

Ground outs_____

Runs_____ER_____

IP_____LOB_____

Figure D.1 Standard pitching chart.

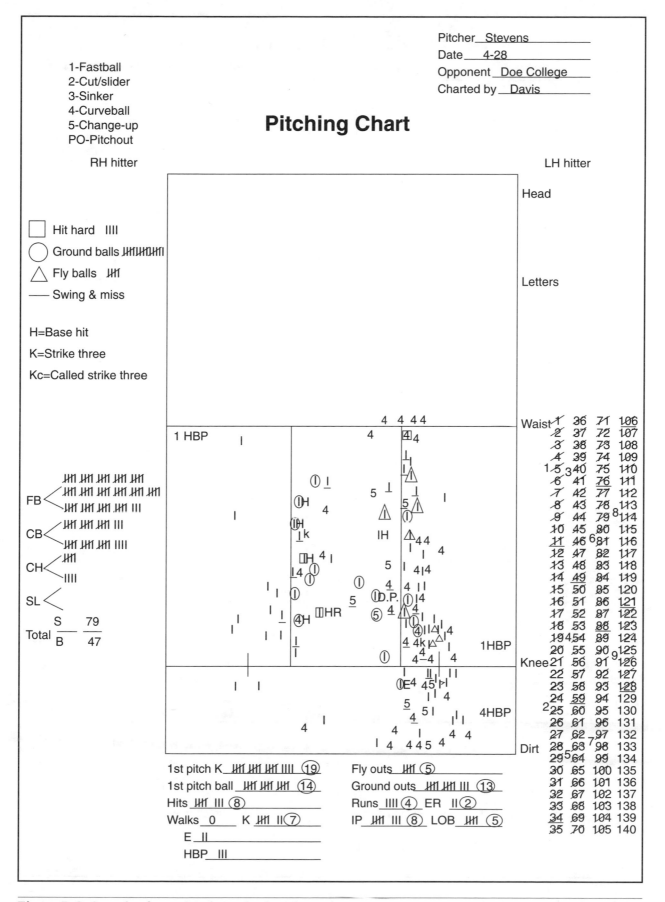

Figure D.2 Sample of completed standard pitching chart.

Pitch Total Chart

Pitcher	Mon	Tue	Wed	Thu	Fri	Sat	Sun	Total

Enter: Game-G, Bullpen-B, Batting practice-BP, or Long-toss-LT into chart with pitch totals.

Figure D.3 Pitch total chart.

Pitcher's Performance Chart

Pitcher	Date	P-G-BP	Pitch Total	K/B Ratio	K FB	K CB	K SL	K CH	K OT	Hold	Step off	Slide	1.5	IP	H	BB	R	ER	SO	Comments

Figure D.4 Pitcher's performance chart.

Pitcher's Performance Chart

Pitcher	Date	P-G-BP	Pitch Total	K/B Ratio	K FB	K CB	K SL	K CH	K OT	Hold	Step off	Slide	1.5	IP	H	BB	R	ER	SO	Comments
Nichols	3/31	Chapman	60	33/27	27/21				6/6					3		0	3	0	0	Not bad
Schulz	=	=	28	16/12	12/10			1/0	3/2					2		0	1	1	0	Good
Estavil	=	=	24	14/10	10/9		2/0	2/1						2		1	0	0	0	OK
Housley	=	=	26	15/11	13/11		2/0							2		1	2	2	2	so so
Duda	4/2	USD	105	69/37	57/26	9/10		3/1						9		1	1	1	8	nice job
Gregory	4/3	=	57	39/18	30/15	3/2		6/1						$3\frac{2}{3}$		0	2	2	4	hit a bit
Housley	=	=	33	18/14	9/6		9/7	1/1						$3\frac{2}{3}$		0	0	0	1	OK
Le Blanc	=	=	94	58/36	45/24		7/9	2/3	4/0					6		2	4	4	2	OK
Estavil	=	=	48	30/18	27/18			3/0						3		2	5	5	0	Nice
Duda	4/6	CSF	104	74/30	54/17	12/11		8/2						$8\frac{1}{3}$		1	1	1	10	Very Good
Estavil	=	=	10	5/5	5/5									$\frac{1}{3}$		1	0	0	0	OK
Housley	=	=	1	1	1/10									$\frac{1}{3}$		0	0	0	0	OK
Logeais	4/8	INTNA	49	29/20	21/14	6/6		2/0						3		1	2	2	1	Not bad
Miller	=	=	85	48/37	28/20	18/17		2/0						6		2	1	1	0	OK
Doerges	=	=	35	19/16	14/10	2/3		3/3						3		2	0	0	0	OK
Kennedy	=	=	36	27/9	20/7	1/1	6/1							3		0	2	2	1	Not bad
Gibbons	=	=	69	34/35	27/23	4/4	2/2	1/6						3		3	1	1	5	Careless
Workman	=	=	54	32/22	19/8	0/1	10/12		2/1					3		1	3	3	6	UP!
Palaru	=	=	27	16/11	13/4	0/3		3/4						3		0	0	0	0	OK
Duda	4/12	UCLA	63	42/21	34/11	5/7		3/3						$4\frac{1}{3}$		0	1	1	4	Nice job
Moe	=	=	61	32/29	23/21		6/4	3/4						$3\frac{2}{3}$		2	1	1	3	Nice job
Housley	=	=	15	11/4	7/2		2/2	2/0						1		0	1	1	0	Nice job

Figure D.5 Sample of completed pitcher's performance chart.

Appendix E

Scouting Reports

Opponent Scouting Report—Defense

This chart helps you organize a general overview of a particular opponent while scouting. The first four sections enable you to evaluate their defensive capabilities and tendencies. The section titled *Action* allows you to take notice of particular offensive tendencies (see figure E.1).

Opponent Scouting Report—Pitching and Signals

This chart may be used in a scouting role or from your game bench. It is designed almost as a checklist to determine if an opponent gives away any signs and to monitor a pitcher's ability to hold runners (see figure E.2).

Opponent Scouting Report—Hitter Tendencies

This is an additional chart to help keep account of a hitter's tendencies, out/pitch ratio, speed, and so on. Note the numbered grid in the upper right-hand corner, which represents defensive positioning of your outfield with #5 being straight away and normal depth. Each outfielder would play each particular hitter at the appropriate numbered position. For instance, a pull hitter from the right side of the plate would be played 4, 4, 5, representing where your left fielder, center fielder, and right fielder would play respectively (see figure E.3).

Hitter Tendency Chart

This chart may be used to monitor your opponent's hitters as well as your own. Each of the four squares represents a particular at-bat in a game (see figure E.4). The example shown is for four at-bats by one of my Pepperdine players, Ryan Christiansen, in a particular game (see figure E.5). In at-bat 1 Ryan struck out looking on a curveball down and away on a 2-2 pitch. This happened in inning #1. In inning #3 Ryan singled up the middle on a fastball, low and in the middle of the plate; the count was 0-1. In the 6th inning Ryan flied out to center field on a 1-0 fastball, a high strike in the middle of the plate. In the 8th inning against a relief pitcher by the name of Davis, Ryan took a 3-2 slider for ball 4 with the runner at first base. Notice that we are able to chart that Davis threw less than 85 miles an hour and was right-handed. This chart can be used for a hitter and coach to review at-bats following each game and for reference purposes when facing the opponent again.

Opponent Scouting Report—Defense

Team: _____   **Opponent:** _____

Date & place: _____   **Charter:** _____

Outfielders   **Rating 1-5**

#	Name	Pos.	Arm	Speed	Depth	Comments:

Infielders

#	Name	Pos.	Arm	Range	Bunt?	Comments:

Catchers

#	Name	Arm	Time	Snap	Block	Bunt?	Comments:

Pitchers

#	Name	Arm	Time	Slide	Move	Bunt?	Comments:

Action

B-S	Play	Outs	Inn.	Hitter	Runner	Situation:

Figure E.1 Opponent scouting report—defense.

Opponent Scouting Report—Pitching and Signals

Opponents: **Date:**   **Charter:**

Pitchers Name and #=				
Tips pitches				
Comments				

Pickoff move
    Max looks
    Time
    # of throws
    Step off
    Tips move				

Comments				

Catchers
    Name and #:
    Tips pitches
    Base coaches see signs
    Time
    Signs while on second				

Fielders
    Relay to OF
    Shifting
    Bunt
    Delay
    Comments				

Pitching coach's signs				
Dugout coach's signs				
Offensive signs				

OF positioning

#	LF CF RF	**Comments**

		1	2	3	4	5	6	7	8	9	10	R/H/E
	Home											
	Visitors											

Figure E.2 Opponent scouting report—pitching and signals.

Opponent Scouting Report—Hitter Tendencies

Team:_____   **Opponent:**_____

Date & place:_____   **Charter:**_____

1	2	3
4	5	6
7	8	9

#	Name	Bats	Stance	Swing	Hands	Comments	LF	CF	RF

Figure E.3 Opponent scouting report—hitter tendencies.

Hitter Tendency Chart

Player_____ #_____   Date _____

Starting pitcher_____ #____

Team _____   (85 -- 85 +)(L - R)

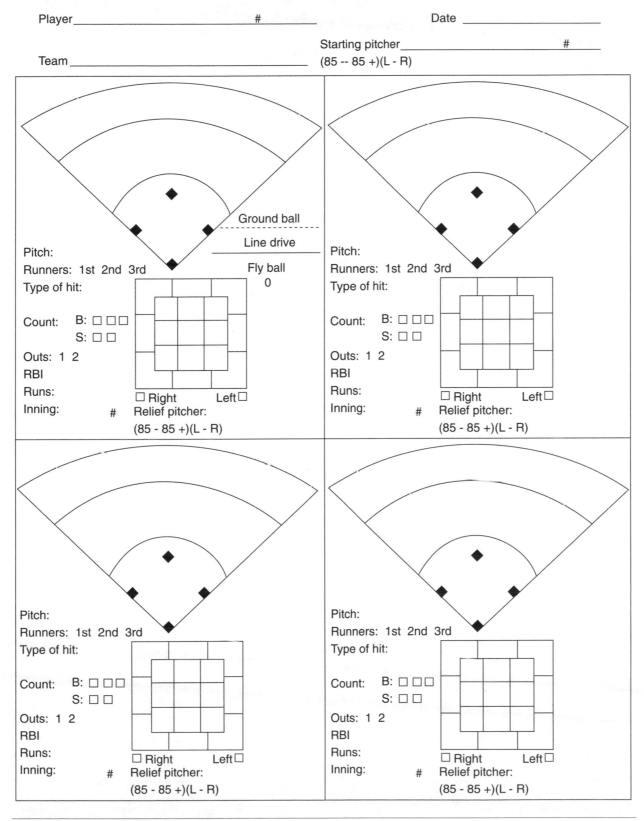

Figure E.4 Hitter tendency chart.

Figure E.4 was originally created by Joe Moeller with the "Eye in the Sky" computer program.

Hitter Tendency Chart

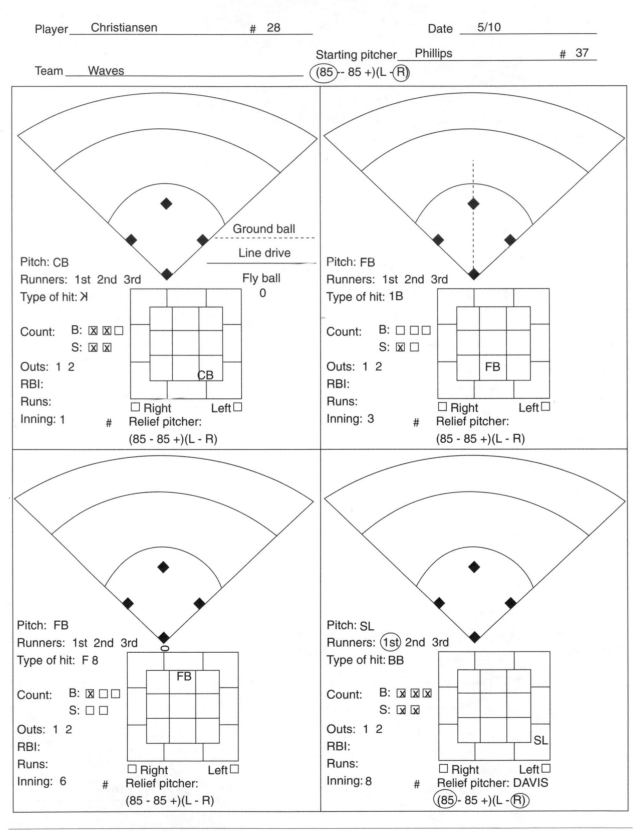

Player___Christiansen_____ #__28____   Date___5/10_____

                                        Starting pitcher___Phillips_____ #__37__
Team___Waves_____   (85)- 85 +)(L -(R))

Pitch: CB
Runners: 1st 2nd 3rd
Type of hit: ⅄
Count: B: ⊠ ⊠ ☐
        S: ⊠ ⊠
Outs: 1 2
RBI:
Runs:
Inning: 1   #

Ground ball
- - - - - - -
Line drive
_____
Fly ball
0

CB
☐ Right   Left ☐
Relief pitcher:
(85 - 85 +)(L - R)

Pitch: FB
Runners: 1st 2nd 3rd
Type of hit: 1B
Count: B: ☐ ☐ ☐
        S: ⊠ ☐
Outs: 1 2
RBI:
Runs:
Inning: 3   #

FB
☐ Right   Left ☐
Relief pitcher:
(85 - 85 +)(L - R)

Pitch: FB
Runners: 1st 2nd 3rd
Type of hit: F 8
Count: B: ⊠ ☐ ☐
        S: ☐ ☐
Outs: 1 2
RBI:
Runs:
Inning: 6   #

FB
☐ Right   Left ☐
Relief pitcher:
(85 - 85 +)(L - R)

Pitch: SL
Runners: (1st) 2nd 3rd
Type of hit: BB
Count: B: ⊠ ⊠ ⊠
        S: ⊠ ⊠
Outs: 1 2
RBI:
Runs:
Inning: 8   #

SL
☐ Right   Left ☐
Relief pitcher: DAVIS
(85)- 85 +)(L -(R))

Figure E.5 Sample of completed hitter tendency chart.

Figure E.5 was originally created by Joe Moeller with the "Eye in the Sky" computer program.

Index

Note: Page numbers in bold refer to appendixes.

About the Authors

Andy Lopez

John Kirkgard

Andy Lopez has been a head baseball coach since 1978, putting together an impressive string of winning ball clubs at three different levels. He began his career at Mira Costa High School in Manhattan Beach, California, where his team was a frequent participant in the California Interscholastic Federation (CIF) playoffs. In 1982 his squad was runner-up in the CIF finals played at Dodger Stadium.

Andy moved up to the NCAA Division II level the following year, becoming head coach at California State University at Dominguez Hills, in Carson. His teams clinched three conference championships and finished third place in the 1987 College World Series. In 1988 Andy stepped up to the NCAA Division I level when he was named head baseball coach at Pepperdine University in Malibu, California. Under his leadership, Pepperdine teams won four conference championships and captured the 1992 NCAA National Championship. Today, he is head baseball coach at the University of Florida in Gainesville.

Andy has received numerous honors as coach of the year, including the 1992 NCAA Division I National Coach of the Year Award. He was inducted into the University of Cali-

fornia at Los Angeles (UCLA) Athletic Hall of Fame in 1994. A graduate of UCLA, Andy is a member of the American Baseball Coaches Association and Fellowship of Christian Athletes. In his leisure time, he enjoys spending time with his family, reading, and jogging.

John Kirkgard's unique perspective as both a longtime friend of Andy Lopez and a colleague in the coaching ranks brought special insights to this book. He helped Andy put his thoughts on paper and added his own expertise. A successful coach in his own right, John has managed the baseball team at Westmont College in Santa Barbara, California, since 1984. His teams have won three Golden State Athletic Conference championships and one NAIA District 3 championship.

John is baseball chairman of the NAIA's Far West Region. He was named NAIA Far West Region Coach of the Year in 1994 and NAIA District 3 Coach of the Year in 1988, 1989, and 1994. In 1986 he received an MBA from California Lutheran University in Thousand Oaks, California. A member of the American Baseball Coaches Association and Fellowship of Christian Athletes, John resides in Santa Barbara, California.

ASEP's *SportCoach* Curriculum

The American Sport Education Program (ASEP) believes that the single most important step in improving amateur sport is to educate coaches. For this reason, ASEP offers its *SportCoach* curriculum at three levels:

- **Volunteer Level**, for coaches who work with youth sport programs
- **Leader Level**, for coaches in interscholastic or club sport
- **Master Level**, for coaches who have completed Leader Level courses and seek further professional development

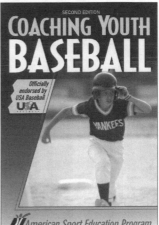

Volunteer Level

One of the *SportCoach* courses for educating youth sport coaches is the Rookie Coaches Course. This course is for anyone who is coaching children's sports for the first time and has no formal training as a coach. *Coaching Youth Baseball*, an excellent reference for new baseball coaches, serves as a text for the course.

Leader Level

ASEP's Leader Level *SportCoach* curriculum consists of three courses: the Coaching Principles Course, Sport First Aid Course, and Drugs and Sport Course. These courses teach coaches to form a sportsmanship-based coaching philosophy, communicate better with athletes, plan and teach sport skill progressions, manage risks effectively, provide appropriate first aid for sport injuries, and help coaches tackle the problem of drug use among athletes.

Master Level

At the Master Level, coaches can choose from 9 *SportCoach* courses: Sport Psychology, Sport Physiology, Teaching Sport Skills, Sport Injuries, Sport Rehabilitation, Nutrition/Weight Control, Sport Law, Time Management, and Sport Administration.

For more information about ASEP's *SportCoach* curriculum, call the ASEP National Center toll-free at 1-800-747-5698. Let ASEP help you expand your coaching skills and knowledge. Your athletes will be glad you did!

American Sport Education Program

P.O. Box 5076 • Champaign, IL 61825-5076 • Toll-free phone: 1-800-747-5698 • http // www.humankinetics.com

Additional Baseball Resources

MAXIMIZING BASEBALL PRACTICE

John Winkin
with Jay Kemble & Michael Coutts

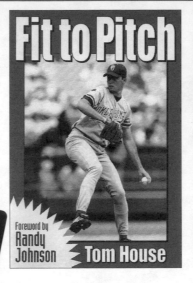

Fit to Pitch

Foreword by Randy Johnson

Tom House

OFFENSIVE BASEBALL DRILLS

68 Hitting, Baserunning, & Team Drills

FOREWORD BY Tommy Lasorda

Rod Delmonico

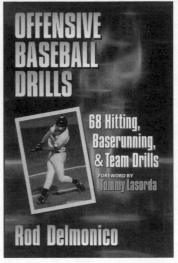

Foreword by Tommy Lasorda

1995 • Paper • 152 pp
Item PWIN0430
ISBN 0-87322-430-2
$17.95 ($23.95 Canadian)

(88-minute videotape)

1995 • 1/2" VHS
Item MWIN0438
ISBN 0-88011-485-1
$29.95 ($44.95 Canadian)

Let John Winkin show you how to get the most out of your practices, even when you have to practice indoors. *Maximizing Baseball Practice* will help you field the most competitive team possible. You'll find everything you need to help you set priorities and plan practices, improve player skills, and develop teamwork. The book contains fifty-nine illustrated drills and more than 160 photos and figures. The video shows drills for improving defensive and offensive skills.

Foreword by Randy Johnson, 1995 American League Cy Young Award Winner

1996 • Paper • Approx 216 pp
Item PHOU0882
ISBN 0-87322-882-0
$17.95 ($25.95 Canadian)

Tom House combines his on-field experiences, training with weight room workouts, and years of research to bring you proven, practical applications that will strengthen your pitching throughout the year. He outlines essential training components to develop more speed, strength, and stamina on the mound; details pitcher-specific workouts for year-round conditioning; and highlights rehabilitation guidelines that help players return to competition faster, safely.

Foreword by Tommy Lasorda

1996 • Paper • 184 pp
Item PDEL0865
ISBN 0-87322-865-0
$14.95 ($20.95 Canadian)

Let Rod Delmonico, *Baseball America*'s 1995 National Division I College Coach of the Year, show you 68 of the offensive drills he uses to take his teams to the top.

Offensive Baseball Drills includes 35 hitting drills, 20 baserunning drills, and 13 team drills for coaches to use in practice or for athletes to do at home. Coach Delmonico also explains the purpose of each drill, equipment needs, proper procedures, coaching points, and how to tailor the drills to older and younger athletes.

Prices subject to change.

Human Kinetics
The Premier Publisher for Sports & Fitness
http://www.humankinetics.com

2335

Place your order using the appropriate telephone number/address found in the front of this book, or call TOLL-FREE in the U.S. 1 800 747-4457.